# LOVE'S
# EXECUTIONER

Irvin D. Yalom

# LOVE'S EXECUTIONER

*And Other Tales of Psychotherapy*

BASIC BOOKS

*A Member of the Perseus Books Group*
*New York*

Hardcover first published by Basic Books, A Member of the Perseus Books Group
Paperback published in 2012 by Basic Books

A hardcover edition of this book was first published in 1989 by Basic Books.
A paperback edition was first published in 1990 by HarperPerennial, an imprint of
HarperCollins Publishers.

Cataloging-in-Publication data for the hardcover edition of this book are available
from the Library of Congress.

ISBN (Basic Books hardcover): 978-0-465-0420-7
LCCN: 89042522

ISBN (HarperCollins paperback): 978-0-06-095834-3
ISBN (Basic Books paperback): 978-0-465-02011-9
ISBN (Basic Books e-book): 978-0-465-03160-3

*To my family:*
*my wife, Marilyn,*
*and my children, Eve, Reid, Victor, and Ben*

# CONTENTS

# ACKNOWLEDGMENTS

❧❧❧

*Most of this book was written during a well-traveled sabbatical year. I am grateful* to many individuals and institutions who hosted me and facilitated my writing: the Stanford University Humanities Center, the Rockefeller Foundation Bellagio Study Center, Drs. Mikiko and Tsunehito Hasegawa in Tokyo and Hawaii, the Caffé Malvina in San Francisco, the Bennington College Creative Writing Program.

I am grateful to my wife, Marilyn (always my toughest critic and staunchest support); to my Basic Books editor, Phoebe Hoss, an enabling editor in this as in my previous books at Basic; and to my project editor at Basic Books, Linda Carbone. Thanks also to many, many colleagues and friends who did not bolt when they saw me approaching, a new story in hand, and offered criticism, encouragement, or consolation. The process has been long and I've no doubt lost names along the way. But my gratitude to: Pat Baumgardner, Helen Blau, Michele Carter, Isabel Davis, Stanely Elkin, John Felstiner, Albert Guerard, Maclin Guerard, Ruthellen Josselson, Herant Katchadourian, Stina Katchadourian, Marguerite Lederberg, John L'Heureux, Morton Lieberman, Dee Lum, K. Y. Lum, Mary Jane Moffatt, Nan Robinson, my sister Jean Rose, Gena Sorensen, David Spiegel, Winfried Weiss, my son Benjamin Yalom, the 1988 class of Stanford residents and psychology interns, my secretary Bea Mitchell who, for ten years, typed the clinical notes and ideas from which these stories spring. As always, I am grateful to Stanford University for providing me with the support, academic freedom, and intellectual community so essential for my work.

I owe a great debt to the ten patients who grace these pages. Each read every line of his or her story (except for one patient who died before I finished) and gave me approval for publication. Each checked and approved the disguise, many offered editorial help, one (Dave) gave me the title of his story, some commented that the disguise was unnecessarily extensive and urged me to be more accurate, a couple were unsettled by my personal self-revelation or by some of the dramatic liberties I took but, nonetheless, in the hope that the tale would be useful to therapists and/or other patients, gave me both their consent and their blessing. To all, my deepest gratitude.

These are true stories, but I have had to make many changes to protect the identity of the patients. I have often made symbolically equivalent substitutes for aspects of a patient's identity and life circumstances; occasionally I have grafted part of another patient's identity onto the protagonist. Often dialogue is fictional, and my personal reflections post hoc. The disguise is deep, penetrable in each case only by the patient. Any readers who believe they recognize one of the ten will, I am certain, be mistaken.

# PROLOGUE

❧❧❧

*Imagine this scene: three to four hundred people, strangers to each other, are told* to pair up and ask their partner one single question, "What do you want?" over and over and over again.

Could anything be simpler? One innocent question and its answer. And yet, time after time, I have seen this group exercise evoke unexpectedly powerful feelings. Often, within minutes, the room rocks with emotion. Men and women—and these are by no means desperate or needy but successful, well-functioning, well-dressed people who glitter as they walk—are stirred to their depths. They call out to those who are forever lost—dead or absent parents, spouses, children, friends: "I want to see you again." "I want your love." "I want to know you're proud of me." "I want you to know I love you and how sorry I am I never told you." "I want you back—I am so lonely." "I want the childhood I never had." "I want to be healthy—to be young again. I want to be loved, to be respected. I want my life to mean something. I want to accomplish something. I want to matter, to be important, to be remembered."

So much wanting. So much longing. And so much pain, so close to the surface, only minutes deep. Destiny pain. Existence pain. Pain that is always there, whirring continuously just beneath the membrane of life. Pain that is all too easily accessible. Many things—a simple group exercise, a few minutes of deep reflection, a work of art, a sermon, a personal crisis, a loss—remind us that our deepest wants can never be fulfilled: our wants for youth, for a halt to aging, for the return of vanished ones, for eternal love, protection, significance, for immortality itself.

It is when these unattainable wants come to dominate our lives that we turn for help to family, to friends, to religion—sometimes to psychotherapists.

In this book I tell the stories of ten patients who turned to therapy, and in the course of their work struggled with existence pain. This was not the reason they came to me for help; on the contrary, all ten were suffering the common problems of everyday life: loneliness, self-contempt, impotence, migraine headaches, sexual compulsivity, obesity, hypertension, grief, a consuming love obsession, mood swings, depression. Yet somehow (a "somehow" that unfolds differently in each story), therapy uncovered deep roots of these everyday problems—roots stretching down to the bedrock of existence.

"I want! I want!" is heard throughout these tales. One patient cried, "I want my dead darling daughter back," as she neglected her two living sons. Another insisted, "I want to fuck every woman I see," as his lymphatic cancer invaded the crawl spaces of his body. And another pleaded, "I want the parents, the childhood I never had," as he agonized over three letters he could not bring himself to open. And another declared, "I want to be young forever," as she, an old woman, could not relinquish her obsessive love for a man thirty-five years younger.

I believe that the primal stuff of psychotherapy is always such existence pain—and not, as is often claimed, repressed instinctual strivings or imperfectly buried shards of a tragic personal past. In my therapy with each of these ten patients, my primary clinical assumption—an assumption on which I based my technique—is that basic anxiety emerges from a person's endeavors, conscious and unconscious, to cope with the harsh facts of life, the "givens" of existence.*

---

*For a detailed discussion of this existential perspective and the theory and practice of a psychotherapy based upon it, see my *Existential Psychotherapy* (New York: Basic Books, 1980).

I have found that four givens are particularly relevant to psychotherapy: the inevitability of death for each of us and for those we love; the freedom to make our lives as we will; our ultimate aloneness; and, finally, the absence of any obvious meaning or sense to life. However grim these givens may seem, they contain the seeds of wisdom and redemption. I hope to demonstrate, in these ten tales of psychotherapy, that it is possible to confront the truths of existence and harness their power in the service of personal change and growth.

Of these facts of life, death is the most obvious, most intuitively apparent. At an early age, far earlier than is often thought, we learn that death will come, and that from it there is no escape. Nonetheless, "everything," in Spinoza's words, "endeavors to persist in its own being." At one's core there is an ever-present conflict between the wish to continue to exist and the awareness of inevitable death.

To adapt to the reality of death, we are endlessly ingenious in devising ways to deny or escape it. When we are young, we deny death with the help of parental reassurances and secular and religious myths; later, we personify it by transforming it into an entity, a monster, a sandman, a demon. After all, if death is some pursuing entity, then one may yet find a way to elude it; besides, frightening as a death-bearing monster may be, it is less frightening than the truth—that one carries within the spores of one's own death. Later, children experiment with other ways to attenuate death anxiety: they detoxify death by taunting it, challenge it through daredevilry, or desensitize it by exposing themselves, in the reassuring company of peers and warm buttered popcorn, to ghost stories and horror films.

As we grow older, we learn to put death out of mind; we distract ourselves; we transform it into something positive (passing on, going home, rejoining God, peace at last); we deny it with sustaining myths; we strive for immortality through imperishable works, by projecting our seed into the future through our children, or by embracing a religious system that offers spiritual perpetuation.

Many people take issue with this description of death denial. "Nonsense!" they say. "We don't deny death. Everyone's going to die.

We know that. The facts are obvious. But is there any point to dwelling on it?"

The truth is that we know but do not know. We know *about* death, intellectually we know the facts, but we—that is, the unconscious portion of the mind that protects us from overwhelming anxiety—have split off, or dissociated, the terror associated with death. This dissociative process is unconscious, invisible to us, but we can be convinced of its existence in those rare episodes when the machinery of denial fails and death anxiety breaks through in full force. That may happen only rarely, sometimes only once or twice in a lifetime. Occasionally it happens during waking life, sometimes after a personal brush with death, or when a loved one has died; but more commonly death anxiety surfaces in nightmares.

A nightmare is a failed dream, a dream that, by not "handling" anxiety, has failed in its role as the guardian of sleep. Though nightmares differ in manifest content, the underlying process of every nightmare is the same: raw death anxiety has escaped its keepers and exploded into consciousness. The story "In Search of the Dreamer" offers a unique backstage view of the escape of death anxiety and the mind's last-ditch attempt to contain it: here, amidst the pervasive, dark death imagery of Marvin's nightmare is one life-promoting, death-defying instrument—the glowing white-tipped cane with which the dreamer engages in a sexual duel with death.

The sexual act is seen also by the protagonists of other stories as a talisman to ward off diminishment, aging, and approaching death: thus, the compulsive promiscuity of a young man in the face of his killing cancer ("If Rape Were Legal . . . "); and an old man's clinging to yellowing thirty-year-old letters from his dead lover ("Do Not Go Gentle").

In my many years of work with cancer patients facing imminent death, I have noted two particularly powerful and common methods of allaying fears about death, two beliefs, or delusions, that afford a sense of safety. One is the belief in personal specialness; the other, the belief in an ultimate rescuer. While these are delusions in that they rep-

resent "fixed false beliefs," I do not employ the term *delusion* in a pejo-
rative sense: these are universal beliefs which, at some level of consciousness, exist in all of us and play a role in several of these tales.

*Specialness* is the belief that one is invulnerable, inviolable—beyond
the ordinary laws of human biology and destiny. At some point in life,
each of us will face some crisis: it may be serious illness, career failure,
or divorce; or as happened to Elva in "I Never Thought It Would Happen to Me," it may be an event as simple as a purse snatching, which
suddenly lays bare one's ordinariness and challenges the common assumption that life will always be an eternal upward spiral.

While the belief in personal specialness provides a sense of safety
from within, the other major mechanism of death denial—*belief in an
ultimate rescuer*—permits us to feel forever watched and protected by an
outside force. Though we may falter, grow ill, though we may arrive at
the very edge of life, there is, we are convinced, a looming, omnipotent
servant who will always bring us back.

Together these two belief systems constitute a dialectic—two diametrically opposed responses to the human situation. The human
being either asserts autonomy by heroic self-assertion or seeks safety
through fusing with a superior force: that is, one either emerges or
merges, separates or embeds. One becomes one's own parent or remains the eternal child.

Most of us, most of the time, live comfortably by uneasily avoiding
the glance of death, by chuckling and agreeing with Woody Allen when
he says, "I'm not afraid of death. I just don't want to be there when it
happens." But there is another way—a long tradition, applicable to
psychotherapy—that teaches us that full awareness of death ripens our
wisdom and enriches our life. The dying words of one of my patients
(in "If Rape Were Legal . . .") demonstrate that though the *fact*, the
physicality, of death destroys us, the *idea* of death may save us.

⟿

Freedom, another given of existence, presents a dilemma for several
of these ten patients. When Betty, an obese patient, announced that

she had binged just before coming to see me and was planning to binge again as soon as she left my office, she was attempting to give up her freedom by persuading me to assume control of her. The entire course of therapy of another patient (Thelma in "Love's Executioner") revolved around the theme of surrender to a former lover (and therapist) and my search for strategies to help her reclaim her power and freedom.

Freedom as a given seems the very antithesis of death. While we dread death, we generally consider freedom to be unequivocally positive. Has not the history of Western civilization been punctuated with yearnings for freedom, even driven by it? Yet freedom from an existential perspective is bonded to anxiety in asserting that, contrary to everyday experience, we do not enter into, and ultimately leave, a well-structured universe with an eternal grand design. Freedom means that one is responsible for one's own choices, actions, one's own life situation.

Though the word *responsible* may be used in a variety of ways, I prefer Sartre's definition: to be responsible is to "be the author of," each of us being thus the author of his or her own life design. We are free to be anything but unfree: we are, Sartre would say, condemned to freedom. Indeed, some philosophers claim much more: that the architecture of the human mind makes each of us even responsible for the structure of external reality, for the very form of space and time. It is here, in the idea of self-construction, where anxiety dwells: we are creatures who desire structure, and we are frightened by a concept of freedom which implies that beneath us there is nothing, sheer groundlessness.

Every therapist knows that the crucial first step in therapy is the patient's assumption of responsibility for his or her life predicament. As long as one believes that one's problems are caused by some force or agency outside oneself, there is no leverage in therapy. If, after all, the problem lies out there, then why should one change oneself? It is the outside world (friends, job, spouse) that must be changed—or exchanged. Thus, Dave (in "Do Not Go Gentle"), complaining bitterly of being locked in a marital prison by a snoopy, possessive wife-warden, could not proceed in therapy until he recognized how he himself was responsible for the construction of that prison.

Since patients tend to resist assuming responsibility, therapists must develop techniques to make patients aware of how they themselves create their own problems. A powerful technique, which I use in many of these cases, is the here-and-now focus. Since patients tend to re-create *in the therapy setting* the same interpersonal problems that bedevil them in their lives outside, I focus on what is going on at the moment between a patient and me rather than on the events of his or her past or current life. By examining the details of the therapy relationship (or, in a therapy group, the relationships among the group members), I can point out on the spot how a patient influences the responses of other people. Thus, though Dave could resist assuming responsibility for his marital problems, he could not resist the immediate data he himself was generating in group therapy: that is, his secretive, teasing, and elusive behavior was activating the other group members to respond to him much as his wife did at home.

In similar fashion, Betty's ("Fat Lady") therapy was ineffective as long as she could attribute her loneliness to the flaky, rootless California culture. It was only when I demonstrated how, in our hours together, her impersonal, shy, distancing manner re-created the same impersonal environment in therapy, that she could begin to explore her responsibility for creating her own isolation.

While the assumption of responsibility brings the patient into the vestibule of change, it is not synonymous with change. And it is change that is always the true quarry, however much a therapist may court insight, responsibility assumption, and self-actualization.

Freedom not only requires us to bear responsibility for our life choices but also posits that change requires an act of will. Though *will* is a concept therapists seldom use explicitly, we nonetheless devote much effort to influencing a patient's will. We endlessly clarify and interpret, assuming (and it is a secular leap of faith, lacking convincing empirical support) that understanding will invariably beget change. When years of interpretation have failed to generate change, we may begin to make direct appeals to the will: "Effort, too, is needed. You have to try, you know. There's a time for thinking and analyzing but there's also a time for action." And when direct exhortation fails, the therapist is reduced, as these stories bear witness, to employing any known means by which one person can influence another. Thus, I may advise, argue, badger, cajole, goad, implore, or simply endure, hoping that the patient's neurotic worldview will crumble away from sheer fatigue.

It is through *willing*, the mainspring of action, that our freedom is enacted. I see willing as having two stages: a person initiates through wishing and then enacts through deciding.

Some people are wish-blocked, knowing neither what they feel nor what they want. Without opinions, without impulses, without inclinations, they become parasites on the desires of others. Such people tend to be tiresome. Betty was boring precisely because she stifled her wishes, and others grew weary of supplying wish and imagination for her.

Other patients cannot decide. Though they know exactly what they want and what they must do, they cannot act and, instead, pace tormentedly before the door of decision. Saul, in "Three Unopened Letters," knew that any reasonable man would open the letters; yet the fear they invoked paralyzed his will. Thelma ("Love's Executioner") knew that her love obsession was stripping her life of reality. She *knew* that she was, as she put it, living her life eight years ago, and that, to regain it, she would have to give up her infatuation. But that she could not, or would not, do and fiercely resisted all my attempts to energize her will.

Decisions are difficult for many reasons, some reaching down into the very socket of being. John Gardner, in his novel *Grendel*, tells of a wise man who sums up his meditation on life's mysteries in two simple but terrible postulates: "Things fade: alternatives exclude." Of the first postulate, death, I have already spoken. The second, "alternatives exclude," is an important key to understanding why decision is difficult. Decision invariably involves renunciation: for every yes there must be a no, each decision eliminating or killing other options (the root of the word *decide* means "slay," as in *homicide* or *suicide*). Thus, Thelma clung to the infinitesimal chance that she might once again revive her relationship with her lover, renunciation of that possibility signifying diminishment and death.

Existential isolation, a third given, refers to the unbridgeable gap between self and others, a gap that exists even in the presence of deeply gratifying interpersonal relationships. One is isolated not only from other beings but, to the extent that one constitutes one's world, from world as well. Such isolation is to be distinguished from two other types of isolation: interpersonal and intrapersonal isolation.

One experiences *interpersonal* isolation, or loneliness, if one lacks the social skills or personality style that permit intimate social interactions. *Intrapersonal* isolation occurs when parts of the self are split off, as when one splits off emotion from the memory of an event. The most extreme, and dramatic, form of splitting, the multiple personality, is relatively rare (though growing more widely recognized); when it does occur, the therapist may be faced, as was I in the treatment of Marge ("Therapeutic Monogamy"), with the bewildering dilemma of which personality to cherish.

While there is no solution to existential isolation, therapists must discourage false solutions. One's efforts to escape isolation can sabotage one's relationships with other people. Many a friendship or marriage has failed because, instead of relating to, and caring for, one another, one person uses another as a shield against isolation.

A common, and vigorous, attempt to solve existential isolation, which occurs in several of these stories, is fusion—the softening of one's boundaries, the melting into another. The power of fusion has been demonstrated in subliminal perception experiments in which the message "Mommy and I are one," flashed on a screen so quickly that the subjects cannot consciously see it, results in their reporting that they feel better, stronger, more optimistic—and even in their responding better than other people to treatment (with behavioral modification) for such problems as smoking, obesity, or disturbed adolescent behavior.

One of the great paradoxes of life is that self-awareness breeds anxiety. Fusion eradicates anxiety in a radical fashion—by eliminating self-awareness. The person who has fallen in love, and entered a blissful state of merger, is not self-reflective because the questioning lonely *I* (and the attendant anxiety of isolation) dissolve into the *we*. Thus one sheds anxiety but loses oneself.

This is precisely why therapists do not like to treat a patient who has fallen in love. Therapy and a state of love-merger are incompatible because therapeutic work requires a questioning self-awareness and an anxiety that will ultimately serve as guide to internal conflicts.

Furthermore, it is difficult for me, as for most therapists, to form a relationship with a patient who has fallen in love. In the story "Love's Executioner," Thelma would not, for example, relate to me: her energy was completely consumed in her love obsession. Beware the powerful exclusive attachment to another; it is not, as people sometimes think, evidence of the purity of the love. Such encapsulated, exclusive love—feeding on itself, neither giving to nor caring about others—is destined to cave in on itself. Love is not just a passion spark between two people; there is infinite difference between falling in love and standing in love. Rather, love is a way of being, a "giving to," not a "falling for"; a mode of relating at large, not an act limited to a single person.

Though we try hard to go through life two by two or in groups, there are times, especially when death approaches, that the truth—that we are born alone and must die alone—breaks through with chilling clarity. I have heard many dying patients remark that the most awful thing about dying is that it must be done alone. Yet, even at the point of death, the willingness of another to be fully present may penetrate the isolation. As a patient said in "Do Not Go Gentle," "Even though you're alone in your boat, it's always comforting to see the lights of the other boats bobbing nearby."

Now, if death is inevitable, if all of our accomplishments, indeed our entire solar system, shall one day lie in ruins, if the world is contingent (that is, everything could as well have been otherwise), if human beings must construct the world and the human design within that world, then what enduring meaning can there be in life?

This question plagues contemporary men and women, and many seek therapy because they feel their lives to be senseless and aimless. We are meaning-seeking creatures. Biologically, our nervous systems are organized in such a way that the brain automatically clusters incoming stimuli into configurations. Meaning also provides a sense of mastery: feeling helpless and confused in the face of random, unpatterned events, we seek to order them and, in so doing, gain a sense of control over them. Even more important, meaning gives birth to values and, hence, to a code of behavior: thus the answer to *why* questions (Why do I live?) supplies an answer to *how* questions (How do I live?).

There are, in these ten tales of psychotherapy, few explicit discussions of meaning in life. The search for meaning, much like the search for pleasure, must be conducted obliquely. Meaning ensues from meaningful activity: the more we deliberately pursue it, the less likely are we to find it; the rational questions one can pose about meaning will always outlast the answers. In therapy, as in life, meaningfulness is a by-product of engagement and commitment, and that is where therapists must direct their efforts—not that engagement provides the rational answer to questions of meaning, but it causes these questions not to matter.

This existential dilemma—a being who searches for meaning and certainty in a universe that has neither—has tremendous relevance for the profession of psychotherapist. In their everyday work, therapists, if they are to relate to their patients in an authentic fashion, experience considerable uncertainty. Not only does a patient's confrontation with unanswerable questions expose a therapist to these same questions, but also the therapist must recognize, as I had to in "Two Smiles," that the experience of the other is, in the end, unyieldingly private and unknowable.

Indeed, the capacity to tolerate uncertainty is a prerequisite for the profession. Though the public may believe that therapists guide patients systematically and sure-handedly through predictable stages of therapy to a foreknown goal, such is rarely the case: instead, as these stories bear witness, therapists frequently wobble, improvise, and grope for direction. The powerful temptation to achieve certainty through embracing an ideological school and a tight therapeutic system is treacherous: such belief may block the uncertain and spontaneous encounter necessary for effective therapy.

This encounter, the very heart of psychotherapy, is a caring, deeply human meeting between two people, one (generally, but not always, the patient) more troubled than the other. Therapists have a dual role: they must both observe and participate in the lives of their patients. As observer, one must be sufficiently objective to provide necessary rudimentary guidance to the patient. As participant, one enters into the life of the patient and is affected and sometimes changed by the encounter.

In choosing to enter fully into each patient's life, I, the therapist, not only am exposed to the same existential issues as are my patients but must be prepared to examine them with the same rules of inquiry. I must assume that knowing is better than not knowing, venturing than not venturing; and that magic and illusion, however rich, however alluring, ultimately weaken the human spirit. I take with deep seriousness Thomas Hardy's staunch words: "If a way to the Better there be, it exacts a full look at the Worst."

The dual role of observer and participant demands much of a therapist and, for me in these ten cases, posed harrowing questions. Should I, for example, expect a patient, who asked me to be the keeper of his love letters, to deal with the very problems that I, in my own life, have avoided? Was it possible to help him go further than I have gone? Should I ask harsh existential questions of a dying man, a widow, a bereaved mother, and an anxious retiree with transcendent dreams—questions for which I have no answers? Should I reveal my weakness and my limitations to a patient whose other, alternative personality I found so seductive? Could I possibly form an honest and a caring relationship with a fat lady whose physical appearance repelled me?

Should I, under the banner of self-enlightenment, strip away an old woman's irrational but sustaining and comforting love illusion? Or forcibly impose my will on a man who, incapable of acting in his best interests, allowed himself to be terrorized by three unopened letters?

Though these tales of psychotherapy abound with the words *patient* and *therapist*, do not be misled by such terms: these are everyman, everywoman stories. Patienthood is ubiquitous; the assumption of the label is largely arbitrary and often dependent more on cultural, educational, and economic factors than on the severity of pathology. Since therapists, no less than patients, must confront these givens of existence, the professional posture of disinterested objectivity, so necessary to scientific method, is inappropriate. We psychotherapists simply cannot cluck with sympathy and exhort patients to struggle resolutely with their problems. We cannot say to them *you* and *your* problems. Instead, we must speak of *us* and *our* problems, because our life, our existence, will always be riveted to death, love to loss, freedom to fear, and growth to separation. We are, all of us, in this together.

# 1

## Love's Executioner

*I do not like to work with patients who are in love. Perhaps it is because of* envy—I, too, crave enchantment. Perhaps it is because love and psychotherapy are fundamentally incompatible. The good therapist fights darkness and seeks illumination, while romantic love is sustained by mystery and crumbles upon inspection. I hate to be love's executioner.

Yet Thelma, in the opening minutes of our first interview, told me that she was hopelessly, tragically in love, and I never hesitated, not for one moment, to accept her for treatment. Everything I saw in my first glance—her wrinkled seventy-year-old face with that senile chin tremor, her thinning, bleached, unkempt yellow hair, her emaciated blue-veined hands—told me she had to be mistaken, that she could not be in love. How could love ever choose to ravage that frail, tottering old body, or house itself in that shapeless polyester jogging suit?

Moreover, where was the aura of love bliss? Thelma's suffering did not surprise me, love being always contaminated by pain; but her love was monstrously out of balance—it contained *no* pleasure at all, her life wholly a torment.

So I agreed to treat her because I was certain she was suffering, not from love, but from some rare variant which she mistook for love. Not only did I believe that I could help Thelma but I was intrigued by the idea that this counterfeit love could be a beacon that might illuminate some of the deep mystery of love.

Thelma was remote and stiff in our first meeting. She had not returned my smile when I greeted her in the waiting room, and followed a step or two behind me as I escorted her down the hall. Once we entered my office, she did not inspect her surroundings but immediately sat down. Then, without waiting for any comment from me and without unbuttoning the heavy jacket she wore over her jogging suit, she took a sharp deep breath and began:

"Eight years ago I had a love affair with my therapist. Since then he has never left my mind. I almost killed myself once and I believe I will succeed the next time. You are my last hope."

I always listen carefully to first statements. They are often preternaturally revealing and foreshadow the type of relationship I will be able to establish with a patient. Words permit one to cross into the life of the other, but Thelma's tone of voice contained no invitation to come closer.

She continued: "In case you have a hard time believing me, perhaps these will help!"

She reached into a faded red drawstring purse and handed me two old photographs. The first was of a young beautiful dancer wearing a sleek black leotard. I was startled, when I looked into the face of that dancer, to meet Thelma's large eyes peering out at me across the decades.

"That one," Thelma informed me when she saw me turning to the second photo, of a sixty-year-old handsome but stolid woman, "was taken about eight years ago. As you see"—she ran her fingers through her uncombed hair—"I no longer tend to my appearance."

Though I had difficulty imagining this shabby old woman having an affair with her therapist, I had said nothing about not believing her. In fact, I had said nothing at all. I had tried to maintain complete objectivity but she must have noticed some evidence of disbelief, some small cue, perhaps a minuscule widening of my eyes. I decided not to protest her accusation that I did not believe her. This was no time for gallantry and there *was* something incongruous in the idea of a disheveled seventy-year-old infatuated, lovesick woman. She knew that, I knew it, and she knew I knew it.

I soon learned that over the last twenty years she had been chronically depressed and in psychiatric treatment almost continuously. Much of her therapy had been obtained at the local county mental health clinic, where she had been treated by a series of trainees.

About eleven years before, she began treatment with Matthew, a young, handsome psychology intern, and met weekly with him for eight months at the clinic and continued to see him in his private practice for another year. The following year, when Matthew took a full-time position at a state hospital, he had to terminate therapy with all his private patients.

It was with much sadness that Thelma said goodbye to him. He was, by far, the best therapist she had ever had, and she had grown fond of him, very fond, and for those twenty months looked forward all week to her therapy hour. Never before had she been as totally open with anyone. Never before had a therapist been so scrupulously honest, direct, and gentle with her.

Thelma rhapsodized about Matthew for several minutes. "He had so much caring, so much loving. I've had other therapists who tried to be warm, to put you at ease, but Matthew was different. He *really* cared, he *really* accepted me. No matter what I did, what horrid things I thought, I knew he'd accept it and still—what's the word?—confirm me—no, *validate* me. He helped me in the way therapists usually do, but he did a lot more."

"For example?"

"He introduced me to the spiritual, religious dimension of life. He taught me to care for all living things. He taught me to think about the reasons I was put here on earth. But he didn't have his head in the clouds. He was right in there with me."

Thelma was highly animated—she snapped her words off and pointed down to the earth and up to the clouds as she spoke. I could see she liked talking about Matthew. "I loved the way he tangled with me. He didn't let me get away with anything. He always called me on my shitty habits."

This phrase startled me. It didn't fit with the rest of her presentation. Yet she chose her terms so deliberately that I assumed they had been Matthew's words, maybe an example of his fine technique! My negative feelings toward him were rapidly growing, but I kept them to myself. Thelma's words told me clearly that she would not look kindly at any criticism of Matthew.

After Matthew, Thelma started therapy with other therapists, but none ever reached her or helped her value her life the way he had.

Imagine, then, how pleased she was, a year after their last meeting, to run into him late one Saturday afternoon at Union Square in San Francisco. They chatted and, to escape the swirl of shoppers, had coffee together in the café at the St. Francis Hotel. There was so much to talk about, so much that Matthew wanted to know about Thelma's past year, that their coffee hour extended into the dinner hour, and they walked over to Scoma's on Fisherman's Wharf for crab cioppino.

Somehow it all seemed so natural, as if they had shared meals like this countless times before. In reality, they had had a strictly professional relationship which had in no way splashed over the formal patient-therapist boundary. They had learned to know each other in weekly segments of precisely fifty minutes, no more, no less.

But that evening, for reasons Thelma, even now, cannot comprehend, she and Matthew slipped outside everyday reality. Neither looked at the time; they silently colluded in pretending that there was nothing unusual about talking personally or sharing coffee or dinner. It seemed natural for her to adjust the crumpled collar of his shirt, to brush the lint from his jacket, to take his arm as they climbed Nob Hill. It seemed natural for Matthew to describe his new "pad" in the Haight, and so very natural for Thelma to say she was dying to see it. They had chuckled when Thelma said that her husband was out of town: Harry, a member of the advisory board of the Boy Scouts of America, spoke at Boy Scout functions somewhere in America almost every night of the week. Matthew was amused that nothing had changed; there was no need to explain anything to him—after all, he knew everything about her.

"I don't remember," Thelma continued, "much about the rest of the evening, about how things happened, about who touched who first, about how we decided to go to bed. We didn't make any decisions, everything just happened effortlessly and spontaneously. What I do remember most clearly was that lying in Matthew's arms was transporting—one of the greatest moments in my life."

"Tell me about what happened next."

"The next twenty-seven days, June 19 to July 16, were magical. We spoke on the phone several times a day and saw one another fourteen times. I floated, I glided, I danced."

Thelma's voice had a lilt to it now, and she rocked her head in rhythm to a melody of eight years past. Her eyes were almost closed, sorely trying my patience. I don't like to feel invisible.

"That was the peak of my life. I have never before or since been so happy. Whatever has happened since then can never erase what he gave me then."

"What *has* happened since then?"

"The last time I saw him was at twelve-thirty p.m. on July 16. For two days I hadn't been able to reach him on the phone, so I popped in unannounced at his office. He was eating a sandwich and had about twenty minutes before he had to lead a therapy group. I asked about why he hadn't returned my calls and he said simply, 'It's not right, we both know it.'" She paused and wept silently.

A great time for him to discover that it's not right, I thought. "Can you go on?"

"I asked him, 'Suppose I call you next year or in five years? Would you see me? Could we take another walk across the Golden Gate Bridge? Would I be allowed to hug you?' Matthew answered my questions by taking my hand, pulling me into his lap, and hugging me tightly for several minutes.

"I've called him countless times since and left messages on his tape machine. At first he returned some of my calls, but then I stopped hearing from him at all. He cut me off. Complete silence."

Thelma turned away and looked out the window. The lilt was gone from her voice. She was speaking more deliberately, in a bitter, forlorn tone, but there were no more tears. I thought that now she was closer to ripping or gouging than to crying.

"I never could find out *why*—*why* it was over, just like that. In one of our last talks he said that we have to return to our real lives, and then added that he was involved with a new person." I suspected, silently, that the new person in Matthew's life was another patient.

Thelma wasn't sure whether the new person was a man or a woman. She suspected Matthew was gay: he lived in one of San Francisco's gay enclaves, and was beautiful in the way many gay men are, with his neatly combed mustache, boyish face, and Mercury-like body. This possibility occurred to her a couple of years later when, while taking an out-of-town guest sightseeing, she warily entered a gay bar on Castro Street and was astounded to see fifteen Matthews sitting at the bar—fifteen slim, attractive, neatly mustached young men.

To be suddenly cut off from Matthew was devastating; and not to know *why*, unbearable. Thelma thought about him continuously, not an hour passing without some prolonged fantasy about him. She became obsessed with *why? Why* had he rejected her and cast her out? *Why* then? *Why* would he not see her or even speak to her on the phone?

Thelma grew deeply despondent after all attempts to contact Matthew failed. She stayed home all day staring out the window; she could not sleep; her movements and speech slowed down; she lost her enthusiasm for any activities. She stopped eating, and soon her depression had passed beyond the reach of psychotherapy or antidepressive medication. By consulting three different doctors for her insomnia and obtaining from each a prescription for sleeping medication, she soon collected a lethal amount. Precisely six months after her chance meeting with Matthew in Union Square, she left a goodbye note to her husband, Harry, who was out of town for the week, waited until his goodnight phone call from the East Coast, took the phone off the hook, swallowed all the tablets, and went to bed.

Harry, unable to sleep that night, phoned Thelma back and grew alarmed at the continual busy signal. He called his neighbors, who banged, in vain, on Thelma's door and windows. Soon they called the police, who stormed into the house to find her close to death.

Thelma's life was saved only by heroic medical efforts. The first call she made upon regaining consciousness was to Matthew's tape machine. She assured him she would keep their secret and pleaded with him to visit her in the hospital. Matthew came to visit but stayed only fifteen minutes and his presence, Thelma said, was worse than his silence: he evaded any allusions she made to their twenty-seven days of love and insisted on remaining formal and professional. Only once did he step out of role: when Thelma asked him how the relationship with the new person in his life was going, Matthew snapped, "You have no need to know that!"

"And that was that!" Thelma turned her face directly toward me for the first time and added, in a resigned, weary voice, "I've never seen him again. I call to leave taped messages for him on important dates: his birthday, June 19 (our first date), July 17 (our last date), Christmas, and New Year's. Every time I switch therapists, I call to let him know. He never calls back.

"For eight years I haven't stopped thinking about him. At seven in the morning I wonder if he's awake yet, and at eight I imagine him eating his oatmeal (he loves oatmeal—he grew up on a Nebraska farm). I keep looking for him when I walk down the street. I often mistakenly think I see him, and rush up to greet some stranger. I dream about him. I replay in my mind each of our meetings together during those twenty-seven days. In fact, most of my life goes on in these daydreams—I scarcely take note of what's happening in the present. My life is being lived eight years ago."

*My life is being lived eight years ago*—an arresting phrase. I stored it for future use.

"Tell me about the therapy you've had in the last eight years—since your suicide attempt."

"During that time I've never been without a therapist. They gave me lots of antidepressants, which don't do much except allow me to sleep. Not much other therapy has gone on. Talking treatments have never helped. I guess you could say I didn't give therapy much chance since I made a decision to protect Matthew by never mentioning him or my affair to any other therapist."

"You mean that in *eight years* of therapy you've never talked about Matthew!"

Bad technique! A beginner's error—but I could not suppress my astonishment. A scene I hadn't thought of in decades entered my mind: I was a student in a medical school interviewing class. A well-meaning but blustering and insensitive student (later, mercifully, to become an orthopedic surgeon) was conducting an interview before his classmates and attempting to use the early Rogerian technique of coaxing the patient along by repeating the patient's words, usually the last word of the statement. The patient, who had been enumerating ghastly deeds committed by his tyrannical father, ended by commenting, "And he eats raw hamburger!" The interviewer, who had struggled hard to maintain his neutrality, was no longer able to contain his outrage, and bellowed back, "*Raw hamburger?*" For the rest of that year, the phrase "raw hamburger" was often whispered in lectures and invariably cracked up the class.

I, of course, kept my reverie to myself. "But today, you've made a decision to come to see me and to be honest about yourself. Tell me about that decision."

"I checked you out. I called five former therapists and told them I was going to give therapy one last chance and asked them who I should see. Your name appeared on four of their lists—they said you were a good 'last ditch' therapist. So that was one thing in your favor. But I also knew they were your former students, so I checked you out some more. I went to the library and checked out one of your books. I was impressed by two things: you were clear—I could understand your writing—and you were willing to speak openly about death. And I'm going to be open with you: I'm almost certain I will eventually commit suicide. I'm here to make one final attempt in therapy to find a way to live with some iota of happiness. If not, I hope you'll help me die and help me find a way to cause as little pain as possible to my family."

I told Thelma that I thought we could work together, but I suggested we have another consultation hour to consider things further and also to let her assess whether she could work with me. I was going to say more when Thelma looked at her watch and said, "I see that my fifty minutes are up and, if nothing else, I've learned not to overstay my welcome in therapy."

I was musing on the tone of this final comment—not quite sardonic, not quite coquettish—when Thelma got up, telling me on her way out that she would schedule the next hour with my secretary.

After this session I had much to think about. First, there was Matthew. He infuriated me. I've seen too many patients badly damaged by therapists using them sexually. It's *always* damaging to a patient.

Therapists' excuses are invariably patent and self-serving rationalizations—for example, that the therapist is accepting and affirming the patient's sexuality. While plenty of patients may need sexual affirmation—those who are markedly unattractive, extremely obese, surgically disfigured—I have yet to hear of a therapist affirming one of *them* sexually. It's always the attractive woman who gets chosen for affirmation. It is, of course, the offending therapists who are in need of sexual affirmation and lack the resources or resourcefulness to obtain it in their own personal lives.

But Matthew presented somewhat of an enigma. When he seduced Thelma (or permitted himself to be seduced—same thing), he had just finished graduate school and thus must have been in his late twenties or early thirties. So *why*? Why does an attractive, presumably accomplished young man select a sixty-two-year-old woman who has been lifeless and depressed for many years? I thought about Thelma's speculation that he was gay. Perhaps the most reasonable hypothesis was that Matthew was working on (or acting out) some personal psychosexual issues—and using his patient(s) to do it.

It's precisely for this reason that we urge trainees to be in prolonged personal therapy. But today, with brief training courses, less

supervision, a relaxation of training standards and licensure require-
ments, therapists often refuse, and many patients have suffered from
a therapist's lack of self-knowledge. I feel little charity for the irresponsible professionals and have urged many patients to report sexually offending therapists to professional ethics boards. I considered,
momentarily, what recourse I had with Matthew, but supposed he was
beyond the statute of limitations. Still, I wanted him to know about
the damage he had done.

I turned my attention to Thelma and dismissed, for the time being,
the question of Matthew's motivation. But I was to struggle with that
question many times before the dénouement of this therapy, and could
not have guessed then that, of all the riddles in the case of Thelma, it
was the riddle of Matthew I was destined to solve most fully.

I was struck by the tenacity of her love obsession, which had pos-
sessed her for eight years with no external reinforcement. The obsession filled her entire life space. She was right: she *was* living her life
eight years ago. The obsession must draw part of its strength from the
impoverishment of the rest of her existence. I doubted whether it
would be possible to separate her from her obsession without first
helping her to enrich other realms of her life.

I wondered about the amount of intimacy in her daily life. From
what she had so far told me of her marriage, there was apparently little
closeness between her and her husband. Perhaps the function of the
obsession was simply to provide intimacy: it bonded her to another—
but not to a real person, to a fantasy.

My best hope might be to establish a close, meaningful relationship
between the two of us and then use that relationship as a solvent in
which to dissolve her obsession. But that would not be easy. Her account of therapy was chilling. Imagine being in therapy for eight years
and not talking about the real problem! That takes a special type of
person, someone who can tolerate considerable duplicity, someone
who embraces intimacy in fantasy but may avoid it in life.

Thelma began the next session by telling me that it had been an
awful week. Therapy always presented a paradox for her. "I know I need

to be seen, I can't manage without it. And yet every time I talk about what's happened, I have a miserable week. Therapy sessions always just stir the pot. They never resolve anything—they always make things worse."

I didn't like the sound of that. Were these previews of coming attractions? Was Thelma telling me why she would ultimately leave therapy?

"This week has been one long crying jag. Matthew's been on my mind nonstop. I can't talk to Harry because I've got only two things on my mind—Matthew and suicide—and both topics are off limits.

"I will never, never talk about Matthew to my husband. Years ago I told him that I briefly saw Matthew once by chance. I must have talked too much because later Harry stated that he believed that Matthew was in some way responsible for my suicide attempt. If he ever were to know the truth, I honestly believe he would kill Matthew. Harry is full of Boy Scout honor slogans—the Boy Scouts, that's all he thinks about—but underneath he's a violent man. He was a British commando officer during the Second World War and specialized in teaching methods of hand-to-hand killing."

"Tell me some more about Harry." I was struck by the vehemence in Thelma's voice when she said that Harry would kill Matthew if he knew about what had happened.

"I met Harry in the thirties when I was dancing professionally on the Continent. I've always lived for two things only: making love and dancing. I refused to stop dancing to have children, but I was forced to stop thirty-one years ago because I got gout in my large toe—not a good disease for a ballerina. As for love, when I was younger I had many, many lovers. You saw that picture of me—be honest, tell the truth, was I not beautiful?" She continued, without waiting for my response. "But once I married Harry, love was over. Very few men (though there were some) were brave enough to love me—everyone was terrified of Harry. And Harry gave up sex twenty years ago (he's good at giving things up). We hardly ever touch now—probably my fault as much as his."

I was about to ask about Harry being good at giving things up, but Thelma raced on. She wanted to talk, yet still without seeming to be talking to me. She gave no evidence of wanting a response from me. Her gaze was averted. Usually she looked upward, as though lost in recollection.

"The other thing I think about, but can't talk about, is suicide. Sooner or later I know that I will do it, it's the only way out. But I never breathe a word of this to Harry. It almost killed him when I attempted suicide. He suffered a small stroke and aged ten years right before my eyes. When, to my surprise, I woke up alive in the hospital, I did a lot of thinking about what I had done to my family. Then and there I made some resolutions."

"What sort of resolutions?" No real need for my question, since Thelma had been on the verge of describing the resolutions, but I had to have some exchange with her. I was getting plenty of information, but we were not making contact. We might as well have been in separate rooms.

"I resolved never to say or do anything which could possibly cause Harry pain. I resolved to give him everything, to give in to him on every issue. He wants to build a new room for his exercise equipment—O.K. He wants Mexico for vacation—O.K. He wants to meet people at church socials—O.K."

Noticing my quizzical look about church socials, Thelma explained, "For the last three years, ever since I knew I would eventually commit suicide, I haven't wanted to meet anyone new. New friends only mean more farewells to say and more people to hurt."

I have worked with many people who have truly tried to kill themselves; but usually their experience is in some way transformational, and they ripen into new maturity and new wisdom. A real confrontation with death usually causes one to question with real seriousness the goals and conduct of one's life up to then. So also with those who confront death through a fatal illness: how many people have lamented, "What a pity I had to wait till now, when my body is riddled with cancer, to know how to live!" Yet Thelma was different. Rarely have I encountered anyone who came so close to death yet learned so little from it. Those resolutions she made when she regained consciousness after her overdose: Could she really believe that she would make Harry happy by rubber-stamping his every request and keeping her own wishes and thoughts concealed? And what could be worse for Harry than for his wife to cry last week and share nothing with him? This was a woman steeped in self-deception.

Her self-deception was particularly evident when she discussed Matthew. "He has a gentleness about him that touches the life of everyone who comes into contact with him. The secretaries all loved him. He said something caring to each of them, he knew all their children's names, he brought in doughnuts for them three or four mornings a week. Whenever we went out during the twenty-seven days, he never failed to say something that would make the waiter or the store clerk feel good. Do you know anything about Buddhist meditation practice?"

"Well, yes, as a matter of fact, I—" But Thelma didn't wait to hear the rest of my sentence.

"Then you know about 'loving-kindness' meditation. He did that twice a day and taught me the practice as well. That's exactly why I would never, not in a hundred years, dream that he would treat me like this. His silence is killing me. Sometimes when I get deep into thought, I feel that it would not be possible for him—the person who taught me to be open—to devise a more terrible punishment than total silence. More and more these days"—here Thelma lowered her voice almost to a whisper—"I believe he is intentionally trying to drive me to suicide. Does that sound like a crazy thought?"

"I don't know if it's crazy, but it sounds like a desperate and terribly painful thought."

"He's trying to drive me to suicide. I'd be out of his hair for good. It's the only possible explanation!"

"Yes, thinking that, you have still protected him all these years. Why?"

"Because, more than anything in the world, I want Matthew to think well of me. I don't want to jeopardize my only chance for some kind of happiness!"

"But Thelma, it's been *eight* years. You haven't heard from him for *eight years!*"

"But there's a chance—a small one. But a two-percent or even a one-percent chance is better than no chance at all. I don't expect Matthew to love me again, I just want him to care about my being on this planet. It's not too much to ask—when we walked in Golden Gate Park, he almost sprained his ankle trying to avoid disturbing an anthill. Surely he can send some of that loving-kindness my way!"

So much inconsistency, so much anger, almost mockery, standing cheek by jowl with such reverence. Though I was gradually entering her experiential world and growing accustomed to hyperbolic assessments of Matthew, I was truly staggered by her next comment.

"If he would call me once a year, talk to me for even five minutes, ask about me, show me his concern, then I could live happily. Is that too much to ask?"

Never had I encountered one person giving another more power. Imagine—she claimed that one five-minute phone call a year would cure her. I wondered whether it would. I remember thinking that if everything else failed, I wasn't beyond trying to set up that experiment! I recognized that the chances for success in therapy were not good: Thelma's self-deception, her lack of psychological mindedness, her resistance to introspection, her suicidality—all signalled, "Be careful!"

Yet her problem fascinated me. Her love obsession—what else could one call it?—was powerful and tenacious, having dominated eight years of her life. Still, the roots of the obsession seemed extraordinarily friable. A little effort, a little ingenuity should suffice to yank the whole weed out. And then? Underneath obsession, what would I find? Would I discover the brutal facts of human experience that the enchantment concealed? Then I might really learn something about the function of love. Medical researchers discovered, in the early days of nineteenth-century medical research, that the best way to understand the purpose of an endocrine organ is to remove it and observe the subsequent physiological functioning of the laboratory animal. Though I was chilled by the inhumaneness of my metaphor, I wondered: *Might not the same principle hold here?* So far it was apparent that Thelma's love for Matthew was, in reality, something else—perhaps an escape, a shield against aging and isolation. There was little of Matthew in it, nor—if love is a caring, giving, need-free relationship—much love.

Other prognostic signs clamored for my attention, but I chose to ignore them. I could have, for example, given more serious consideration to Thelma's *twenty years* of psychiatric care! When I was a student at the Johns Hopkins Psychiatric Clinic, the staff had many "back room" indices of chronicity. One of the most irreverent of these was poundage: the heavier the patient's clinical chart, the worse the prognosis. Thelma would have been a seventy-year-old "ten pounder" at least, and no one, absolutely no one, would have recommended psychotherapy.

As I look back on my state of mind at that time, I realize that I simply rationalized away these concerns.

Twenty years of therapy? Well, the last eight can't be counted as therapy because of Thelma's secretiveness. No therapy has a chance if the patient conceals the main issues.

The ten years of therapy before Matthew? Well, that was a long time ago! Besides, most of her therapists were young trainees. Surely, I could offer her more. Thelma and Harry, with limited financial means, had never been able to afford to see anyone other than student therapists. But I was currently funded by a research institute to study the psychotherapy of the elderly and could see Thelma for a minimal fee. Surely this was an unusual opportunity for her to obtain therapy from an experienced clinician.

My real reasons for taking on Thelma lay elsewhere: first, I was fascinated by encountering a love obsession at once deeply rooted and in a vulnerable, exposed state, and I was not to be swayed from digging it out and investigating it; second, I was afflicted by what I now recognize

as hubris—I belived that I could help any patient, that no one was beyond my skills. The pre-Socratics defined *hubris* as "insubordination to
divine law"; I was insubordinate, of course, not to divine law but to natural law, the laws that govern the flow of events in my professional field.
I think I had a premonition at the time that, before my work with
Thelma was over, I would be called to account for hubris.

At the end of our second hour, I discussed a treatment contract
with Thelma. She had made it clear that she would not commit herself
to long-term treatment; and, besides, I thought that I should know
within six months whether I could help her. So we agreed to meet once
a week for six months (with the possibility of a six-month extension,
if we thought it necessary). Her commitment was to attend regularly
and to participate in a psychotherapy research project, which entailed
a research interview and a battery of psychological tests to measure
outcome, to be completed twice, at the beginning of therapy and six
months after termination.

I took pains to inform her that therapy would undoubtedly be unsettling, and attempted to get her to promise to stick with it.

"Thelma, this continual rumination about Matthew—for shorthand,
let's call it an obsession——"

"Those twenty-seven days were a great gift," she said, bristling.
"That's one of the reasons I haven't talked about them to other therapists—I don't want them to be treated as a disease."

"No, Thelma, I'm not talking about eight years ago. I'm talking
about now and about how you cannot live life because you continually
replay past history over and over. I thought you came to see me because you wanted to stop tormenting yourself."

She sighed, closed her eyes, and nodded. She had given me the
warning she wanted, and now she leaned back in her chair.

"What I was going to say was that this obsession—let's find a better
word if *obsession* offends you——"

"No, it's O.K. I understand what you're saying now."

"Well, this obsession has been a central part of your mind for eight
years. It'll be difficult to dislodge it. I'll need to challenge some of your

beliefs, and therapy might be stressful. I need your commitment to hang in there with me."

"You have it. When I make a resolution, I never go back on it."

"Also, Thelma, I can't work well with a suicide threat hanging over-head. I need a solemn promise from you that for the next six months you will do nothing physically self-destructive. If you feel on the verge, call me. Phone me at any time and I'll be there for you. But if you make any attempt—no matter how slight—then our contract is broken, and I will not continue to work with you. Often I put this down on paper and ask for a signature, but I respect your claim to always honor your resolutions."

To my surprise, Thelma shook her head. "There is no way I can promise you this. I get into moods when I know it's the only way out. I'm not going to close off this option."

"I'm talking about the next six months only. I'm not asking for any longer commitment, but I won't start without this. Do you want to think some more about it, Thelma, and we'll schedule another meeting next week?"

She immediately became conciliatory. I don't think she had ex-pected me to take such a firm stand. Even though she gave no evidence of it, I believe she was relieved.

"I can't wait another week. I want us to make a decision now and to start therapy right away. I'll agree to do my best."

"Do my best"—I didn't feel that this was enough, yet hesitated to get into a control struggle so quickly. So I said nothing but simply raised my eyebrows.

After a minute or a minute and a half (a long silence in therapy), Thelma stood up, offered me her hand, and said, "You have my promise."

Next week we commenced our work. I decided to maintain a sharp focus on relevant and immediate issues. Thelma had had suffi-cient time (twenty years of therapy!) to explore her developmental years; and the last thing I wanted to focus on were events dating back sixty years.

She was highly ambivalent about therapy: although she regarded it as her only hope, she never had a satisfying session. Over the first ten weeks I learned that, if we analyzed her feelings toward Matthew, her obsession tormented her for the next week. If, on the other hand, we explored other themes, even such important issues as her relationship with Harry, she considered the session a waste of time because we had ignored the major problem of Matthew.

As a result of her discontent, our time together became ungratifying for me as well. I learned not to expect any personal rewards from my work with Thelma. I never experienced pleasure from being in her presence and, as early as the third or fourth session, realized that any gratification for me in this therapy would have to issue from the intellectual realm.

Most of our time together we devoted to Matthew. I inquired about the precise content of her daydreams, and Thelma seemed to enjoy talking about them. The ruminations were highly repetitious: most were a fairly faithful replay of any one of their meetings during the twenty-seven days. The most common was their first encounter—the chance meeting in Union Square, the coffee at the St. Francis, the walk to Fisherman's Wharf, the view of the bay from Scoma's restaurant, the excitement of the drive to Matthew's "pad"; but often she simply thought of one of his loving phone conversations.

Sex played a minor role in these thoughts: rarely did she experience any sexual arousal. In fact, though there had been considerable sexual caressing during her twenty-seven days with Matthew, they had had intercourse only once, the first evening. They had attempted intercourse two other times, but Matthew was impotent. I was becoming more convinced that my hunch about his behavior was correct: namely, that he had major psychosexual problems which he had acted out on Thelma (and probably other unfortunate patients).

There were so many rich leads that it was hard to select and concentrate on one. First, however, it was necessary to establish to Thelma's satisfaction that the obsession had to be eradicated. For a love obsession drains life of its reality, obliterating new experience, both good and bad—as I know from my own life. Indeed, most of my deeply held beliefs about therapy, and my areas of keenest psycholog-ical interest, have arisen from personal experience. Nietzsche claimed that a philosopher's system of thought always arises from his autobi-ography, and I believe that to be true for all therapists—in fact, for anyone who thinks about thought.

At a conference approximately two years prior to meeting Thelma, I had encountered a woman who subsequently invaded my mind, my thoughts, my dreams. Her image took up housekeeping in my mind and defied all my efforts to dislodge it. But, for a time, that was all right: I liked the obsession and savored it afresh again and again. A few weeks later, I went on a week's vacation with my family to a beautiful Caribbean island. It was only after several days that I realized I was missing everything on the trip—the beauty of the beach, the lush and exotic vegetation, even the thrill of snorkeling and entering the un-derwater world. All this rich reality had been blotted out by my ob-session. I had been absent. I had been encased in my mind, watching replays over and over again of the same and, by then, pointless fantasy. Anxious and thoroughly fed up with myself, I entered therapy (yet again), and after several hard months, my mind was my own again and I was able to return to the exciting business of experiencing my life *as it was happening.* (A curious thing: my therapist eventually became a close friend and years later told me that, at the time he was treating me, he himself was obsessed with a lovely Italian woman whose attention was riveted to someone else. And so, from patient to therapist to patient goes *La Ronde* of obsessional love.)

So, in my work with Thelma, I stressed to her how her obsession was vitiating her life, and often repeated her earlier comment that she was living her life eight years before. No wonder she hated being alive! Her life was being stifled in an airless, windowless chamber ventilated only by those long-gone twenty-seven days.

But Thelma never found this thesis persuasive—with, I now think, good reason. Generalizing from my experience to hers, I had mistak-enly assumed her life to have richness that she was missing because of her obsession. Thelma felt, though she did not explicitly say so at the time, that the obsession contained infinitely more vitality than her lived experience. (Later we were to explore, also with minimal impact, the reverse of that formula—that it was *because* of the impoverishment of her life that she embraced the obsession in the first place.)

By approximately the sixth session, I had worn her down and—to humor me, I believe—she agreed that the obsession was the enemy and had to be extirpated. We spent session after session simply reconnoitering the obsession. It seemed to me that the source of its hold on her was the power she had given Matthew. Nothing could be done until we diminished that power.

"Thelma, this feeling that the only thing that matters is for Matthew to think well of you—tell me everything you know about it."

"It's hard to put into words. The idea of him hating me is unbearable. He's the one person who has ever known *everything* about me. So the fact that he could still love me, despite everything he knew, meant so much."

This, I thought, is precisely the reason therapists should not become emotionally involved with patients. By virtue of their privileged role, their access to deep feelings and secret information, their reactions always assume larger-than-life meanings. It is almost impossible for patients to see therapists as they really are. My anger toward Matthew grew.

"But, Thelma, he's just a person. You haven't seen him for eight years. What *difference* does it make what he thinks of you?"

"I can't tell you why. I know it doesn't make sense but, to the bottom of my soul, I believe that I'd be all right, I'd be happy, if he thought well of me."

This thought, this core false belief, was the enemy. I had to dislodge it. I made an impassioned plea.

"You are you, you have your own existence, you continue to be the person you are from moment to moment, from day to day. Basically your existence is impervious to the fleeting thoughts, to the electro-

magnetic ripples occurring in some unknown mind. Try to see that. All
this power that Matthew has—you've given it to him—every bit of it!"

"I get sick in my stomach at the thought of his despising me."

"What goes on in another person's mind, someone you never even
see, who probably isn't even aware of your existence, who is caught
up in his own life struggles, doesn't change the person you are."

"Oh, he's aware of my existence, all right. I leave a lot of messages
on his telephone-answering tape. In fact, I left a message last week to
let him know I was seeing you. I think he ought to know that I'm talking
about him to you. Over the years I've always called him whenever I've
changed therapists."

"But I thought you did not discuss him with all these therapists."

"I didn't. I promised him that, even though he never asked it, and
I kept that promise—until now. Even though I didn't talk about him
all those years, I still thought he should know which therapist I was
seeing. Many of them were from his school. They might have even
been his friends."

Because of my vindictive feelings toward Matthew, I was not displeased with Thelma's words. On the contrary, I was amused when I
imagined his discomfiture over the years when listening to Thelma's
ostensibly solicitous messages on his tape. I began to relinquish my
ideas of striking back at Matthew. This lady knew how to punish him
and needed no help from me in that task.

"But, Thelma, go back to what I was saying earlier. Can't you see
that you're doing this to yourself? His thoughts really can't change the
kind of person you are. You *let* him influence you. He's just a person
like you or me. If *you* think poorly of a person with whom you never
have any contact, will *your* thoughts—those mental images circulating
in your brain and known only to you—affect *that* person? The only
way that can happen is through voodoo influence. Why do you surrender your power to Matthew? He's a person like anyone else, he
struggles to live, he'll age, he'll fart, he'll die."

No response from Thelma. I upped the ante.

"You said before that one could hardly have deliberately designed behavior more likely to hurt you. You've thought that maybe he was trying to drive you to suicide. He is not interested in your welfare. So what sense does it make to elevate him so? To believe that nothing in life is more important than that he think well of you?"

"I don't really believe he's trying to drive me to suicide. It's just a thought I have sometimes. I flip back and forth quickly in my feelings about Matthew. Most of the time what's important is that he would wish me well."

"But why is his wish so all-important? You've elevated him to a superhuman position. Yet he seems to be a particularly screwed-up person. You yourself mention his significant sexual problems. Look at the whole issue of integrity—at his code of ethics. He's violated the basic code of any helping profession. Look at the distress he's caused you. We both know it is simply wrong for a professional therapist, who is sworn to act in the best interests of his patient, to hurt anyone the way he has hurt you."

But I might as well have been talking to the wind.

"It was only *when* he started acting professionally, *when* he went back into a formal role, that he hurt me. When we were simply two human beings in love he gave me the most precious gift in the world."

It was deeply frustrating. *Obviously*, Thelma was responsible for her own life predicament. *Obviously*, it was a fiction that Matthew had any real power over her. *Obviously*, she gave him that power in an effort to deny her own freedom and her responsibility for the constitution of her own life. Far from wanting to take back her freedom from Matthew, she had a lust for submission.

From the beginning, of course, I had known that the pure forcefulness of my argument would not penetrate deep enough to effect any change. It almost never does. It's never worked for me when I've been in therapy. Only when one feels an insight *in one's bones* does one own it. Only then can one act on it and change. Pop psychologists forever talk about "responsibility assumption," but it's all words: it is extraordinarily hard, even terrifying, to own the insight that you and only you construct your own life design. Thus, the problem in therapy is always how to move from an ineffectual intellectual appreciation of a truth about oneself to some emotional *experience* of it. It is only when therapy enlists deep emotions that it becomes a powerful force for change.

And powerlessness was the problem in my therapy with Thelma. My attempts to generate power were shamefully inelegant and consisted mainly of fumbling, nagging, and repetitively circling her obsession and bashing away at it.

How I long at such junctures for the certainty that orthodoxy offers. Psychoanalysis, to take the most catholic of the psychotherapy ideological schools, always posits such strong convictions about the necessary technical procedures—indeed, analysts seem more certain of *everything* than I am of *anything*. How comforting it would be to feel, just once, that I know exactly what I'm doing in my psychotherapeutic work—for example, that I am dutifully traversing, in proper sequence, the precise stages of the therapeutic process.

But, of course, it is all illusion. If they are helpful to patients at all, ideological schools with their complex metaphysical edifices succeed because they assuage the *therapist's*, not the patient's, anxiety (and thus permit the therapist to face the anxiety of the therapeutic process). The more the therapist is able to tolerate the anxiety of not knowing, the less need there is for the therapist to embrace orthodoxy. The creative members of an orthodoxy, *any* orthodoxy, ultimately outgrow their disciplines.

Though there is something reassuring about an omniscient therapist who is always in control of every situation, there can be something powerfully engaging about a fumbling therapist, a therapist willing to flounder with the patient until they, together, stumble upon an enabling discovery. Alas, however, as Thelma was to teach me before this case was over, much wonderful therapy may be wasted on a patient!

In my search for power, I pushed to the limits. I tried to rattle and shock her.

"Suppose, for a moment, that Matthew died! Would that release you?"

"I've tried to imagine that. When I imagine him dead, a great sadness descends. I'd be living in an empty world. I never can think past that."

"How can you release yourself from this? How could you be released? Could Matthew release you? Have you ever imagined a conversation in which he releases you?"

Thelma smiled at this question. She looked at me with what I imagined to be more respect—as though she were impressed with my mind-reading abilities. I had obviously tapped into an important fantasy.

"Often, very often."

"Share it with me. How would it go?" I don't rely on role-playing or chair-switching, but this seemed the perfect place for it. "Let's try role-playing it. Would you move to the other chair, play the role of Matthew, and talk to Thelma here in this chair?"

Since Thelma had opposed everything else I suggested, I was preparing my argument to convince her when, to my surprise, she enthusiastically agreed. Perhaps, in her twenty years of therapy, she had worked with gestalt therapists who had employed these techniques; perhaps it was her stage experience shining through. She almost leaped out of her chair, cleared her voice, pantomimed putting on a necktie and buttoning a suit jacket, assumed a saintly smile and a delightfully exaggerated expression of benevolent magnanimity, cleared her voice, sat down in the other chair, and became Matthew.

"Thelma, I came to you remembering you pleasantly from the work we did together in therapy and wanting you as a friend. I enjoyed the give-and-take. I enjoyed the joking about your shitty habits. I was truthful. I meant the things I said to you, every one of them. And then an event occurred which I chose not to tell you about and which caused me to change my mind. It was nothing that you did—there was nothing about you that was obnoxious, although we didn't have enough to build a lasting relationship. What happened was that a woman, Sonia——"

Here Thelma broke role for a minute and said in a loud stage whisper, "Dr. Yalom, Sonia was my stage name when I was a dancer."

She became Matthew again and continued. "This woman, Sonia, entered on the scene, and I realized that a life with her was the proper way for me. I tried to stay away, tried to tell you to quit calling, and—I'll be honest—it annoyed me that you wouldn't. After your suicide attempt, I knew I had to be very careful with what I said, and *that's* why I became so distant. I saw a shrink, and it was *he* who advised complete silence. You are someone I'd love to have as a friend, but there is no way to do it on an open basis. There is your Harry, and there is my Sonia."

She stopped and sank into her chair. Her shoulders slumped, her benevolent smile vanished, and, entirely spent, she became Thelma again.

We sat in silence together. As I thought about the words she'd put in Matthew's mouth, I could easily understand their appeal and why she had no doubt replayed them so often: they confirmed her view of reality, they absolved Matthew of any responsibility (after all, it was his shrink who advised him to be silent), and they confirmed that there was nothing wrong with her or incongruous about their relationship; it was only that Matthew had a greater obligation to another. That the other woman was Sonia, herself as a young woman, suggested I needed to spend more time looking at Thelma's feelings about her age.

I was fascinated with the idea of release. *Would those words from Matthew really release her?* There flashed into my mind an interaction with a patient from my first year of residency (these first clinical experiences stay with one, as through an imprinting in one's professional infancy). The patient, who was very paranoid, insisted that I was not Dr. Yalom but an FBI agent, and demanded proof of my identification. When, at the next session, I artlessly presented him with my birth certificate, driver's license, and passport, he announced that I had proved him correct: only FBI connections could have produced forgeries so quickly. If a system is infinitely expanding, one cannot *not* be encircled by it.

Not, of course, that Thelma was paranoid, but I wondered whether she, too, would defeat any releasing statements, even ones from Matthew, by infinitely demanding more proof and reassurance. Nonetheless, in looking back over this case, I believe that it was at this moment that I first began to consider seriously whether to involve Matthew in the therapy process—not her idealized Matthew, but the real-life, flesh-and-blood Matthew.

"How do you feel about the role-playing, Thelma? What did it stir up in you?"

"I felt like an idiot! It's ridiculous for someone of my age to act like a foolish adolescent."

"Is there a question in there for me? Do you think I feel that way about you?"

"To be honest, that's another reason (in addition to my promise to Matthew) that I haven't talked about him to therapists or anyone else. I know they'll say that it's an infatuation or a crush or transference. 'Everybody falls in love with their therapist'—I can hear it now. Or else they'll talk about it as—what is it called when the therapist transfers something to the patient?"

"Countertransference."

"Yes, countertransference. In fact, you were suggesting that last week when you talked about Matthew 'working out' his personal problems in his therapy with me. I'll be frank (like you tell me to be in therapy): that grates on me. It's as though I didn't matter, as though I were some innocent bystander in something he was playing out with his mother."

I held my tongue. She was right; those were exactly my thoughts. You and Matthew *are* both "innocent bystanders." Neither of you were really relating to the other but to some fantasy of the other. You fell in love with Matthew because of what he represented to you: someone who would love you totally and unconditionally; who would be entirely devoted to your welfare, to your comfort and growth; who would undo your aging and love you as the young, beautiful Sonia; who provided you the opportunity to escape the pain of being separate and offered you the bliss of selfless merger. You may have been "in love," but one thing's for sure: you didn't love Matthew; you have never known Matthew.

And Matthew? Who or what was he loving? I didn't know yet, but I didn't think he was either "in love" *or* loving. He wasn't loving you, Thelma, he was using you. He had no genuine care for Thelma, for the flesh-and-blood Thelma! Your comment about his playing something out with his mother probably isn't a bad guess.

As though she were reading my mind, Thelma continued, lifting her chin and projecting her words as to a large audience. "When people think that we really hadn't loved one another, it belittles the love that we had. It takes away the depth—it makes it into nothing. The love was, and is, *real. Nothing has ever been more real to me.* Those twenty-seven days were the high point of my life. Those were twenty-seven days of paradise, and I'd give anything to have them back!"

A powerful lady, I thought. She had drawn the line effectively:

"Don't take away the high point of my life. Don't take away the only real thing that has ever happened to me." Who could bear to do that to *anyone,* much less a depressed, suicidal, seventy-year-old woman?

But I had no intention of being blackmailed in that fashion. To yield to her now would render me absolutely ineffective. So I continued in a matter-of-fact tone. "Tell me about the euphoria, all that you remember."

"It was an out-of-the-body experience. I had no weight. It was as though I wasn't there, or at least the part of me that hurts and pulls me down. I just stopped thinking and worrying about me. I became a *we.*"

The lonely *I* ecstatically dissolving into the *we.* How often I've heard that! It's the common denominator of every form of bliss—romantic, sexual, political, religious, mystical. Everyone wants and welcomes this blissful merger. But it's different with Thelma—it's not that she *wants* it, but that she *has to have it in order to escape some danger.*

"That fits with what you told me about sex with Matthew—that it wasn't important that he be *in* you. What was important was that he connect or even fuse with you."

"That's right. That's what I meant when I said you were making too much out of the sexual relationship. Sex, itself, didn't play too important a role."

"This helps us understand the dream you had a couple of weeks ago."

Two weeks ago Thelma had reported an anxiety dream—the only dream she reported during the entire therapy:

*I was dancing with a large black man. Then he turned into Matthew. We were lying on the dance floor having sex. Just as I started to come, I whispered, "Kill me," into his ear. He vanished, and I was all alone on the dance floor.*

"It's as though you want to get rid of your separateness, to lose yourself (which the dream symbolizes by 'Kill me'), and Matthew is to be the instrument by which that happens. Any thoughts about this happening on a dance floor?"

"I said earlier that it was only those twenty-seven days that I ever felt euphoric. That's not entirely true. I often felt euphoric when I was dancing. Often everything disappeared then, me and everything else, there was just the dance and the moment. When I dance in my dreams, it means I'm trying to make everything that's bad disappear. I think it also means being young again."

"We've talked very little about your feelings about being seventy. How much do you think about it?"

"I guess I'd have a different slant on therapy if I were forty rather than seventy. I'd have something to look forward to. Wouldn't psychiatrists rather work with younger people?"

I knew that there was rich material here. I felt strongly that Thelma's fear of aging and death fueled her obsession. One of the reasons she wanted to merge in love, and be obliterated by it, was to escape the terror of facing obliteration by death. Nietszche said, "The final reward of the dead—to die no more." Yet here was also a wonderful opportunity to work on our relationship. Although the two themes we had been exploring (the flight from freedom and from the isolation of separateness) constituted, and would continue to constitute, the *content* of our discourse, I felt that my best chance to help Thelma lay in the development of a meaningful relationship with her. I hoped that the establishment of an intimate bond with me might sufficiently attenuate her bond with Matthew so that she could pry herself loose from him. Only then would we turn to the identification and removal of the obstacles that were preventing her from establishing intimate relationships in her social life.

"Thelma, when you ask whether psychiatry doesn't prefer to work with younger patients, it sounds to me that there is a personal question in there."

Thelma, as usual, avoided the personal. "It stands to reason that there is more to be gained in working with, say, a young mother with three children. She has her whole life ahead of her, and her improved mental condition would benefit her children and her children's children."

I persisted. "What I meant was that I thought there was a question, a personal question, you might be asking me, something involving you and me."

"Wouldn't psychiatrists rather treat a thirty-year-old patient than a seventy-year-old patient?"

"Can we focus on *you* and *me* rather than on *psychiatry, psychiatrists, and patients*? Aren't you asking this question: 'How do *you*, Irv'"— Thelma smiled here. She rarely addressed me by name, either given name or surname—"'feel about treating me, Thelma, a woman who is seventy years old?'"

No answer. She stared out the window. Her head shook ever so slightly. Damn, she was stubborn!

"Am I right? Is that the question?"

"That's *a* question, not necessarily *the* question. But if you had just answered my question the way I first put it, I would have gotten the answer to the question you just asked."

"You mean you would have learned my opinion about how psychiatry, in general, feels about the treatment of the average elderly patient, and then you would have assumed that that was the way I felt about treating you."

Thelma nodded.

"But that's so roundabout. And it may be inaccurate. My general comment may have been a guess about the whole field and not an expression of *my* personal feelings about *you*. What stops you from directly asking me the real question?"

"This is the kind of thing I worked on with Matthew. This is exactly what he called my shitty habits."

That gave me pause. Did I want to ally myself in any way with Matthew? Yet I was certain this was the correct trail to follow.

"Let me try to answer your questions—the general one you asked and the personal one you didn't. I'll start with the more general one. I, personally, like to work with older patients. As you know from all those questionnaires you filled out before we started, I'm in the midst of a research project and work with a lot of patients in their sixties and seventies. I'm learning that they do as well in therapy as younger patients, maybe better, and I get just as much gratification from the work.

"I appreciate your question about the young mother and her potential influence, but I see it differently. You, too, have much influence. All younger people with whom you come into contact will look upon you as a guide or model for their next stages of life. And from your individual standpoint, I believe it is possible at seventy to discover a new perspective that will permit you to flood retroactively, as it were, your whole earlier life with new meaning and significance. I know that that's difficult to see now—but, trust me, it often happens.

"Now let me answer the personal part of the question—how do *I* feel about working with *you*? I *want* to see you. I think I understand your pain, and I have a lot of empathy for it—I've experienced that kind of pain in the past myself. I'm interested in the problem you're struggling with, and I think I can help you. In fact, I'm committed to helping you. The hardest part for me in our work together is the frustration I have at the amount of distance you put between us. Earlier you said you can find out (or at least make a good guess about) the answer to a personal question by asking an impersonal one. But consider the effect of that on the other person. When you keep asking me impersonal questions, as you did a few minutes ago, I feel pushed away."

"This is exactly the sort of thing Matthew used to say."

I smiled and silently ground my teeth. I could think of nothing constructive to say. This frustrating, laborious interaction was prototypical. We were to have many similar exchanges.

It was hard and unrewarding work. Week after week I chipped away. I tried to teach her the ABCs of the language of intimacy: for example, how to use the pronouns *I* and *you*, how to identify feelings (starting with the difference between feelings and thoughts), how to "own" and to express feelings. I tutored her in the basic feelings (*bad, sad, mad,* and *glad*). I provided sentences to complete: for example, "Irv, when you say that, I feel _____ toward you."

She had an impressive repertory of distancing operations. She would, for example, introduce what she was about to say with a lengthy, boring preamble. When I pointed this out to her, she acknowledged that I was right, but then launched into an account of how, when someone asks her for the time, she gives a lecture on watchmaking. Several minutes later when she finished that anecdote (complete with a full historical account of how she and her sister first developed the habit of telling long tangential stories), we were hopelessly removed from our starting place and I had been effectively distanced.

On one occasion she acknowledged that she had a significant problem with expressing herself. She had been herself, in a fully spontaneous way, in only two situations in her adult life—when she danced and when she and Matthew had been in love for twenty-seven days. That's an important part of the reason Matthew's acceptance of her loomed so large: "He knew me as very few people ever have—as I really am, completely open, nothing held back."

When I asked about how we were doing today, or asked her to describe all the feelings she had experienced toward me in the session so far that day, she rarely responded. Usually she denied having any feelings, but sometimes she disarmed me completely by saying that she had felt very intimate that hour—an hour when I experienced her as particularly evasive and distant. Exploring the discrepancy in our views was treacherous because then she was likely to feel rebuffed.

As the evidence mounted that no meaningful relationship was developing between us, I felt baffled and rejected. Insofar as I could tell, I was making myself available to her. Yet she remained indifferent to me. I tried to raise this question with her but, no matter how I put it, I felt that I was whining, "Why don't you like me as much as Matthew?"

"You know, Thelma, there's something else going on alongside your letting Matthew's opinion of you mean everything, and that is you refuse to let my opinion mean anything at all to you. After all, like Matthew, I know a great deal about you. I, too, am a therapist—in fact I am twenty years more experienced and probably wiser than Matthew. I wonder why what I think and feel about you doesn't count?"

She responded to the content but not to the emotion. She mollified me: "It's not you. I'm sure you know your business. I'd be this way with any therapist in the world. It's just that I've been so hurt by Matthew that I'm not going to make myself vulnerable again to another therapist."

"You've got good answers for everything, but what it all adds up to is 'Don't get close.' You can't get close to Harry because you don't want to hurt him by telling him your intimate thoughts about Matthew and suicide. You can't become intimate with friends lest you hurt them when you ultimately commit suicide. You can't be intimate with me because another therapist, eight years ago, hurt you. The words are different in each case, but the music is the same."

Finally, by the fourth month, there were signs of progress. Thelma stopped battling on every point and, to my surprise, began one session by telling me that she had spent many hours during the last week making a list of all her close relationships and what happened to each. She realized that whenever she got really close to someone, she managed, in one way or another, to break off the relationship.

"Maybe you're right, maybe I do have a serious problem with getting close to people. I don't think I've had a good girlfriend for thirty years. I'm not sure whether I've *ever* had one."

This insight could have been a turning point in our therapy: for the first time, Thelma identified and took responsibility for a specific problem. I was hopeful now of plunging into real work. Instead, the opposite occurred: she withdrew even more, claiming that her problem with intimacy doomed our work in therapy.

I tried mightily to persuade her that it was a positive, not a negative, thing that had emerged in therapy. Again and again, I explained that intimacy difficulties are not extraneous static that just happen to get in the way of treatment, but are the core issue. It was a *positive*, not a negative, development that it had surfaced here and now where we could examine it.

Yet her despair deepened. Now every week was a bad week. She obsessed more, she wept more, she withdrew more from Harry, she spent much time planning how she would commit suicide. More and more frequently did I hear criticisms of therapy. She claimed that our sessions succeeded only in "stirring the pot," in increasing her discomfort, and she regretted having committed herself to six full months of therapy.

Time was running out. We were now beginning the fifth month; and, though Thelma assured me she would honor her commitment, she made it clear that she would not be willing to continue longer than six months. I felt discouraged: all my strenuous efforts had been ineffective. I had not even managed to establish a solid therapeutic alliance with her: her emotional energy, every dram of it, was riveted to Matthew, and I had found no way to pry it loose. The moment had come to play my final card.

"Thelma, ever since that hour a couple of months ago when you role-played Matthew and spoke the words that would release you, I've been deliberating about inviting him into my office and having a three-way session—you, me, and Matthew. We've only got seven more sessions, unless you reconsider your decision to stop"—Thelma shook her head firmly. "I think we need some help to move along further. I'd like your permission to phone Matthew and invite him to join us. I think just a single three-way session would be sufficient, but we ought to do it soon because I think we'll need several hours afterward to integrate what we learn."

Thelma, who had been apathetically slumped in her chair, suddenly bolted upright. Her string purse fell from her lap onto the floor, but she ignored it to listen wide-eyed to me. Finally, finally, I had gotten her attention, and she sat silently for several minutes contemplating my words.

Although I had not fully thought through my proposal, I believed that Matthew would agree to meet with us. I hoped that my reputation in the field would intimidate him into cooperating. Moreover, eight years of Thelma's taped phone messages *had* to be getting to him, and I was confident that he, too, longed for release.

I was not certain what would happen in this extraordinary three-way meeting, yet I felt strangely confident that all would be for the best. *Any* information would help. *Any* introduction of reality should help me release Thelma from her fixation on Matthew. Regardless of the depth of his character flaw—and I had no doubt that it was a trench of considerable magnitude—I was sure he would do nothing in my presence to encourage her fantasies of ultimate reunion.

After an unusually long silence, Thelma stated that she needed more time to think about it. "So far," she said, "I see more cons than pros——"

I sighed and settled back into my chair. I knew that Thelma would take the rest of the hour spinning obsessional webs.

"On the positive side I guess it would give Dr. Yalom some firsthand observations."

I sighed even more deeply. This was going to be worse than usual; she was speaking of me in the third person. I started to point out that she was speaking as though I weren't in the same room with her, but couldn't summon the energy—she had worn me down.

"On the negative side, I can think of several possibilities. First, your call would alienate him from me. I've got a one- or two-percent chance now that he'll come around. Your call would drop my chances to zero, or less."

I was definitely growing irritated and thought, "*Eight years* have gone by, Thelma, can't you get the message? And besides, how can your chances be less than zero, you ninny?" This really *was* my final card and I was beginning feel that she would trump it. But I kept silent.

"His only motivation to participate would be professional—helping a sickie who's too incompetent to run her own life. Number three,——"

My God! She was talking in lists again. I couldn't stand it.

"Number three, Matthew will probably tell the truth, but the wording will be patronizing and would be heavily influenced by Dr. Yalom's presence. I don't think I could take being patronized. Number four, this is going to put him in a very compromising and embarrassing position professionally. He will never forgive me for it."

"But, Thelma, he's a therapist. He knows that in order for you to get well, you've got to talk about him. If he's the spiritually minded person you think him to be, then surely he's experienced much guilt at your distress and would take pleasure in helping."

But Thelma was too involved in developing her list to hear my words.

"Number five, what possible help could I get from a three-way meeting? There is almost no chance he'll say what I hope he'll say. I don't even care if he means it, I just want him to say he cares about me. If I'm not going to get what I want and need, why should I expose myself to the pain? I've been hurt enough. Why should I do it?" Thelma got out of her chair and walked over to the window.

Now I was deeply concerned. Thelma was getting herself worked up into an irrational frenzy and was going to block my last chance to help her. I took my time and thought out my words carefully.

"The best answer I can give to all the questions you've raised is that speaking to Matthew will bring us closer to the truth. Surely you want that?" She had her back to me, but I thought I could see a slight nod of agreement. "You can't go on living a lie or an illusion!

"You know, Thelma, you've many times asked me questions about my theoretical orientation. I often haven't answered because I thought that talking about schools of therapy would get us away from the personal discourse we needed to have. But let me give you one answer to that question now. Perhaps the single most important therapeutic credo that I have is that 'the unexamined life is not worth living.' Getting Matthew into this office might be the key to a true examination and understanding of what's been happening to you these past eight years."

My answer soothed Thelma. She walked back to her chair and sat down.

"This is stirring up a lot of stuff in me. My head is spinning. Let me think about it for a week. But you must promise me one thing—that you won't call Matthew without my permission."

I promised that unless I heard from her, I would not call Matthew during the next week, and we parted. I wasn't about to give a guarantee that I would *never* call—but fortunately she didn't ask for that.

Thelma came in for the next session looking ten years younger and with a spring to her step. She had had her hair done and was attractively dressed in an argyle wool skirt and stockings, instead of her usual polyester slacks or jogging suit. She immediately took her seat and got down to business.

"I've spent all week thinking about a meeting with Matthew. I've gone over all the pros and cons, and I now believe you are right—I'm in such bad shape that it's not likely anything could make me worse!"

"Thelma, those aren't my words. I said that——"

But Thelma was not interested in my words and spoke over me. "But your plan of phoning him was not a good idea. It would have been a shock to get an out-of-the-blue call from you. So I decided to call him to prepare him for your call. Of course, I didn't reach him, but I told his telephone-answering tape about your proposal, and I said for him to phone me or you and—and——"

Here, with a big grin on her face, she paused to let the suspense build.

I was astonished. I had never before seen her play. "And?"

"Well, you've got more clout than I thought. For the first time in eight years, he returned my call and we had a twenty-minute friendly chat."

"How did it feel to talk to him?"

"Wonderful! I can't tell you how wonderful. It was like we had just talked the previous day. He was the old gentle, caring Matthew. He asked all about me. He was concerned about my depression. He was glad I was seeing you. We had a good talk."

"Can you tell me what you discussed?"

"God, I don't know. We just chattered away."

"About the past? The present?"

"You know, it sounds crazy, but I don't remember!"

"Can you remember any of it?" A lot of therapists, at this point, would have made an interpretation about the way she was shutting me out. Perhaps I should have, but I couldn't wait. I was so damn curious! It was typical of Thelma not to think that I might have some wishes, too.

"You know, I'm not trying to conceal anything. I just can't remember. I was too excited. Oh, yes, he told me he had been married and divorced and that he had gone through a lot of turmoil about the divorce.

"But the main thing is that he is willing to come in for a three-way meeting. You know, it's funny, he even sounded eager—as though it has been me avoiding him. I told him to come in to your office at my regular hour next week, but he told me to ask you if we could make it sooner. Now that we've decided to do it, he wants to do it as soon as possible. I guess I feel the same way."

I suggested a time two days hence, and Thelma said she'd inform Matthew. Following that, we reviewed her phone conversation once again and planned the next hour. Thelma never did recall all the details of her phone conversation but she did remember what they had *not* talked about. "Ever since I hung up the phone, I've been kicking myself for chickening out and not having asked Matthew the two really important questions. First, what *really* happened eight years ago? Why did you break off? Why have you remained silent? Second, how do you really feel about me now?"

"Let's be certain that you don't also finish our three-way meeting wanting to kick yourself for something you didn't ask. I promise to help you ask all the questions you want to ask, all the questions that might release you from the power you've given Matthew. That's going to be my main job in the session."

During the rest of the hour, Thelma repeated a lot of old material: she talked about her feelings toward Matthew, how they were *not* transference, how Matthew had given her the best days of her life. It seemed to me that she droned on interminably, went off into tangent after tangent, and, moreover, said everything to me as though for the first time. I became aware of how little she had changed and how much depended on something dramatic happening the next session.

Thelma arrived twenty minutes early for the session. I was doing correspondence that morning and passed her in the waiting room a couple of times as I conferred with my secretary. She was dressed in an attractive, tight royal-blue knit dress—a daring outfit for a seventy-year-old woman, but I thought she pulled it off well. Later, when I invited her into my office, I complimented her on it and she told me, with a conspiratorial hush and a finger crossing her lips, that she had spent most of the week shopping for it. It was the first new dress she had bought in eight years. As she touched up her lipstick she told me that Matthew would arrive in a minute or two, precisely on time. He had told her that he didn't want to spend too much time in the waiting room because he wanted to minimize the possibility of running into colleagues who might be passing by. I could not blame him for that.

Suddenly, she stopped talking. I had left my door ajar, and we could hear that Matthew had arrived and was speaking to my secretary.

"I came to some lectures here when the department was in the old building. . . . When did you move? . . . I really like the light, airy feel of this building, do you?"

Thelma put her hand to her breast as though to still her heartbeat and whispered, "You see? You see how naturally his caring comes?"

Matthew entered. It was the first time he had seen Thelma in eight years, and if he was in any way startled by the physical aging she had undergone, his boyish, good-natured smile gave no evidence of it. He was older than I expected, perhaps in his early forties, and conservatively dressed in an un-Californian three-piece suit. Otherwise, he was much as Thelma had described him—slender, mustached, well tanned.

I was prepared for his directness and sincerity and, therefore, not thrown off by it. (Sociopaths often present themselves well, I thought.) I began by briefly thanking him for coming.

He immediately rejoined, "I've been wanting a session like this for years. It's *my* place to thank *you* for bringing it to pass. Besides, I've read your books for years. It's an honor to meet you."

He's not without some charm, I thought, but I did not want to get involved in a distracting personal or professional discussion with Matthew: it was best for me to keep a low profile in this session and for Thelma and Matthew to interact as much as possible. I turned the session over to them: "We've got a lot to talk about today. Where to start?"

Thelma began: "It's funny, I haven't increased my medication." She turned to Matthew. "I'm still on antidepressants. It's eight years later—my goodness, eight years, that's hard to believe—but it's eight years later, I've probably tried eight new antidepressants and they *still* don't work. But the interesting thing is that all the side effects are greater today. My mouth is so dry I can hardly talk. Now why should that be? Does stress increase side effects?"

Thelma continued to ramble and to consume huge chunks of our precious time with preambles to preambles. I was in a dilemma: under ordinary circumstances, I might have attempted to clarify the consequences of her indirect discourse. For example, I might point out that she was staking out a role of fragility that would immediately discourage the open discussion she said she wished. Or that she had invited Matthew here to speak freely and yet immediately mobilized his guilt by reminding him that she had been on antidepressants since he left her. But such interpretations would only result in most of the hour being used as a conventional individual therapy session—exactly what none of the three of us wanted. Besides, if I were in any way to label her behavior as problematic, she would feel humiliated and would never forgive me for that.

But too much was riding on this hour. I could not bear for Thelma to waste this opportunity with indirect meanderings. This was her chance to ask the questions that had plagued her for eight years. This was her chance to be released.

"I'm going to interrupt you for a minute, Thelma, if I may. I'd like, if you two agree, to have the role of timekeeper today and to keep us focused. Can we spend a minute or two establishing our agenda?"

There was silence for a short time until Matthew punctured it.

"I'm here today to be helpful to Thelma. I know she has been going through bad times, and I know that I bear the responsibility for that. I'll be as open as possible to any questions."

That was Thelma's perfect cue. I gave her a starting glance. She caught it and began.

"There is nothing worse than to feel bereft, to feel that you are absolutely alone in the world. When I was a child, one of my favorite books—I used to take it to Lincoln Park in Washington, D.C., to read on the benches there—was———"

Here I shot Thelma the sharpest, nastiest look I could muster. She got it.

"I'll get to the point. I guess the bottom line is"—and she slowly and carefully turned to Matthew—"what do you feel about me?"

Atta girl! I positively beamed at her.

Matthew's answer made me gasp. He looked straight at her and said, "I've thought about you every day for the last eight years! I care about you. I care a great deal. I want to know what happens to you. I wish that there were some way in the world of our meeting every few months so I could catch up on you. I don't want to be cut off."

"Then," Thelma asked, "why have you been silent all these years?"

"Sometimes caring can be best expressed by silence."

Thelma shook her head. "That's like one of your Zen riddles that I could never understand."

Matthew continued, "Whenever I tried to talk to you, it made things worse. You asked for more and more until it reached the point when I couldn't find a way to give any more. You called me a dozen times a day. You showed up time and time again in my office waiting room. Then when you almost killed yourself, I knew—and my therapist agreed—that the best thing was to cut it off completely."

Matthew's statement, I thought, bore an uncanny resemblance to the releasing scenario Thelma had shared in our role-playing session.

"But," Thelma commented, "it's natural for a person to be bereft if something so important is taken away so suddenly."

Matthew nodded understandingly to Thelma and briefly put his hand on top of hers. Then he turned to me. "I think it's important for you to know exactly what happened eight years ago. I'm speaking to you now rather than to Thelma because I've already told her this story, more than once." He turned to her. "Sorry you have to hear this whole thing yet again, Thelma."

Then Matthew, ingenuously, turned to me and began: "This is not easy for me. The best way to do it is simply to do it. So here goes.

"Eight years ago, about a year after I finished my training, I had a serious psychotic break. During that time I was heavily into Buddhism and was sitting Vipassana—that's a form of Buddhist meditation—" When Matthew saw me nod, he interrupted his story. "You seem familiar with it—I'd be very interested to know your opinion of it. But today I guess I'd better continue. . . . I was sitting Vipassana for three to four hours a day. I considered becoming a Buddhist monk and went to India for a thirty-day meditation retreat in Igapuri, a small village north of Bombay. The regimen was too severe for me—total silence, total isolation, sitting meditation for fourteen hours a day—and I began to lose my ego boundaries. By the third week I was hallucinating and thought that I could see through walls and had total access to both my past and future lives. The monks took me to Bombay, and an Indian doctor put me on antipsychotic medication and called my brother, who flew to India to take me home. I was hospitalized for about four weeks in Los Angeles. After I was discharged I immediately flew back to San Francisco, and it was the following day that I met Thelma, sheerly by chance, in Union Square.

"I was still in a very fragmented state of mind. I had turned the Buddhist doctrines into a real craziness and believed I was in a state of oneness with everybody. I was glad to run into Thelma—into *you*, Thelma," turning to her. "I was glad to see you. It helped me feel anchored again."

Matthew turned back to me and, until he finished his story, did not again look at Thelma.

"I had nothing but good feelings for her. I felt one with Thelma. I wanted her to have everything she wanted in life. More than that—I thought her quest for happiness was my quest as well. It was the same quest, she and I were the same. I took the Buddhist credo of universal oneness and egolessness very literally. I didn't know where I ended and another started. I gave her everything she wanted. She wanted me to be close to her, she wanted to come home with me, she wanted sex— I was willing to give her everything in a state of perfect oneness and love.

"But she wanted more and I couldn't give more. I grew more disturbed. After three or four weeks my hallucinations returned, and I had to re-enter the hospital—this time for six weeks. I hadn't been out very long when I heard about Thelma's suicide attempt. I didn't know what to do. It was catastrophic. It was the worst thing that had ever happened to me. I've been haunted by it for eight years. I answered her calls at first, but they kept coming. My psychiatrist finally advised me to sever all contact, to be totally silent. He said that would be necessary for my own sanity, and he was certain that it would be best for Thelma as well."

As I listened to Matthew, my head began to spin. I had developed a variety of hypotheses about his behavior, but I was not remotely prepared for the story I had just heard.

First, was it true? Matthew was a charmer. He was smooth. Was he staging all this for me? No, I had no doubt that things were as he described them: his words had the unmistakable ring of truth. He freely offered the names of hospitals and his treating physicians if I should want to call. Furthermore, Thelma, to whom he said he had told this in the past, had listened with rapt attention and offered no demurral whatsoever.

I turned to look at Thelma, but she averted her glance. After Matthew finished talking, she began to stare out the window. Was it possible that she knew all this from the start and had concealed it from me? Or had she been so absorbed with her own distress and her own needs that, throughout, she had been completely unaware of Matthew's mental state? Or had she known for some brief period and then repressed the knowledge because it clashed with her own vital lie?

Only Thelma could tell me. But which Thelma? The Thelma who deceived me? The Thelma who deceived herself? Or the Thelma who was deceived by herself? I doubted that I would find the answers to these questions.

Primarily, though, my attention was fixed on Matthew. Over the last several months, I had constructed a vision—or, rather, several alternative visions—of him: an irresponsible, sociopathic Matthew who exploited his patients; a callous and sexually confused Matthew who acted out his personal conflicts (with women in general or mother in particular); an errant, grandiose young therapist who mistook the love desired for the love required.

Yet he was none of these. He was something else, something I had never anticipated. But what? I wasn't certain. A well-intentioned victim? A wounded healer, a Christ figure who had sacrificed his own integrity for Thelma? Certainly, I no longer viewed him as an offending therapist: he was as much a patient as Thelma and, furthermore (I could not help thinking, glancing toward Thelma, who was still staring out the window), a *working* patient, a patient after my own heart.

I remember feeling dislocated—so many constructs exploded in so few minutes. Gone forever was the construct of Matthew as sociopath or exploiter-therapist. Instead there arose a haunting question: *In this relationship, who had exploited whom?*

This was all the information I could handle (and all that I thought I needed). I have only a dim recollection of the rest of the hour. I remember that Matthew encouraged Thelma to ask more questions. It was as though he, too, sensed that she could be released only by information, that her illusions could not endure the beam of truth. And I think, too, that he realized that only through Thelma's release could he obtain his own. I remember that Thelma and I both asked many questions, each of which he answered fully. His wife had left him four years ago. She and he had increasingly diverging views about religion, and she could not follow his conversion into a fundamentalist Christian sect.

No, he was not gay. Nor had he ever been, though Thelma had often asked him about that. It was only at this moment that his smile narrowed and a trace of irritation entered his voice ("I kept telling you, Thelma, that straight people live in the Haight, too").

No, he had never had a personal relationship with any other patient. In fact, as a result of his psychosis and what had happened with Thelma, he had, several years ago, realized that his psychological problems posed an insurmountable barrier, and he had stopped being a therapist. But, committed to a life of service, he did psychological testing for a few years; then he worked in a biofeedback lab; and, more recently, he had become the administrator of a Christian health maintenance organization.

I was musing about Matthew's professional decision, even wondering whether he had evolved to the point where he should go back to doing therapy—perhaps he now might make an exceptional therapist—when I noticed that our time was almost up.

I inquired whether we had covered everything. I asked Thelma to project herself into the future and to imagine how she might feel several hours from now. Would she be left with unasked questions?

To my surprise, she began sobbing so forcefully that she could not catch her breath. Tears poured down upon her new blue dress until Matthew, outracing me, handed her the box of tissues. As her sobbing subsided, Thelma's words grew audible.

"I *don't* believe, I simply *can't* believe that Matthew really cares about what happens to me." Her words were directed neither to Matthew nor to me but to some point between us in the room. I noted with some satisfaction that I wasn't the only one she addressed in the third person.

I tried to help Thelma talk. "Why? Why don't you believe him?"

"He's saying that because he has to. It's the right thing to say. It's the only thing he can say."

Matthew did his best, but communication was difficult because of her sobbing. "I mean exactly what I said. I've thought about you every day these eight years. I care about what happens to you. I care about you a great deal."

"But your caring—what does it mean? I know about your caring. You care about the poor, about ants and plants and ecological systems. I don't want to be one of your ants!"

We had run twenty minutes over and had to stop even though Thelma had still not regained her composure. I gave her an appointment for the following day not only to be supportive but also because it would be best to see her again quickly, while the details of this hour were still fresh in her mind.

The three of us ended the hour with round-robin handshakes and parted. A few minutes later, as I was getting some coffee, I noticed Thelma and Matthew chatting in the corridor. He was trying to make a point to her, but she was looking away from him. Shortly afterward, I saw them walk away in different directions.

Thelma had not recovered by the next day and was exceptionally labile throughout our session. She wept often and, at times, flashed into anger. First, she lamented that Matthew had such a low opinion of her. She had worked and worried Matthew's statement that he "cared" for her until it now seemed an insult. He had, she noted, mentioned none of her positive features, and Thelma convinced herself that his basic posture to her had been "unfriendly."

Furthermore, she was convinced that, probably because of my presence, he had adopted a pseudo-therapeutic voice and manner which she had found patronizing. Thelma rambled a great deal and swerved back and forth between her reconstruction of the hour and her reaction to it.

"I feel like an amputation has taken place. Something has gone from me. Despite Matthew's high-sounding ethics, I believe I am more honest than he. Especially in his account of who seduced who."

Thelma remained cryptic on this matter, and I did not press her for explication. Although I would have relished finding out what "really" happened, her reference to "amputation" intrigued me even more.

"I haven't had any more fantasies about Matthew," she went on. "I'm not daydreaming any more. But I want to. I want to sink into the embrace of some warm daydream. It's cold out and I feel empty. Now, there is just nothing."

Like a drifting boat torn loose from its mooring, I thought—but a sentient boat desperately searching for a berth, any berth. Now, between obsessions, Thelma was in a rare free-floating state. This was the time I had been waiting for. Such states don't last long: the unbonded obsessional, like nascent oxygen, quickly melds with some mental image or idea. This moment, this brief interval between obsessions, was the crucial time for us to work—before Thelma re-established her equilibrium by latching onto something or someone. Most likely she would reconstruct the hour with Matthew so that her version of reality could once again support her fusion fantasy.

It seemed to me that real progress had occurred: the surgery was complete, and now my task was to prevent her from preserving the amputated limb and quickly stitching it back on again. My opportunity arrived soon, as Thelma proceeded to lament her loss.

"My predictions of what might happen have come true. I don't have any more hope, I'll never have any more satisfaction. I could live with that one-percent chance. I've lived with it a long time."

"What was the satisfaction, Thelma? A one-percent chance for what?"

"For what? For those twenty-seven days. Until yesterday there was always a chance that Matthew and I could go back to that time. We were there, the feeling was real, I know love when I feel it. As long as Matthew and I were alive, we always had the chance to return to it. Until yesterday. In your office."

There were still a few threads of illusion to be severed. I'd almost totally destroyed the obsession. It was time to finish the job.

"Thelma, what I have to say now is not pleasant, but I think it's important. Let me try to get my thoughts out clearly. If two people share a moment or share a feeling between them, if they both feel the same thing, then I can see how it might be possible for them, as long as they are alive, to re-establish that precious feeling between the two of them. It would be a delicate procedure—after all, people change, and love never stays—but still, perhaps, it is within the realm of possibility. They could communicate fully, they could try to achieve a deep authentic relationship which, since authentic love is an absolute state, should approximate what they had before.

*"But suppose it was never a shared experience! Suppose the two people had widely different experiences. And suppose one of them mistakenly thought her experience was the same as his?"*

Thelma's eyes were fixed on me. I was certain that she understood me perfectly.

I continued. "What I heard in the session with Matthew was precisely that. His experience and your experience were very different. Can you see how impossible it would be for each of you to re-create the particular mental state you were in? The two of you can't help one another with this because *it was not a shared state*.

"He was in one place and you were in another. He was lost in a psychosis. He didn't know where his boundaries were—where he ended and you began. He wanted you to be happy because he thought he was the same as you. He wasn't having a love experience, because he didn't know who he was. Your experience was very different. You cannot re-create a state of shared romantic love, of the two of you being deeply in love with one another *because it was never there in the first place.*"

I don't think I've ever said a crueler thing, but to make myself heard, I had to speak in words so strong and so stark that they could be neither twisted nor forgotten.

There was no doubt my comment struck home. Thelma had stopped crying and just sat there stock still considering my words. I broke the heavy silence after several minutes:

"How do you feel about what I said, Thelma?"

"I can't feel anything any more. There's nothing else to feel. I have to find a way to live out my time. I feel numb."

"You've been living and feeling one way for eight years, and now suddenly in twenty-four hours all that is pulled away from you. These next few days are going to feel very disorienting. You're going to feel lost. But we have to expect that. How could it be otherwise?"

I said this because often the best way to prevent a calamitous reaction is to predict it. Another way is to help the patient get outside of it and move into the observer role. So I added, "It will be important this week to be an observer and recorder of your own inner state. I'd like you to check in on your internal state every four hours, when you are awake, and jot down your observations. We'll go over them next week."

But the next week Thelma, for the first time, missed her appointment. Her husband called to apologize for his wife, who had overslept, and we agreed upon a meeting two days later.

When I went to the waiting room to greet Thelma, I was dismayed at her physical deterioration. She was back in her green jogging suit and had obviously not combed her hair or made any other attempts to groom herself. Moreover, for the first time, she was accompanied by her husband, Harry, a tall, white-haired man with a large bulbous nose, who sat there squeezing a grip strengthener in each hand. I remembered Thelma's telling me about his teaching hand-to-hand combat in wartime. I could picture him strangling someone.

I thought it was odd that he accompanied her that day. In spite of her age, Thelma is physically fit and had always driven herself to my office. My curiosity was piqued even more by her comment in the waiting room that Harry wanted to meet with me today. I had met him once before: in the third or fourth session I saw him together with Thelma for a fifteen-minute discussion—primarily to see what kind of person he was and to learn about the marriage from his perspective. Never before had he asked to meet with me. Obviously something important was up. I agreed to speak to him for the last ten minutes of Thelma's hour and also made it clear that I would feel free to report back to her the entirety of our discussion.

Thelma looked weary. She slumped into her chair and spoke slowly and softly in a resigned tone.

"My week has been a horror, sheer hell! My obsession has gone or almost gone, I guess. Rather than ninety percent of the time, I spend less than twenty percent of my waking time thinking about Matthew, and even that twenty percent is different.

"But what have I been doing instead? Nothing. Absolutely nothing. I've been sleeping twelve hours a day. All I do is sleep and sit and sigh. I'm all dried up, I can't cry any more. Harry, who is almost never critical of me, said to me last night as I picked at my dinner—I've hardly eaten anything this week—'Are you feeling sorry for yourself again?'"

"How do you explain what's happening to you?"

"It's like I've been in a magic show and now I've come outside—and it's very gray outside."

I felt goose bumps. I had never before heard Thelma speak metaphorically; it was as though someone else were speaking.

"Say some more about how you feel."

"I feel old, really old. For the first time I know I'm seventy years old, seven zero—that's older than ninety-nine percent of the people walking around. I feel like a zombie, run out of gas, my life's a void, a dead end. Nothing to do but live out my time."

These words were said quickly, but the cadence slowed for the last sentence. Then she turned to me and fixed her eyes on mine. That in itself was unusual, for she had seldom ever looked directly at me. Maybe I was wrong, but I think her eyes said, "Are you satisfied now?" I did not comment on her gaze.

"All of this followed our session with Matthew. What happened in that hour to throw you like this?"

"What a fool I was to have protected him for eight years!"

Thelma's anger enlivened her. She took her string purse from her lap, placed it on the floor, and put a lot of energy into her words. "What reward did I get? I'll tell you. A kick in the teeth! If I hadn't kept his secret from my therapists all these years, maybe the dominoes might have fallen differently."

"I don't understand. What was the kick in your teeth?"

"You were there. You saw it. You saw his callousness. He didn't say hello or goodbye to me. He didn't answer my questions. How much effort would it have taken him? He *still* hasn't told me why he cut me off!"

I tried to describe to her how I had seen things differently, and how, in my view, Matthew had been warm to her and had gone into lengthy and painful detail about why he had broken off with her.

But Thelma rushed on, not listening to my comments. "He was clear about only one thing—Matthew Jennings is sick and tired of Thelma Hilton. You tell me: What's the perfect scenario to drive an ex-lover to suicide? *Sudden dismissal with no reasons given*—that's exactly what he's done to me!

"In one of my daydreams yesterday, I could see Matthew, eight years ago, bragging to one of his friends (and placing a bet on it) that he could use his psychiatric knowledge to first seduce me and then totally destroy me in twenty-seven days!"

Thelma leaned over, opened her purse and pulled out a newspaper clipping about murder. She waited a couple of minutes for me to read it. She had underlined with red pencil a paragraph that claimed that suicides are, in actuality, double homicides.

"I saw that in last Sunday's paper. Could that have been true for me? Maybe when I tried to commit suicide, I really wanted to kill Matthew? You know, it feels right. Right here." She pointed to her heart. "I never thought of it that way before!"

I fought to keep my equilibrium. Naturally, I was concerned about her depression. And yet, *of course,* she was in despair. How could it be otherwise? Only the deepest despair could have generated an illusion with the strength and the tenacity to have endured for eight years. And if I eradicated the illusion, then I had to be prepared to encounter the despair it had concealed. So, bad as it was, Thelma's distress was a good sign, a homing signal that we were on target. Everything was going well. The preparation was finally complete, and the real therapy could now begin.

In fact, it had already begun! Thelma's surprising outbursts, her sudden eruption of anger toward Matthew was a sign that the old defenses were no longer holding. She was in a fluid state. Every severely obsessional patient has a core of anger, and I was not unprepared for its emergence in Thelma. All in all, I considered her anger, despite its irrational components, an excellent development.

I was so preoccupied with these thoughts and with plans for our future work that I missed the first part of Thelma's next comment—but I heard the ending of the sentence all too clearly.

" . . . and *that's* why I have to stop therapy!"

I scrambled to respond. "Thelma, how can you even consider that? This is the worst possible time to stop therapy. Now is the time you can make some real progress."

"I don't want to be in therapy any more. I've been a patient for twenty years, and I'm tired of being treated like a patient. Matthew treated me like a patient, not a friend. You treat me like a patient. I want to be like everyone else."

I no longer remember the sequence of my words. I only know that I pulled out all stops and placed the utmost pressure on her to reconsider. I reminded her of the six-month commitment, of which five weeks remained.

But she countered, "Even you would agree that that there's a time when you have to protect yourself. A little more of this 'treatment' would be unendurable." She added, with a grim smile, "A little more treatment would kill the patient."

All of my arguments met a similar fate. I insisted that we had made real progress. I reminded her that she had originally come to see me to free her mind from her preoccupation, and we had made great strides toward that. Now was the time we could address the underlying sense of emptiness and futility that had fueled the obsession.

Her response was, in effect, that her losses had been too great—more than she could bear. She had lost her hope for the future (by that she meant she had lost her "one-percent chance" of reconciliation); she had also lost the best twenty-seven days of her life (if, as I had shown her, they weren't "real," then she had lost this sustaining memory of her life's highest point); and she had also lost eight years of sacrifice (if she had been protecting an illusion, then her sacrifice had been meaningless).

So powerful were Thelma's words that I found no effective way to counter them, other than to acknowledge her losses and say that there was much mourning that she had to do and that I wanted to be with her to help her mourn. I tried, also, to point out that regret was extraordinarily painful to endure once it was in place, but that we could do much to prevent further regret from taking root. For example, consider the decision facing her at this moment: Would she not—a month, a year from now—deeply regret her decision to stop treatment?

Thelma replied that, though I was probably right, she had made a promise to herself to stop therapy. She compared our three-way session to a visit with the doctor when you suspect you have cancer. "You've been in great turmoil—so frightened that you've put this visit off time and again. The doctor confirms that you do have cancer, and all your turmoil about not knowing is ended—but what are you left with?"

As I tried to sort out my feelings, I realized that one of my first responses clamoring for attention was, "How can you do this to me?"

Though, no doubt, my outrage derived in part from my own frustration, I was also certain I was responding to Thelma's feeling toward me. *I* was the person responsible for all three losses. The three-way meeting had been *my* idea and I had been the one who stripped her of her illusions, I was the disillusioner. It occurred to me that I was performing a thankless task. Even the word *disillusion*, with its negative, nihilistic connotation, should have warned me. I thought of O'Neill's *The Iceman Cometh* and the fate of Hickey, the disillusioner. Those whom he tries to restore to reality ultimately turn against him and re-enter the life of illusion.

I remembered my discovery a few weeks before that Thelma knew how to punish and didn't need my help. I think her suicide try *was* a murder attempt, and I now believed that her decision to stop therapy was also a form of double homicide. She considered termination to be an attack upon me—and she was right! She had perceived how critically important it was to me to succeed, to satisfy my intellectual curiosity, to follow everything through until the very end.

Her revenge upon me was to frustrate each of these aims. No matter that the cataclysm she meant for me would engulf her as well: in fact, her sadomasochistic trends were so pronounced that she was attracted by the idea of dual immolation. I noted wryly that my resorting to professional diagnostic jargon meant I must really be angry with her.

I tried to explore these ideas with Thelma. "I hear your anger toward Matthew, but I'm also wondering if you're not upset with me, too. It would make a lot of sense if you were angry—very angry, indeed—with me. After all, in some ways you must feel that I got you into the fix you are in now. It was my idea to invite Matthew, my idea to ask him the questions you did." I thought I saw her nod her head.

"If that's so, Thelma, what better place to work on it than right here and now in therapy?"

Thelma nodded her head more vigorously. "My head tells me that you're right. But sometimes you've got to do what you've got to do. I promised myself not to be a patient any more, and I'm going to keep that promise."

I gave up. I was facing a stone wall. Our hour was long over, and I had yet to see Harry, to whom I had promised ten minutes. Before parting, I extracted some commitments from Thelma: she agreed to think more about her decision and to meet with me again in three weeks, and she promised to honor her commitment to the research project by meeting, six months hence, with the research psychologist and completing the battery of questionnaires. I ended the session thinking that, though she might fulfill her research commitment, there was little chance she would resume therapy.

Her pyrrhic victory safely in her grasp, she could afford a little gen- erosity and, as she was leaving my office, she thanked me for my efforts and said that if she ever went back into therapy, I would be her first choice as a therapist.

I escorted Thelma to the waiting room and Harry to my office. He was brisk and direct: "I know what it is to run a tight ship, Doc—I did it in the army for thirty years—and I see that you're running late. That means you'll be running late all day, doesn't it?"

I nodded but assured him that I had time to meet with him.

"Well, I can keep it very brief. I'm not like Thelma. I never beat around the bush. I'll come right to the point. Give me back my wife, Doctor, the old Thelma—just the way she used to be."

Harry's voice was pleading rather than threatening. Just the same, he had my full attention—and, as he spoke, I could not help glancing at his large, strangler's hands. He proceeded, and now reproach en- tered his voice, to describe how Thelma had gotten progressively worse since she and I had started working together. After hearing him out, I tried to offer some support by stating that a long depression is almost as hard on the family as it is on the patient. Ignoring my gambit, he responded that Thelma had always been a good wife and that per- haps he had aggravated her problem by being on the go and traveling too much. Finally, when I informed him of Thelma's decision to termi- nate, he seemed relieved and gratified: he had been urging her in this direction for several weeks.

After Harry left my office, I sat there tired and stunned and angry. God, what a couple! Deliver me from both of them! The irony of it all. The old fool wants his "old Thelma back again." Has he been so "absent" he hasn't noticed that he never *had* the old Thelma? The old Thelma was never home: for the last eight years she has spent ninety percent of her life lost in the fantasy of a love she never had. Harry, no less than Thelma, chose to embrace illusion. Cervantes asked, "Which will you have: wise madness or foolish sanity?" It was clear which choice Harry and Thelma were making!

But I got little solace from pointing my finger at Thelma and Harry or from lamenting the weakness of the human spirit—that feeble wraith unable to survive without illusion, without enchantment or pipe dreams or vital lies. It was time to face the truth: I had botched this case beyond belief, and I could not transfer blame to the patient, or her husband, or the human condition.

My next few days were filled with self-recrimination and worry about Thelma. At first concerned about suicide, I ultimately soothed myself with the thought that her anger was so overt and so outwardly directed that it was unlikely she would turn it against herself.

To combat my self-recriminations, I attempted to persuade myself that I had employed a proper therapeutic strategy: Thelma *was* in extremis when she consulted me and something *had* to be done. Although she was in bad shape now, she was no worse than when she started. Who knows, maybe she was better, maybe I had successfully disillusioned her, and she needed to lick her wounds in solitude for a while before proceeding with any form of therapy? I *had* tried a more conservative approach for four months and had resorted to a radical intervention only when it was apparent I had no other choice.

But this was all self-deception. I knew that I had good reason to be guilty. I had, once again, fallen prey to the grandiose belief that I can treat anyone. Swept along by hubris and by my curiosity, I had disregarded twenty years of evidence at the outset that Thelma was a poor candidate for psychotherapy, and had subjected her to a painful confrontation which, in retrospect, had little likelihood of success. I had stripped away defenses without building anything to replace them.

Perhaps Thelma was right in protecting herself from me at this point. Perhaps she was right in saying that "a little more treatment would kill the patient!" All in all, I deserved Thelma and Harry's criticism. I had also embarrassed myself professionally. In describing her psychotherapy at a teaching conference a couple of weeks before, I had aroused considerable interest. I cringed now at the prospect of colleagues and students asking me in the weeks to come, "Fill us in. How did it all turn out?"

As I had expected, Thelma did not keep her next appointment three weeks later. I phoned her and had a brief but remarkable conversation. Though she was adamant in reaffirming her intention to quit the realm of patienthood, I detected less rancor in her voice. Not only was she turned off therapy, she volunteered, but she had no further need of it: she had been feeling much better, certainly far better than three weeks ago! Seeing Matthew yesterday, she told me offhandedly, had helped immeasurably!

"What? Matthew? How did that come about?" I asked.

"Oh, I had a pleasant talk with him over coffee. We've agreed to meet for a chat every month or so."

I was in a frenzy of curiosity and questioned her closely. First, she responded in a teasing way ("I told you all along that's what I needed"). Then she simply made it clear that I no longer had the right to make personal inquiries. Eventually I realized I would learn no more, and said my final goodbye. I went through the ritual of telling her that I was available as a therapist should she ever change her mind. But she apparently never again developed an appetite for my type of treatment, and I did not hear from her again.

Six months later, the research team interviewed Thelma and readministered the battery of psychological instruments. When the final research report was issued, I turned quickly to their review of the case of Thelma Hilton.

In summary, T.H. is a 70-year-old married Caucasian woman who, as a result of a five-month, once-weekly course of therapy, improved significantly. In fact, of the twenty-eight geriatric subjects involved in this study, she had the most positive outcome.

She is significantly less depressed. Her suicidality, extremely high at the onset, was reduced to the point where she may no longer be considered a suicidal risk. Self-esteem improved and there was corresponding significant improvement on several other scales: anxiety, hypochondriacal, psychoticism, and obsessionalism.

The research team is not entirely clear about the nature of the therapy which produced these impressive results because the patient continues to be unaccountably secretive about the details of therapy. It appears that the therapist successfully employed a pragmatic symptom-oriented treatment plan designed to offer relief rather than deep insight or personality change. In addition, he effectively employed a systems approach and introduced, into the therapy process, both her husband and a lifelong friend (from whom she had been long estranged).

Heady stuff! Somehow it afforded me little comfort.

# 2

# "If Rape Were Legal . . ."

*"Your patient is a dumb shit and I told him so in the group last night—in just those words."* Sarah, a young psychiatric resident, paused here and glared, daring me to criticize her.

Obviously something extraordinary had occurred. Not every day does a student charge into my office and, with no trace of chagrin—indeed, she seemed proud and defiant—tell me she has verbally assaulted one of my patients. Especially a patient with advanced cancer.

"Sarah, would you sit down and tell me about it? I've got a few minutes before my next patient arrives."

Struggling to keep her composure, Sarah began, "Carlos is the grossest, most despicable human being I have ever met!"

"Well, you know, he's not my favorite person either. I told you that before I referred him to you." I had been seeing Carlos in individual treatment for about six months and, a few weeks ago, referred him to Sarah for inclusion in her therapy group. "But go on. Sorry for stopping you."

"Well, as you know, he's been generally obnoxious—sniffing the women as though he were a dog and they bitches in heat, and ignoring everything else that goes on in the group. Last night, Martha—she's a really fragile borderline young woman, who has been almost mute in the group—started to talk about having been raped last year. I don't think she's ever shared that before—certainly not with a group. She was so scared, sobbing so hard, having so much trouble saying it, that it was incredibly painful. Everyone was trying to help her talk and, rightly or wrongly, I decided it would help Martha if I shared with the group that I had been raped three years ago—"

"I didn't know that, Sarah."

"No one else has known either!"

Sarah stopped here and dabbed her eyes. I could see it was hard for her to tell me this—but at this point I couldn't be sure what hurt worse: telling me about the rape, or how she had excessively revealed herself to her group. (That I was the group therapy instructor in the program must have complicated things for her.) Or was she most upset by what she had still to tell me? I decided to remain matter-of-fact about it.

"And then?"

"Well, that's when your Carlos went into action."

*My* Carlos? Ridiculous! I thought. As though he's my child and I have to answer for him. (Yet it was true that I had urged Sarah to take him on: she had been reluctant to introduce a patient with cancer into her group. But it was also true that her group was down to five, and she needed new members.) I had never seen her so irrational—and so challenging. I was afraid she'd be very embarrassed about this later, and I didn't want to make it worse by any hint of criticism.

"What did he do?"

"He asked Martha a lot of factual questions—when, where, what, who. At first that helped her talk, but as soon as I talked about my attack, he ignored Martha and started doing the same thing with me. Then he began asking us both for more intimate details. Did the rapist tear our clothing? Did he ejaculate inside of us? Was there any moment when we began to enjoy it? This all happened so insidiously that there was a time lag before the group began to catch on that he was getting off on it. He didn't give a damn about Martha and me, he was just getting his sexual kicks. I know I should feel more compassion for him— but he is such a creep!"

"How did it end up?"

"Well, the group finally wised up and began to confront him with his insensitivity, but he showed no remorse whatsoever. In fact, he became more offensive and accused Martha and me (and all rape victims) of making too much of it. 'What's the big deal?' he asked, and then claimed he personally wouldn't mind being raped by an attractive woman. His parting shot to the group was to say that he would welcome a rape attempt by any woman in the group. That's when I said, 'If you believe that, you're fucking ignorant!'"

"I thought your therapy intervention was calling him a dumb shit?" That reduced Sarah's tension, and we both smiled.

"That, too! I really lost my cool."

I stretched for supportive and constructive words, but they came out more pedantic than I'd intended. "Remember, Sarah, often extreme situations like this can end up being important turning points *if* they're worked through carefully. Everything that happens is grist for the mill in therapy. Let's try to turn this into a learning experience for him. I'm meeting with him tomorrow, and I'll work on it hard. But I want you to be sure to take care of yourself. I'm available if you want someone to talk to—later today or anytime this week."

Sarah thanked me and said she needed time to think about it. As she left my office, I thought that even if she decided to talk about her own issues with someone else, I would still try to meet with her later when she settled down to see if we could make this a learning experience for *her* as well. That was a hell of a thing for her to have gone through, and I felt for her, but it seemed to me that she had erred by trying to bootleg therapy for herself in the group. Better, I thought, for her to have worked on this first in her personal therapy and then, even if she still chose to talk about it in the group—and that was problematic—she would have handled it better for all parties concerned.

Then my next patient entered, and I turned my attention to her. But I could not prevent myself from thinking about Carlos and wondering how I should handle the next hour with him. It was not unusual for him to stray into my mind. He was an extraordinary patient; and ever since I had started seeing him a few months earlier, I thought about him far more than the one or two hours a week I spent in his presence.

"Carlos is a cat with nine lives, but now it looks as if he's coming to the end of his ninth life." That was the first thing said to me by the oncologist who had referred him for psychiatric treatment. He went on to explain that Carlos had a rare, slow-growing lymphoma which caused problems more because of its sheer bulk than its malignancy. For ten years the tumor had responded well to treatment but now had invaded his lungs and was encroaching upon his heart. His doctors were running out of options: they had given him maximum radiation exposure and had exhausted their pharmacopeia of chemotherapy agents. How honest should they be? they asked me. Carlos didn't seem to listen. They weren't certain how honest he was willing to be with himself. They did know that he was growing deeply depressed and seemed to have no one to whom he could turn for support.

Carlos was indeed isolated. Aside from a seventeen-year-old son and daughter—dizygotic twins, who lived with his ex-wife in South America—Carlos, at the age of thirty-nine, found himself virtually alone in the world. He had grown up, an only child, in Argentina. His mother had died in childbirth, and twenty years ago his father succumbed to the same type of lymphoma now killing Carlos. He had never had a male friend. "Who needs them?" he once said to me. "I've never met anyone who wouldn't cut you dead for a dollar, a job, or a cunt." He had been married only briefly and had had no other significant relationships with women. "You have to be crazy to fuck any woman more than once!" His aim in life, he told me without a trace of shame or self-consciousness, was to screw as many different women as he could.

No, at my first meeting I could find little endearing about Carlos's character—or about his physical appearance. He was emaciated, knobby (with swollen, highly visible lymph nodes at elbows, neck, behind his ears) and, as a result of the chemotherapy, entirely hairless. His pathetic cosmetic efforts—a wide-brimmed Panama hat, painted-on eyebrows, and a scarf to conceal the swellings in his neck—succeeded only in calling additional unwanted attention to his appearance.

He was obviously depressed—with good reason—and spoke bitterly and wearily of his ten-year ordeal with cancer. His lymphoma, he said, was killing him in stages. It had already killed most of him—his energy, his strength, and his freedom (he had to live near Stanford Hospital, in permanent exile from his own culture).

Most important, it had killed his social life, by which he meant his sexual life: when he was on chemotherapy, he was impotent; when he finished a course of chemotherapy, and his sexual juices started to flow, he could not make it with a woman because of his baldness. Even when his hair grew back, a few weeks after chemotherapy, he said he still couldn't score: no prostitute would have him because they thought his enlarged lymph nodes signified AIDS. His sex life now was confined entirely to masturbating while watching rented sado-masochistic videotapes.

It was true—he said only when I prompted him—that he was isolated and, yes, that did constitute a problem, but only because there were times when he was too weak to care for his own physical needs. The idea of pleasure deriving from close human (nonsexual) contact seemed alien to him. There was one exception—his children—and when Carlos spoke of them real emotion, emotion that I could join with, broke through. I was moved by the sight of his frail body heaving with sobs as he described his fear that they, too, would abandon him: that their mother would finally succeed in poisoning them against him, or that they would become repelled by his cancer and turn away from him.

"What can I do to help, Carlos?"

"If you want to help me—then teach me how to hate armadillos!"

For a moment Carlos enjoyed my perplexity, and then proceeded to explain that he had been working with visual imaging—a form of self-healing many cancer patients attempt. His visual metaphors for his new chemotherapy (referred to by his oncologists as BP) were giant B's and P's—Bears and Pigs; his metaphor for his hard cancerous lymph nodes was a bony-plated armadillo. Thus, in his meditation sessions, he visualized bears and pigs attacking the armadillos. The problem was that he couldn't make his bears and pigs be vicious enough to tear open and destroy the armadillos.

Despite the horror of his cancer and his narrowness of spirit, I was drawn to Carlos. Perhaps it was generosity welling out of my relief that it was he, and not I, who was dying. Perhaps it was his love for his children or the plaintive way he grasped my hand with both of his when he was leaving my office. Perhaps it was the whimsy in his request: "Teach me to hate armadillos."

Therefore, as I considered whether I could treat him, I minimized potential obstacles to treatment and persuaded myself that he was more *un*socialized than malignantly antisocial, and that many of his noxious traits and beliefs were soft and open to being modified. I did not think through my decision clearly and, even after I decided to accept him in therapy, remained unsure about appropriate and realistic treatment goals. Was I simply to escort him through this course of chemotherapy? (Like many patients, Carlos became deathly ill and despondent during chemotherapy.) Or, if he were entering a terminal phase, was I to commit myself to stay with him until death? Was I to be satisfied with offering sheer presence and support? (Maybe that would be sufficient. God knows he had no one else to talk to!) Of course, his isolation was his own doing, but was I going to help him to recognize or to change that? Now? In the face of death, these considerations seemed immaterial. Or did they? Was it possible that Carlos could accomplish something more "ambitious" in therapy? No, no, no! *What sense does it make to talk about "ambitious" treatment with someone whose anticipated life span may be, at best, a matter of months?* Does anyone, do I, want to invest time and energy in a project of such evanescence?

Carlos readily agreed to meet with me. In his typical cynical mode, he said that his insurance policy would pay ninety percent of my fee, and that he wouldn't turn down a bargain like that. Besides, he was a person who wanted to try everything once, and he had never before spoken to a psychiatrist. I left our treatment contract unclear, aside from saying that having someone with whom to share painful feelings and thoughts always helped. I suggested that we meet six times and then evaluate whether treatment seemed worthwhile.

To my great surprise, Carlos made excellent use of therapy; and after six sessions, we agreed to meet in ongoing treatment. He came to every hour with a list of issues he wanted to discuss—dreams, work problems (a successful financial analyst, he had continued to work throughout his illness). Sometimes he talked about his physical discomfort and his loathing of chemotherapy, but most of all he talked about women and sex. Each session he described all of his encounters with women that week (often they consisted of nothing more than catching a woman's eye in the grocery store) and obsessing about what he might have done in each instance to have consummated a relationship. He was so preoccupied with women that he seemed to forget that he had a cancer that was actively infiltrating all the crawl spaces of his body. Most likely that was the point of his preoccupation—that he might forget his infestation.

But his fixation on women had long predated his cancer. He had always prowled for women and regarded them in highly sexualized and demeaning terms. So Sarah's account of Carlos in the group, shocking as it was, did not astonish me. I knew he was entirely capable of such gross behavior—and worse.

But how should I handle the situation with him in the next hour? Above all, I wished to protect and maintain our relationship. We were making progress, and right now I was his primary human connection. But it was also important that he continue attending his therapy group. I had placed him in a group six weeks ago to provide him with a community that would both help to penetrate his isolation and also, by identifying and urging him to alter some of his most socially objectionable behavior, help him to create connections in his social life. For the first five weeks, he had made excellent use of the group but, unless he changed his behavior dramatically, he would, I was certain, irreversibly alienate all the group members—if he hadn't done so already!

Our next session started uneventfully. Carlos didn't even mention the group but, instead, wanted to talk about Ruth, an attractive woman he had just met at a church social. (He was a member of a half-dozen churches because he believed they provided him with ideal pickup opportunities.) He had talked briefly to Ruth, who then excused herself because she had to go home. Carlos said goodbye but later grew convinced that he had missed a golden opportunity by not offering to escort her to her car; in fact, he had persuaded himself that there was a fair chance, perhaps a ten- to fifteen-percent chance, he might have married her. His self-recriminations for not having acted with greater dispatch continued all week and included verbal self-assaults and physical abuse—pinching himself and pounding his head against the wall.

I didn't pursue his feelings about Ruth (although they were so patently irrational that I decided to return to her at some point) because I thought it was urgent that we discuss the group. I told him that I had spoken to Sarah about the meeting. "Were you," I asked, "going to talk about the group today?"

"Not particularly, it's not important. Anyway, I'm going to stop that group. I'm too advanced for it."

"What do you mean?"

"Everyone is dishonest and playing games there. I'm the only person there with enough guts to tell the truth. The men are all losers— they wouldn't be there otherwise. They're jerks with no *cojones*, they sit around whimpering and saying nothing."

"Tell me what happened in the meeting from your perspective."

"Sarah talked about the rape, she tell you that?"

I nodded.

"And Martha did, too. That Martha. God, that's one for you. She's a mess, a real sickie, she is. She's a mental case, on tranquilizers. What the hell am I doing in a group with people like her anyway? But listen to me. The important point is that they talked about their rapes, both of them, and everyone just sat there silently with their mouths hanging open. At least I responded. I asked them questions."

"Sarah suggested that some of your questions were not of the helpful variety."

"Someone had to get them talking. Besides, I've always been curious about rape. Aren't you? Aren't all men? About how it's done, about the rape victim's experience?"

"Oh, come on, Carlos, if that's what you were after, you could have read about it in a book. These were real people there—not sources of information. There was something else going on."

"Maybe so, I'll admit that. When I started the group, your instructions were that I should be honest in expressing my feelings in the group. Believe me, I swear it, in the last meeting I was the only honest person in the group. I got turned on, I admit it. It's a fantastic turn-on to think of Sarah getting screwed. I'd love to join in and get my hands on those boobs of hers. I haven't forgiven you for preventing me from dating her." When he had first started the group six weeks ago, he talked at great length about his infatuation with Sarah—or rather with her breasts—and was convinced she would be willing to go out with him. To help Carlos become assimilated in the group, I had, in the first few meetings, coached him on appropriate social behavior. I had persuaded him, with difficulty, that a sexual approach to Sarah would be both futile and unseemly.

"Besides, it's no secret that men get turned on by rape. I saw the other men in the group smiling at me. Look at the porno business! Have you ever taken a good look at the books and videotapes about rape or bondage? Do it! Go visit the porno shops in the Tenderloin— it'd be good for your education. They're printing those things for somebody—there's gotta be a market out there. I'll tell you the truth, *if rape were legal, I'd do it*—once in a while."

Carlos stopped there and gave me a smug grin—or was it a poke-in-the-arm leer, an invitation to take my place beside him in the brotherhood of rapists?

I sat silently for several minutes trying to identify my options. It was easy to agree with Sarah: he *did* sound depraved. Yet I was convinced part of it was bluster, and that there was a way to reach something better, something higher in him. I was interested in, grateful for, his last few words: the "once in a while." Those words, added almost as an after-thought, seemed to suggest some scrap of self-consciousness or shame.

"Carlos, you take pride in your honesty in the group—but were you really being honest? Or only part honest, or easy honest? It's true, you were more open than the other men in the group. You did express some of your real sexual feelings. And you do have a point about how widespread these feelings are: the porno business must be offering something which appeals to impulses all men have.

"But are you being completely honest? What about all the other feelings going on inside you that you *haven't* expressed? Let me take a guess about something: when you said 'big deal' to Sarah and Martha about their rapes, is it possible you were thinking about your cancer and what you have to face all the time? It's a hell of a lot tougher facing something that threatens your life *right now* than something that hap-pened a year or two ago.

"Maybe you'd like to get some caring from the group, but how can you get it when you come on so tough? You haven't yet talked about having cancer." (I had been urging Carlos to reveal to the group that he had cancer, but he was procrastinating: he said he was afraid he'd be pitied, and didn't want to sabotage his sexual chances with the women members.)

Carlos grinned at me. "Good try, Doc! It makes a lot of sense. You've got a good head. But I'll be honest—the thought of my cancer never entered my mind. Since we stopped chemotherapy two months ago, I go days at a time without thinking of the cancer. That's goddamn good, isn't it—to forget it, to be free of it, to be able to live a normal life for a while?"

Good question! I thought. Was it good to forget? I wasn't so sure. Over the months I had been seeing Carlos, I had discovered that I could chart, with astonishing accuracy, the course of his cancer by not-ing the things he thought about. Whenever his cancer worsened and he was actively facing death, he rearranged his life priorities and be-came more thoughtful, compassionate, wiser. When, on the other hand, he was in remission, he was guided, as he put it, by his pecker and grew noticeably more coarse and shallow.

I once saw a newspaper cartoon of a pudgy lost little man saying, "Suddenly, one day in your forties or fifties, everything becomes clear. . . . And then it goes away again!" That cartoon was apt for Carlos, except that he had not one, but *repeated* episodes of clarity—and they always went away again. I often thought that if I could find a way to keep him continually aware of his death and the "clearing" that death effects, I could help him make some major changes in the way he related to life and to other people.

It was evident from the specious way he was speaking today, and a couple of days ago in the group, that his cancer was quiescent again, and that death, with its attendant wisdom, was far out of mind.

I tried another tack. "Carlos, before you started the group I tried to explain to you the basic rationale behind group therapy. Remember how I emphasized that whatever happens in the group can be used to help us work in therapy?" He nodded.

I continued, "And that one of the most important principles of groups is that the group is a miniature world—whatever environment we create in the group reflects the way we have chosen to live? Remember that I said that each of us establishes *in* the group the *same kind of social world we have in our real life?*"

He nodded again. He was listening.

"Now, look what's happening to you in the group! You started with a number of people with whom you might have developed close relationships. And when you began, the two of us were in agreement that you needed to work on ways of developing relationships. That was why you began the group, remember? But now, after only six weeks, all the members and at least one of the co-therapists are thoroughly pissed at you. And it's your own doing. You've done *in* the group what you do *outside* of the group! I want you to answer me honestly: Are you satisfied? Is this what you want from your relationships with others?"

"Doc, I understand completely what you're saying, but there's a bug in your argument. I don't give a shit, not one shit, about the people in the group. They're not real people. I'm never going to associate with losers like that. Their opinion doesn't mean anything to me. I don't *want* to get closer to them."

I had known Carlos to close up completely like this on other occasions. He would, I suspected, be more reasonable in a week or two, and under ordinary circumstances I would simply have been patient. But unless something changed quickly, he would either drop out of the group or would, by next week, have ruptured beyond repair his relationships with the other members. Since I doubted very much, after this charming incident, whether I'd ever be able to persuade another group therapist to accept him, I persevered.

"I hear those angry and judgmental feelings, and I know you really feel them. But, Carlos, try to put brackets around them for a moment and see if you can get in touch with anything else. Both Sarah and Martha were in a great deal of pain. What other feelings did you have about them? I'm not talking about major or predominant feelings, but about any other flashes you had."

"I know what you're after. You're doing your best for me. I want to help you, but I'd be making up stuff. You're putting feelings into my mouth. Right here, this office, is the one place I can tell the truth, and the truth is that, more than anything else, what I want to do with those two cunts in the group is to fuck them! I meant it when I said that if rape were legal, I'd do it! And I know just where I'd start!"

Most likely he was referring to Sarah, but I did not ask. The last thing I wanted to do was enter into that discourse with him. Probably there was some important oedipal competition going on between the two of us which was making communication more difficult. He never missed an opportunity to describe to me in graphic terms what he would like to do to Sarah, as though he considered that we were rivals for her. I know he believed that the reason I had earlier dissuaded him from inviting Sarah out was that I wanted to keep her to myself. But this type of interpretation would be totally useless now: he was far too closed and defensive. If I were going to get through, I would have to use something more compelling.

The only remaining approach I could think of involved that one burst of emotion I had seen in our first session—the tactic seemed so contrived and so simplistic that I could not possibly have predicted the astonishing result it would produce.

"All right, Carlos, let's consider this ideal society you're imagining and advocating—this society of legalized rape. Think now, for a few minutes, about your daughter. How would it be for her living in the community—being available for legal rape, a piece of ass for whoever happens to be horny and gets off on force and seventeen-year-old girls?"

Suddenly Carlos stopped grinning. He winced visibly and said simply, "I wouldn't like that for her."

"But where would she fit, then, in this world you're building? Locked up in a convent? You've got to make a place where she can live: that's what fathers do—they build a world for their children. I've never asked you before—what do you really want for her?"

"I want her to have a loving relationship with a man and have a loving family."

"But how can that happen if her father is advocating a world of rape? If you want her to live in a loving world, then it's up to you to construct that world—and you have to start with your own behavior. You can't be outside your own law—that's at the base of every ethical system."

The tone of the session had changed. No more jousting or crudity. We had grown deadly serious. I felt more like a philosophy or religious teacher than a therapist, but I knew that this was the proper trail. And these were things I should have said before. He had often joked about his own inconsistency. I remember his once describing with glee a dinner-table conversation with his children (they visited him two or three times a year) when he informed his daughter that he wanted to meet and approve any boy she went out with. "As for *you*," pointing to his son, "*you* get all the ass you can!"

There was no question now that I had his attention. I decided to increase my leverage by triangulation, and I approached the same issue from another direction:

"And, Carlos, something else comes to my mind right now. Remember your dream of the green Honda two weeks ago? Let's go back over it."

He enjoyed working on dreams and was only too glad to apply himself to this one and, in so doing, to leave the painful discussion about his daughter.

Carlos had dreamed that he went to a rental agency to rent a car, but the only ones available were Honda Civics—his least favorite car. Of several colors available, he selected red. But when he got out to the lot, the only car available was green—his least favorite color! The most important fact about a dream is its emotion, and this dream, despite its benign content, was full of terror: it had awakened him and flooded him with anxiety for hours.

Two weeks ago we had not been able to get far with the dream. Carlos, as I recall, went off on a tangent of associations about the identity of the female auto rental clerk. But today I saw the dream in a different light. Many years ago he had developed a strong belief in reincarnation, a belief that offered him blessed relief from fears about dying. The metaphor he used in one of our first meetings was that dying is simply trading in your body for another one—like trading in an old car. I reminded him now of that metaphor.

"Let's suppose, Carlos, that the dream is more than a dream about cars. Obviously renting a car is not a frightening activity, not something that would become a nightmare and keep you up all night. I think the dream is about death and future life, and it uses your symbol of comparing death and rebirth to a trade of cars. If we look at it that way, we can make more sense of the powerful fear the dream carried. What do you make of the fact that the only kind of car you could get was a green Honda Civic?"

"I hate green and I hate Honda Civics. My next car is going to be a Maserati."

"But if cars are dream symbols of bodies, why would you, in your next life, get the body, or the life, that you hate above all others?"

Carlos had no option but to respond. "You get what you deserve, depending on what you've done or the way you've lived your present life. You can either move up or down."

Now he realized where this discussion was leading, and began to perspire. The dense forest of crassness and cynicism surrounding him had always shocked and dissuaded visitors. But now it was his turn to be shocked. I had invaded his two innermost temples: his love for his children and his reincarnation beliefs.

"Go on, Carlos, this is important—apply that to yourself and to your life."

He bit off each word slowly. "The dream is saying that I'm not living right."

"I agree, I think that *is* what the dream is saying. Say some more on your thoughts about living right."

I was going to pontificate about what constitutes a good life in any religious system—love, generosity, care, noble thoughts, pursuit of the good, charity—but none of that was necessary. Carlos let me know I had made my point: he said that he was getting dizzy, and that this was a lot to deal with in one day. He wanted time to think about it during the week. Noting that we still had fifteen minutes left, I decided to do some work on another front.

I went back to the first issue he had raised in the hour: his belief that he had missed a golden opportunity with Ruth, the woman he had met briefly at a church social, and his subsequent head pounding and self-recrimination for not having walked her to her car. The function that his irrational belief served was patent. As long as he continued to believe that he was tantalizingly close to being desired and loved by an attractive woman, he could buttress his belief that he was no different from anyone else, that there was nothing seriously wrong with him, that he was not disfigured, not mortally ill.

In the past I hadn't tampered with his denial. In general, it's best not to undermine a defense unless it is creating more problems than solutions, and unless one has something better to offer in its stead.

Reincarnation is a case in point: though I personally consider it a form of death denial, the belief served Carlos (as it does much of the world's population) very well; in fact, rather than undermine it, I had always supported it and in this session buttressed it by urging that he be consistent in heeding all the implications of reincarnation.

But the time had come to challenge some of the less helpful parts of his denial system.

"Carlos, do you really believe that if you had walked Ruth to her car you'd have a ten- to fifteen-percent chance of marrying her?"

"One thing could lead to another. There was something going on between the two of us. I felt it. I know what I know!"

"But you say that every week—the lady in the supermarket, the receptionist in the dentist's office, the ticket seller at the movie. You even felt that with Sarah. Look, how many times have you, or any man, walked a woman to her car and *not* married her?"

"O.K., O.K., maybe it's closer to a one-percent or half-percent chance, but there was still a chance—if I hadn't been such a jerk. I didn't even *think* of asking to walk her to the car!"

"The things you pick to beat yourself up about! Carlos, I'm going to be blunt. What you're saying doesn't make any sense at all. All you've told me about Ruth—you only talked to her for five minutes—is that she's twenty-three with two small kids and is recently divorced. Let's be very realistic—as you say, this is the place to be honest. What are you going to tell her about your health?"

"When I get to know her better, I'll tell her the truth—that I've got cancer, that it's under control now, that the doctors can treat it."

"And—?"

"That the doctors aren't sure what's going to happen, that there are new treatments discovered every day, that I may have recurrences in the future."

"What did the doctors say to you? Did they say *may* have recurrences?"

"You're right—*will* have recurrences in the future, unless a cure is found."

"Carlos, I don't want to be cruel, but be objective. Put yourself in Ruth's place—twenty-three years old, two small children, been through a hard time, presumably looking for some strong support for herself and her kids, having only a layman's knowledge and fear of cancer—do you represent the kind of security and support she's looking for? Is she going to be willing to accept the uncertainty surrounding your health? To risk placing herself in the situation where she might be obligated to nurse you? What really are the chances she would allow herself to know you in the way you want, to become involved with you?"

"Probably not one in a million," Carlos said in a sad and weary voice.

I was being cruel, yet the option of *not* being cruel, of simply humoring him, of tacitly acknowledging that he was incapable of seeing reality, was crueler yet. His fantasy about Ruth allowed him to feel that he could still be touched and cared for by another human. I hoped that he would understand that my willingness to engage him, rather than wink behind his back, was my way of touching and caring.

All the bluster was gone. In a soft voice Carlos asked, "So where does that leave me?"

"If what you really want now is closeness, then it's time to take all this heat off yourself about finding a wife. I've been watching you beat yourself up for months about this. I think it's time to let up on yourself. You've just finished a difficult course of chemotherapy. Four weeks ago you couldn't eat or get out of bed or stop vomiting. You've lost a lot of weight, you're regaining your strength. Stop expecting to find a wife right now, it's too much to ask of yourself. Set a reasonable goal—you can do this as well as I. Concentrate on having a good conversation. Try deepening a friendship with the people you already know."

I saw a smile begin to form on Carlos's lips. He saw my next sentence coming: *"And what better place to start than in the group?"*

Carlos was never the same person after that session. Our next appointment was the day following the next group meeting. The first thing he said was that I would not believe how good he had been in the group. He bragged that he was now the most supportive and sensitive member. He had wisely decided to bail himself out of trouble by telling the group about his cancer. He claimed—and, weeks later, Sarah was to corroborate this—that his behavior had changed so dramatically that the members now looked to him for support.

He praised our previous session. "The last session was our best one so far. I wish we could have sessions like that every time. I don't remember exactly what we talked about, but it helped me change a lot."

I found one of his comments particularly droll.

"I don't know why, but I'm even relating differently to the men in the group. They are all older than me but, it's funny, I have a sense of treating them as though they were my own sons!"

His having forgotten the content of our last session troubled me little. Far better that he forget what we talked about than the opposite possibility (a more popular choice for patients)—to remember precisely what was talked about but to remain unchanged.

Carlos's improvement increased exponentially. Two weeks later, he began our session by announcing that he had had, during that week, two major insights. He was so proud of the insights that he had christened them. The first, he called (glancing at his notes), "Everybody has got a heart." The second was "I am not my shoes."

First, he explained "Everybody has got a heart." "During the group meeting last week, all three women were sharing a lot of their feelings, about how hard it was being single, about loneliness, about grieving for their parents, about nightmares. I don't know why, but I suddenly saw them in a different way! They were like me! They were having the same problems in living that I was. I had always before imagined women sitting on Mount Olympus with a line of men before them and sorting them out—this one to my bedroom, this one not!

"But that moment," Carlos continued, "I had a vision of their naked hearts. Their chest wall vanished, just melted away leaving a square blue-red cavity with rib-bar walls and, in the center, a liver-colored glistening heart thumping away. All week long I've been seeing everyone's heart beating, and I've been saying to myself, 'Everybody has got a heart, everybody has got a heart.' I've been seeing the heart in everyone—a misshapen hunchback who works in reception, an old lady who does the floors, even the men I work with!"

Carlos's comment gave me so much joy that tears came to my eyes. I think he saw them but, to spare me embarrassment, made no comment and hurried along to the next insight: "I am not my shoes."

He reminded me that in our last session we had discussed his great anxiety about an upcoming presentation at work. He had always had great difficulty speaking in public: excruciatingly sensitive to any criticism, he had often, he said, made a spectacle of himself by viciously counterattacking anyone who questioned any aspect of his presentation.

I had helped him understand that he had lost sight of his personal boundaries. It is natural, I had told him, that one should respond adversely to an attack on one's central core—after all, in that situation one's very survival is at stake. But I had pointed out that Carlos had stretched his personal boundaries to encompass his work and, consequently, he responded to a mild criticism of any aspect of his work as though it were a mortal attack on his central being, a threat to his very survival.

I had urged Carlos to differentiate between his core self and other, peripheral attributes or activities. Then he had to "disidentify" with the non-core parts: they might represent what he liked, or did, or valued—but they were not *him*, not his central being.

Carlos had been intrigued by this construct. Not only did it explain his defensiveness at work, but he could extend this "disidentification" model to pertain to his body. In other words, even though his body was imperiled, he himself, his vital essence, was intact.

This interpretation allayed much of his anxiety, and his work presentation last week had been wonderfully lucid and nondefensive. Never had he done a better job. Throughout his presentation, a small mantra wheel in his mind had hummed, "I am not my work." When he finished and sat down next to his boss, the mantra continued, "I am not my work. Not my talk. Not my clothes. None of these things." He crossed his legs and noted his scuffed and battered shoes: "And I'm not my shoes either." He began to wiggle his toes and his feet hoping to attract his boss's attention so as to proclaim to him, "I am not my shoes!"

Carlos's two insights—the first of many to come—were a gift to me and to my students. These two insights, each generated by a different form of therapy, illustrated, in quintessential form, the difference between what one can derive from group therapy, with its focus on communion *between*, and individual therapy, with its focus on communion *within*. I still use many of his graphic insights to illustrate my teaching.

In the few months of life remaining to him, Carlos chose to continue to give. He organized a cancer self-help group (not without some humorous crack about this being the "last stop" pickup joint) and also was the group leader for some interpersonal skills groups at one of his churches. Sarah, by now one of his greatest boosters, was invited as a guest speaker to one of his groups and attested to his responsible and competent leadership.

But, most of all, he gave to his children, who noted the change in him and elected to live with him while enrolling for a semester at a nearby college. He was a marvelously generous and supportive father. I have always felt that the way one faces death is greatly determined by the model one's parents set. The last gift a parent can give to children is to teach them, through example, how to face death with equanimity—and Carlos gave an extraordinary lesson in grace. His death was not one of the dark, muffled, conspiratorial passings. Until the very end of his life, he and his children were honest with one another about his illness and giggled together at the way he snorted, crossed his eyes, and puckered his lips when he referred to his "lymphoooooooooooomma."

But he gave no greater gift than the one he offered me shortly before he died, and it was a gift that answers for all time the question of whether it is rational or appropriate to strive for "ambitious" therapy in those who are terminally ill. When I visited him in the hospital he was so weak he could barely move, but he raised his head, squeezed my hand, and whispered, "Thank you. Thank you for saving my life."

# 3

❧❧❦

# "The Wrong One Died"

*A few years ago, while preparing a research proposal on bereavement, I placed* a brief article in a local newspaper which ended with this message:

> In the first, planning stage of his research, Dr. Yalom wishes to interview individuals who have been unable to overcome their grief. Volunteers who are willing to be interviewed, please call 555-6352.

Of the thirty-five people who phoned for an appointment, Penny was the first. She told my secretary that she was thirty-eight years old and divorced, that she had lost her daughter four years previously, and that it was urgent for her to be seen immediately. Although she worked sixty hours a week as a taxicab driver, she emphasized that she would come in for an interview at any hour of the day or night.

Twenty-four hours later she was sitting opposite me. A rugged, brawny woman: weathered, battered, proud—and trembling. You could tell she had been through a lot. She reminded me of Marjorie Main, the tough-talking movie star of the 1930s, now long dead.

The fact that Penny was in crisis, or said she was, presented me with a dilemma. I could not possibly treat her; I had no hours available to take on a new patient. Every minute of my time was committed to completing a research proposal, and the deadline for the grant application was rapidly approaching. That was the top priority in my life then; that was why I had advertised for volunteers. Furthermore, since

I was leaving on sabbatical in three months, there was insufficient time for a decent course of psychotherapy.

To prevent any misunderstanding, I decided it would be best to clarify at once the issue of therapy—before I got in too deep with Penny, before I even asked why, four years after her daughter's death, she needed to be seen immediately.

So I started by thanking her for volunteering to speak to me for two hours about her bereavement. I informed her that it was important for her to know, before she agreed to proceed, that these were to be research, not therapeutic, interviews. I even added that, though there was a chance that talking might help, it was also possible that talking might be temporarily unsettling. If, however, I thought therapy *were* needed, I would be glad to help her select a therapist.

I paused and looked at Penny. I was entirely satisfied with my words: I had covered myself and had been clear enough to prevent any misunderstandings.

Penny nodded. She rose from her chair. For an instant I was alarmed because I thought she would walk out. But she simply smoothed out her long denim skirt, sat back down, and asked if she could smoke. When I handed her an ashtray, she lit up and, in a strong deep voice, began: "I need to talk, all right, but I can't afford therapy. I'm strapped. I've seen two cheap therapists—one was still a student—at the county clinic. But they were afraid of me. No one wants to talk about a child's dying. When I was eighteen, I went to a counselor at an alcohol clinic who was an ex-alcoholic—she was good, she asked the right questions. Maybe I need a shrink who's lost a kid! Maybe I need a real expert. I have a lot of respect for Stanford University. That's why I jumped when I saw the newspaper story. I always thought my daughter would go to Stanford—if she had lived."

She looked straight at me and spoke right out. I like hard women, and I liked her style. I noticed that I began to speak a little tougher.

"I'll help you talk. And I can ask hard questions. But I ain't going to be around to pick up the pieces."

"I heard you. You just help get me started. I'll take care of me. I was a latchkey kid when I was ten."

"O.K., begin with why you wanted to see me immediately. My secretary said you sounded desperate. What's happened?"

"A few days ago, I was driving home from work—I finish up about one in the morning—and I had a blackout. I woke up and I was driving on the wrong side of the road and screaming like a wounded animal! If there had been any traffic coming the other way, I wouldn't be here today."

That was how we began. I was unnerved by the image of this woman screaming like a wounded animal, and took a few moments to clear it from my mind. Then I started asking questions. Penny's daughter, Chrissie, had developed a rare form of leukemia when she was nine and died four years later, one day before her thirteenth birthday. During those four years Chrissie attempted to stay in school but was bedridden almost half the time and hospitalized every three or four months.

Her cancer and her treatment were both extremely painful. During her four years of illness, many courses of chemotherapy had prolonged her life but left her, each time, bald and agonizingly ill. Chrissie had had dozens of painful bone marrow extractions and so many bloodlettings that finally there were no more veins to be found. During the last year of her life, her physicians had installed a permanent intravenous catheter that permitted easy access to her bloodstream.

Her death, Penny said, was awful—I couldn't imagine how awful. At this point she started to sob. True to my word to ask hard questions, I urged her to tell me about how awful Chrissie's death had been.

Penny had wanted me to get her started; and, by sheer chance, my first question unleashed a torrent of feeling. (Later I was to learn that I would reach deep pain in Penny no matter where I probed.) Chrissie had died, finally, of pneumonia: her heart and lungs had failed; she couldn't breathe and, in the end, drowned in her own fluids.

The worst thing, Penny told me between sobs, was that she couldn't remember her daughter's death: she had blacked out Chrissie's final hours. All she remembered was going to sleep that evening alongside her daughter—during Chrissie's hospitalizations Penny slept on a cot next to her—and, much later, sitting at the head of Chrissie's bed with her arms around her dead daughter.

Penny began to talk about guilt. She was obsessed with the way she had behaved during Chrissie's death. She could not forgive herself. Her voice became louder, her tone more self-accusatory. She sounded like a prosecuting attorney trying to convince me of her dereliction.

"Can you believe," she said, "I can't even remember *when*, I can't remember *how* I learned my Chrissie had died?"

She was certain, and soon convinced me she was correct, that the guilt about her shameful behavior was *the* reason she couldn't let Chrissie go, *the* reason her grief had been frozen for four years.

I was determined to pursue my research plans: to learn as much as possible about chronic bereavement and to design a structured interview protocol. Nonetheless, possibly because there was so much therapy to be done, I found myself forgetting the research and, little by little, slipping into a therapeutic mode. Since guilt seemed to be the primary problem, I set about, for the rest of the two-hour interview, learning as much as possible about Penny's guilt.

"Guilty of what?" I asked. "What are the charges?"

The main charge she brought against herself was that she had not been really present with Chrissie. She had, as she put it, played a lot of fantasy games. She had never allowed herself to believe that Chrissie would die. Even though the doctor had told her that Chrissie was living on borrowed time, that no one had ever recovered from this disease, even though he said, point-blank, when she last entered the hospital, that she could not live much longer, Penny refused to believe that Chrissie would not get well again. She was full of fury when the doctor referred to the final pneumonia as a blessing that should not be interfered with.

In fact, she had not accepted that Chrissie was dead even now, four years later. Just a week previously, she "woke up" to find herself in a drugstore checkout line with a gift for Chrissie in hand, a stuffed animal. And at one point in my interview with her, she said that Chrissie "will be" seventeen next month, instead of "would be."

"Is that such a crime?" I asked. "Is it a crime to keep on hoping? What mother wants to believe her child has to die?"

Penny replied that she hadn't acted out of love for Chrissie but instead had put herself first. How? She had never helped Chrissie talk about her fears and her feelings. How could Chrissie talk about dying to a mother who continued to pretend it wasn't happening? Consequently, Chrissie was forced to be alone with her thoughts. What difference did it make if she slept next to her daughter? She really wasn't there for her. The worst thing that can happen to someone is to die alone, and that was the way she had let her daughter die.

Then Penny told me that she had a deep belief in reincarnation, a belief that began when she was a teenager and miserable and poor and so tormented by the thought that she had been gypped in life that she could find consolation only in the thought that she would have another chance. Penny knew that next time around she would be luckier— perhaps richer. She knew also that Chrissie was going on to another, healthier, happier life.

Yet she hadn't helped Chrissie die. In fact, Penny was convinced that it was *her* fault Chrissie's dying took so long. For her mother's sake, Chrissie had stayed around, prolonging her pain, delaying her release. Though Penny didn't remember the final hours of Chrissie's life, she was certain that she did *not* say what she *should* have said: "Go! Go! It's time for you to go. You do not have to stay here for me any longer."

One of my sons was then in his teens, and, as she spoke, I began to think of him. Could I have done it, let go of his hand, helped him die, told him, "Go! It is time to go"? His sunny face hovered in the eye of my mind and a wave of inexpressible anguish enveloped me.

"No!" I told myself, shaking myself free. Getting inundated with emotion was likely what happened to the others, to the therapists who couldn't help her. I saw that, to work with Penny, I would need to lash myself to the mast of reason.

"So what I hear you say is that you feel guilty about two main things. *First*, because you didn't help Chrissie talk about dying, and *second*, because you didn't let go of her soon enough."

Penny nodded, sobered by my analytic tone, and her sobbing stopped.

Nothing offers more false security in psychotherapy than a crisp summary, especially a summary containing a list. My own words heartened me: the problem seemed suddenly clearer, more familiar, far more manageable. Though I had never before worked with anyone who had lost a child, I ought to be able to help her since much of her grief was reducible to guilt. Guilt and I were old acquaintances, both personal and professional.

Earlier Penny had told me that she was in frequent communion with Chrissie, visiting her daily in the cemetery and spending an hour a day grooming her grave and talking to her. Penny devoted so much energy and attention to Chrissie that her marriage deteriorated, and her husband left for good about two years before. Penny said she hardly noticed his going.

As a memorial to Chrissie, Penny had kept her room unchanged, with all her clothes and possessions in their familiar places. Even her last, unfinished homework assignment lay on the desk. Only one thing had been changed: Penny took Chrissie's bed into her own room and slept on it every night. Later, after I had interviewed more bereaved parents, I would learn how commonplace such behavior was. But then, in my naiveté, I thought it outrageous, unnatural, something that had to be put right.

"So you deal with your guilt now by hanging on to Chrissie, by not getting on with your life?"

"I just can't forget her. You can't throw a switch on and off, you know!"

"Letting go of her is not the same thing as forgetting—and nobody is asking you to throw a switch." I was now convinced it was important to answer Penny right back: when I stayed tough, she got more resilient.

"Forgetting Chrissie is like saying I never loved her. It's like saying that your love for your own daughter was just something temporary—something that fades. I *won't* forget her."

"'*Won't*' forget her. Well that's different from being asked to throw a switch." She had ignored my distinction between forgetting and letting go, but I let it pass. "Before you can let go of Chrissie, you need to *want* to, to be *willing* to. Let's try to understand this together. For the moment, pretend you're hanging on to Chrissie because you *choose* to. What does this do for you?"

"I don't know what you're talking about."

"Yes, you do! Just humor me. What do you get out of hanging on to Chrissie?"

"I deserted her when she was dying, when she needed me. No way I'm going to desert her again."

Though Penny didn't yet understand, she was locked into an irreconcilable contradiction between her determination to stay with Chrissie and her reincarnation beliefs. Penny's grief was stuck, gridlocked. Perhaps, if she confronted this contradiction, she could start grieving again.

"Penny, you talk to Chrissie every day. Where is Chrissie? Where does she exist?"

Penny's eyes widened. No one had ever before asked such blunt questions. "On the day she died, I brought her spirit back home again. I could feel it in the car with me. At first she stayed around me, sometimes at home in her room. Then later I could always make contact in the cemetery. She usually knew what was going on in my life, but she'd want to know about her friends and her brothers. I stayed in touch with all her friends so I could tell her about them." Penny paused.

"And now?"

"Now she's fading. Which is good. It means she's been reborn into another life."

"Does she have any memory of this life?"

"No. She's into another life. I don't believe in this shit about re-membering past lives."

"So she's got to be free to go on to her next life, and yet there's a part of you that won't let her go."

Penny said nothing. She just stared at me.

"Penny, you're a tough judge. You put yourself on trial for the crime of not letting Chrissie go when she was about to die, and you sen-tenced yourself to self-hatred. I personally think you judge yourself too harshly. Show me the parent who could have done otherwise. I'll tell you, if my child were dying I couldn't have. But, even worse, the sentence is so severe—so damn tough on yourself. It sounds like your guilt and grief have already broken up your marriage. And the *length* of the sentence! That's what really blows my mind. It's four years now. How much longer? Another year? Four more? Ten? A life sentence?"

I collected my thoughts, trying to decide how to help her see what she was doing to herself. She sat motionless, a cigarette smoldering in the ashtray in her lap; her gray eyes were fixed on me. She hardly seemed to breathe.

I continued: "I've been sitting here trying to make sense of it and I've just had an idea. You're not punishing yourself for something you did once, four years ago, when Chrissie was dying. *You're punishing yourself for something you're doing now*, something you're continuing to do this very moment. You're holding on to her, trying to keep her in this life when you know she belongs elsewhere. Letting her go wouldn't be a sign of abandoning her or of *not* loving her, but just the opposite, a sign of really loving her—loving her enough *to let her go* to another life."

Penny continued to stare. She didn't speak but seemed moved by what I had said. My words *felt* powerful, and I knew it would be best simply to sit in silence with her. But I decided to say something else. It was probably overkill.

"Go back to that moment, Penny, that moment when you should have let Chrissie go, that moment you've blotted from your memory. Where is that moment now?"

"What do you mean? I don't understand."

"Well, where is it? Where does it exist?"

Penny seemed anxious and a little irritable at being pushed or quizzed. "I don't know what you're getting at. It's past. It's gone."

"Does any memory of it exist? In Chrissie? You say she's forgotten all traces of this life?"

"It's all gone. She don't remember, I don't remember. So——?"

"So you continue to torture yourself about a moment that doesn't exist anywhere—a 'phantom moment.' If you knew of someone else doing that, I think you'd call it dumb."

Looking back now on this interchange, I see much sophistry in my words. But at the moment they felt compelling and profound. Penny, who, in her streetwise way, always had an answer for everything, again just sat silent, as though in shock.

Our two hours were drawing to a close. Although Penny did not ask for more time, it was obvious we had to meet again. Too much had happened: it would have been professionally irresponsible not to offer her an additional hour. She did not seem surprised by my offer and immediately agreed to return next week at the same time.

*Frozen*—the metaphor often applied to chronic grief—is apt. The body is stiff; the face taut; cold, repetitive thoughts clog the brain. Penny was frozen. Would our confrontation break the ice jam? I was optimistic it would. While I couldn't guess what would be set free, I anticipated considerable churning during the week and awaited her next visit with much curiosity.

Penny began that hour by falling heavily into the chair and saying, "Boy, am I glad to see you! It's been quite a week."

She continued, with forced cheerfulness, to tell me that the good news was that for the past week she had felt less guilty and less involved with Chrissie. The bad news was that she had had a violent confrontation with Jim, her older son, and, in response, had been alternating between rage and crying jags all week.

Penny had two surviving children, Brent and Jim. Both had dropped out of school and were heading toward serious trouble. Brent, sixteen, was in juvenile hall detention for participating in a burglary; Jim, nineteen, was a heavy drug user. The current upheaval began the day after our last session when Penny learned that Jim had, for the last three months, not kept up his payment for their cemetery plot.

Cemetery plot? I must have misheard her and asked her to repeat herself. "Cemetery plot" was what she had said, all right. About five years before, when Chrissie was still alive but weakening, Penny signed a contract for an expensive cemetery plot—a plot large enough, she pointed out (as though this should make things self-evident) "to keep the whole family together." Each family member—Penny, her husband, Jeff, and her two sons—agreed, after intense pressure from her, to contribute a share of the cost in payments spread over seven years.

Yet, despite their promises, the whole financial burden of the plot was falling on her shoulders. Jeff had been gone for two years now and wanted nothing more to do with her, alive or dead. Her younger son, now incarcerated, was obviously unable to keep up his share (he had previously contributed a small amount from his after-school job). And now she found that Jim had been lying to her and not making his payments.

I was about to comment on her bizarre expectation that these two young men, who were obviously having enough problems with the enterprise of growing up, should be paying for their burial plot, when Penny continued with her account of the harrowing events of the week.

The night after her run-in with Jim, two men, obviously drug dealers, came to the door asking for him. When Penny told them that he was not home, one of them ordered her to tell Jim to pay the money he owed or he could forget about coming home: there wouldn't be any house left for him to come home to.

Now, there is nothing, Penny told me, more important to her than her house. After her father died when she was eight, her mother had moved her and her sisters from apartment to apartment at least twenty times, often staying for only two or three months until they were evicted for not paying the rent. She made a vow then that some day she would have a real home for her family—a vow she had worked furiously to fulfill. The monthly mortgage payments were high, and after Jeff left she had to carry the whole burden. Even though she was now working long hours, she was barely making it.

So the two men had said the wrong thing. After they left, she stood stunned by the door for a few moments; then she cursed Jim for using his money for drugs rather than his plot payments; and after that, as she put it, she "lost it completely" and tore after them. They had already driven off, but she jumped into her large, souped-up pickup and followed them at high speed down the highway trying to ram them off the road. She careened into them a couple of times, and they escaped only by gunning their BMW to over a hundred miles per hour.

She then notified the police about the threat (but not, of course, about the highway chase), and for the last week her house had been under constant police surveillance. Jim came home later that night and, after hearing about what had happened, hurriedly threw some clothes into his backpack and left town. She had heard nothing from him since. Although Penny voiced no regrets for her behavior—on the contrary, she seemed to relish telling the story—there were, nonetheless, deeper rumblings. Later that night she grew more agitated, slept poorly, and had this powerful dream:

> I was searching through rooms in an old institution. Finally I opened a door and saw two young boys standing on a platform like they were on display. They looked like my two boys, but they had long girls' hair and were wearing dresses. Only everything was wrong: their dresses were dirty and on backward and inside out. Their shoes were on the wrong feet.

I felt overwhelmed. With so many promising leads I didn't know which to choose. First, I thought of Penny's desperate wish to keep everyone together, to create the stable family she never had as a child, and how that was manifested in her fierce resolve to own a house and a cemetery plot. And now it was apparent that the center could not hold. Her plans and her family were shattered: her daughter was dead, her husband gone, one son was in jail, the other in hiding.

All I could do was to share my thoughts and to commiserate with Penny. I very much wanted to save enough time to work on that dream, especially that final part about her two small children. The first dreams that patients bring to therapy, especially rich and detailed ones, are often deeply illuminating.

I asked her to describe the main feelings in the dream. Penny said she woke up crying, but could not put her finger on the sad part of the dream.

"What about the two little boys?"

She said there was something pathetic, maybe sad, about the way they were dressed—shoes on the wrong feet, dirty inside-out clothes. And dresses? What about the long hair and dresses? Penny couldn't make sense of that, except then to say that maybe having the boys at all was a mistake. Maybe she would have wished them to be girls? Chrissie had been a dream child, a good student, beautiful, musically gifted. Chrissie, I surmised, was Penny's hope for the future: it was she who could have rescued the family from its destiny of poverty and crime.

"Yeah," Penny sadly continued, "the dream's right on about my sons—dressed wrong, shoed wrong. Everything wrong about them—always has been. They been nothing but trouble. I had three children: one was an angel, and the other two, look at 'em—one in jail and the other a drug addict. I had three children—*and the wrong one died.*"

Penny gasped and put her hand to her mouth. "I've thought it before but never said it out loud."

"How does it sound?"

She put her head down, almost into her lap. Tears were streaming down her face and onto her denim skirt. "Inhuman."

"No, it's the opposite. I hear only human feelings. Maybe they don't sound good, but that happens to be the way we're built. Given your situation and your three children, what parent wouldn't feel the wrong one died? I sure as hell would!"

I didn't know how to offer her more than that, but she gave no indication of having heard me so I repeated myself. "If I were in your situation, I'd feel the same way."

She kept her head down but nodded almost imperceptibly.

As our third hour drew to a close, there was no longer any point in pretending that Penny was not in therapy with me. So I acknowledged it openly and suggested that we meet six more times and try to do as much as we could. I stressed that it would not be possible, because of other commitments and travel plans, to meet for more than six weeks. Penny accepted my offer but said that money was a big problem for her. Could we arrange to have payments spread out over several months? I reassured her that there would be no fee: since we had started to meet as part of a research venture, at this point I could not, in good conscience, suddenly change our contract and charge her.

In fact, I had no problems about seeing Penny without a fee: I had wanted to learn more about bereavement, and she was proving an excellent teacher. She had that very hour given me a concept that would serve me in good stead in all my future work with the bereaved: *if one is to learn to live with the dead, one must first learn to live with the living.* There seemed much work for Penny to do on her relationships with the living—especially with her sons and perhaps with her husband; and I assumed that would be how we would spend our remaining six hours.

*The wrong one died. The wrong one died.* Our next two hours were to consist of numerous variations on this harsh theme—a procedure referred to in the trade as "working through." Penny expressed deep rage at her sons—rage not only because of the way they lived but rage *that* they lived. Only after she was spent, only after she had dared to say what she had been feeling over the last eight years (since first hearing that her Chrissie had a killing cancer)—that she had given up on both her sons; that Brent, at sixteen, was already beyond help; that she had prayed for years that Jim's body could have been given to Chrissie (What did he need it for? He was going to kill it soon anyway, with drugs, with AIDS. Why should he have a working body and Chrissie, who loved her little body, have hers eaten away by cancer?)—only when Penny had said all these things, could she stop and reflect upon what she had said.

I could only sit and listen and from time to time reassure her that these were human feelings, and that she was only human for thinking them. Finally, it was time to help her turn toward her sons. I posed questions, at first gentle and gradually more challenging.

Had her sons always been difficult? Born difficult? What had happened in their lives that might have pushed them into the choices they made? What had they experienced when Chrissie was dying? How frightened were they? Had anyone talked to *them* about death? How did they feel about buying a burial plot? A plot next to Chrissie? How had they felt about their father abandoning them?

Penny didn't like my questions. At first they startled, then irritated, her. Then she began to realize that she had never considered what had happened in the family from her sons' perspective. She had never had a positive relationship with a man, and it is possible her sons had paid the penalty for that. We considered the men in her life: a father (faded from personal memory but forever reviled by her mother) who deserted her, through death, when she was eight; her mother's lovers—a lineup of unsavory night characters who vanished at daybreak; a first husband who deserted her one month after their wedding, when she was seventeen; and a cloddish, alcoholic second husband who ultimately deserted her in her grief.

Without question she had neglected the boys for the past eight years. When Chrissie was ill, Penny had spent inordinate amounts of time with her. After Chrissie's death, Penny was still unavailable to her sons: the rage she felt toward them, much of it only because they were alive instead of Chrissie, created a silence between them. Her sons had grown hard and distant, but once, before they sealed their feelings from her, they told her they had wanted more from her: they had wanted the hour a day she had spent, for four years, tending Chrissie's gravesite.

The impact of death on her sons? The boys were eight and eleven years old when Chrissie developed a fatal illness. That they might have been frightened by what was happening to their sister; that they, too, might grieve; that they might have begun to become aware of, and to fear, their own death: none of these possibilities had Penny ever considered.

And there was the matter of her sons' bedroom. Penny's small house had three small bedrooms, and the boys had always shared one while Chrissie had her own room. No doubt they resented that arrangement while Chrissie was alive, I suggested, but what of their anger now when Penny refused to let them use their sister's room after her death? And how did they feel about seeing Chrissie's last will and testament on the refrigerator for the past four years, attached with a magnetic metallic strawberry?

And think of how they must have resented her attempt to keep Chrissie's memory alive by continuing, for example, to celebrate Chrissie's birthday every year! And what had she done for *their* birthdays? Penny blushed and responded gruffly to my question by muttering, "The normal things." I knew I was getting through.

Perhaps Penny and Jeff's marriage was destined to fail, but there seemed little question that the final dissolution was hastened by grief. Penny and Jeff had different styles of grieving: Penny immersed herself in memory; Jeff preferred suppression and distraction. Whether they were compatible in other ways seemed immaterial at this point: they were vastly incompatible in their grieving, each preferring an approach that interfered with that of the other. How could Jeff forget when Penny papered the walls with Chrissie's picture, slept on her bed, turned her room into a memorial? How could Penny overcome her grief when Jeff refused even to talk about Chrissie; when (and this had initiated a dreadful row) he refused, six months after her death, to attend the graduation of Chrissie's junior high school class?

During the fifth hour our work on learning to live better with the living was interrupted by Penny's raising a different type of question. The more she thought about her family, her dead daughter and her two sons, the more she began to think: What am I living for? What's the point of it all? Her entire adult life had been guided by one principle: to give her children a better life than the one she had had. But now what did she have to show for the past twenty years? Had she wasted her life? And was there any point now in continuing to waste her life in the same way? Why kill herself to make mortgage payments? What future was there in anything?

So we changed our focus. We turned away from Penny's relationship with her sons and ex-husband and began to consider another important characteristic of parental bereavement—the loss of meaning in life. To lose a parent or a lifelong friend is often to lose the past: the person who died may be the only other living witness to golden events of long ago. But to lose a child is to lose the future: what is lost is no less than one's life project—what one lives for, how one projects oneself into the future, how one may hope to transcend death (indeed, one's child becomes one's immortality project). Thus, in professional language, parental loss is "object loss" (the "object" being a figure who has played an instrumental role in the constitution of one's inner world); whereas child loss is "project loss" (the loss of one's central organizing life principle, providing not only the *why* but also the *how* of life). Small wonder that child loss is the hardest loss of all to bear, that many parents are still grieving five years later, that some never recover.

But we had not progressed very far in our exploration of life purpose (not that progress can be expected: absence of purpose is a problem of *life* rather than of a life) when Penny changed course yet again. By now I had become accustomed to her bringing up a new concern almost every hour. It was not, as I first thought, that she was mercurial and unable to sustain focus. Instead, she was courageously unfolding her multilayered grief. How many more layers would she reveal to me?

She started one session—our seventh, I believe—by reporting two events: a vivid dream and another blackout.

The blackout consisted of her "waking up" in a drugstore (the same store where she had once before awakened holding a stuffed animal) weeping and clasping a high school graduation card.

Though the dream was not a nightmare, it was full of frustration and anxiety:

> *There was a wedding going on. Chrissie was marrying a boy in the neighborhood—a real turkey. I had to change my clothes. I was in this big horseshoe-shaped house, with lots of little rooms, trying one after the other to find the right room to change in. I kept on trying, but I couldn't find the right one.*

And, moments later, a "tagalong" fragment:

> *I was on a big train. We started going faster and then went up into a big arc in the sky. It was very beautiful. Lots of stars. Somewhere in there, maybe a subtitle (but it couldn't be, because I can't spell it) was the word* evolution—*there was a strong feeling about the word.*

At one level the dream related to Chrissie. We talked for a while about the bad marriage she made in the dream. Perhaps the bridegroom was death: it was clearly not the marriage Penny would have wanted for her daughter.

And evolution? Penny had said she was no longer feeling a connection with Chrissie in her cemetery visits (now down to two or three a week). Perhaps evolution, I suggested, signified that Chrissie had indeed left and gone on to another life.

Perhaps, but Penny had a better explanation for the sadness in both the blackout and the dreams. When she woke up from the blackout in the drugstore, she had the strongest sense that the graduation card in her hand was not for Chrissie (who would have graduated from high school at this time) but for herself. Penny had never finished school, and Chrissie was going to do it for both of them (and was also going to attend Stanford for both of them).

The dream about the wedding and the search for a changing room was, Penny thought, about her own bad marriages and her current attempt to change her life. Her associations to the building in the dream corroborated this view: the dream building bore a striking resemblance to the clinic that housed my office.

And *evolution*, too, referred to her, not to Chrissie. Penny was ready to change into something else. She was fiercely determined to evolve and to succeed in the genteel world. For years, between customers in her taxicab, she had listened to self-improvement cassette tapes on vocabulary improvement, great books, and art appreciation. She felt that she was talented but had never developed her talents because, since the age of thirteen, she had had to earn a living. If only she could stop working, do something for herself, finish high school, go to college full-time, study "nonstop," and "take off" from there (*there* was the dream train "taking off" into the air!).

Penny's emphasis began to change. Instead of talking about Chrissie's tragedy, she spent the next two hours describing the tragedy of her own life. As we approached our ninth, and last, hour, I sacrificed the rest of my credibility and offered to see Penny three additional hours, right up to the time of my sabbatical departure. For a number of reasons, I found it difficult to terminate: the sheer enormity of her suffering compelled me to stay with her. I was concerned by her clinical condition and felt responsible for it: week by week, as new material emerged, she had grown progressively more depressed. I was impressed by her use of therapy: I had never had a patient who had worked as productively. Lastly—I might as well be honest—I was transfixed by the unfolding drama, as each week offered a new, exciting, and entirely unpredictable episode.

Penny remembered her childhood in Atlanta, Georgia, as relentlessly bleak and impoverished. Her mother, an embittered, suspicious woman, had been hard-pressed to feed and clothe Penny and her two sisters. Her father made a fair living as a department-store delivery man but was, if her mother's account were to be trusted, a callous, joyless man who died of alcoholism when Penny was eight. When her father died, everything changed. There was no money. Her mother worked twelve hours a day as a laundress and spent most nights drinking and picking up men at a local bar. It was then that Penny's latchkey days began.

Never again did the family have a stable home. They moved from one tenement flat to another, often being evicted for nonpayment of rent. Penny went to work at thirteen, dropped out of school at fifteen, was an alcoholic at sixteen, married and divorced before she was eighteen, remarried and escaped to the West Coast at nineteen, where she proceeded to bear three children, buy a home, bury her daughter, divorce her husband, and put a down payment on a large cemetery plot.

I was particularly struck by two powerful themes in Penny's account of her life. One was that she had been gypped, that the cards were stacked against her by the time she was eight. Her fondest wish for the next life, for both herself and Chrissie, was to be "stinking rich."

Another theme was "escape," not just physical escape from Atlanta, from her family, from the cycle of poverty and alcoholism, but escape from her destiny of becoming a "poor crazy old lady" like her mother, Penny having recently learned that her mother had, over the last several years, had several psychiatric hospitalizations.

The escape from destiny—from social class destiny and from her personal poor-crazy-old-lady destiny—was a major motif in Penny's life. She came to see me to escape becoming crazy. She could take care, she said, of not being poor. Indeed, it was her drive to escape her destiny that fueled Penny's workaholism, that kept her working long grueling hours.

It was ironic, too, that her drive to escape the destiny of poverty and failure was halted only by a deeper destiny—the finitude inherent in life. Penny had, more than most of us, never come to terms with the inescapability of death. She was a quintessentially active person—I thought of her careening down the highway after the drug dealers—and one of the most difficult things to face during Chrissie's death was her own helplessness.

Despite the fact that I was used to Penny's making new major disclosures, I was not prepared for the bombshell she dropped in our eleventh, penultimate, session. We had been talking about the end of therapy, and she described how accustomed she had become to meeting with me and how difficult it would be to say goodbye next week, how losing me would become another in her string of losses, when she mentioned, casually, "Did I ever tell you I had twins when I was sixteen?"

I wanted to shout, "What? Twins? At sixteen? What do you mean 'Did I ever tell you?' You know damn well you didn't tell me!" But, having available only the rest of this session and the next, I had to ignore the way she made this revelation, and deal with the news itself.

"No, you never told me. Fill me in."

"Well, I got pregnant at fifteen. That's why I dropped out of school. I didn't tell anyone till it was too late to do anything about it, so I went ahead and had the baby. Turned out to be girl twins." Pausing, Penny complained of a pain in her throat. Obviously this was much harder to talk about than she pretended.

I asked what happened to the twins.

"The welfare agency said I was an unfit mother—they were right, I guess—but I refused to give 'em up and tried to take care of them but, after about six months, they took them away. I visited them a couple of times—until they got adopted. I never heard anything about them since. Never tried to find out. I left Atlanta and never looked back."

"You think about them much?"

"Not till now. They entered my mind a couple of times right after Chrissie died, but it's only been this last couple of weeks that I dwell on them. I think about where they are, how they're doing, whether they're rich—that was the only favor I asked the adoption agency. They said they'd try. I read stories now in the papers all the time about poor mothers selling their baby to rich families. But what the hell did I know then?"

We spent the rest of this hour and part of our final one exploring the ramifications of this new information. In a curious way her disclosure helped us to deal with the ending of therapy, since it brought us full circle, back to the beginning of therapy, back to that hitherto mysterious first dream in which her two little sons, dressed like girls, were on display in an institution. Chrissie's death and Penny's deep disappointment in her two sons must have kindled her regret at having given up her girls, must have made her feel that not only did the wrong child die, but the wrong children were adopted.

I asked whether she felt guilty over having given up her children. Penny responded matter-of-factly that what she did was best for her and best for them. If she, at the age of sixteen, had kept her two children, she would have been nailed down to the same life her mother had. And it would have been a disaster for the children; she couldn't have given them anything as a single mother—and it was here that I learned more about why Penny withheld telling me about the twins earlier. She was ashamed, ashamed to tell me that she didn't know the identity of the father. She had been highly promiscuous in her teens; in fact, she had been the "school po' white slut" (her term), and the father could have been any of ten boys. No one in her life now, not even her husband, knew about her past, about either her twins or her high school reputation—that, too, was something she had been trying to escape.

She ended the hour by saying, "You're the only person who knows this."

"How does it feel to tell me?"

"Mixed. I've been thinking a lot about telling you. I've been having conversations with you all week."

"How mixed?"

"Scary, good, bad, up, down——" Penny rattled these off. Intolerant of discussing softer feelings, she was growing irritated. She caught herself and slowed down. "'Fraid you'll judge me, I guess. I want to make it through our last session next week with you still having respect for me."

"Do you think I don't?"

"How do I know? All you do is ask questions."

She was right. We were coming to the end of our eleventh hour—no time for me to be withholding.

"Penny, you've got no worries about me. The more I hear from you, the more I like you. I'm full of admiration for what you've overcome and what you've done in life."

Penny burst out crying. She pointed to her watch to remind me our time was up and rushed from the office with her face buried in Kleenex.

A week later, at our final meeting, I learned that the tears had continued most of the week. On her way home from the previous session, she stopped at the cemetery, sat next to Chrissie's grave and, as she often did, wept for her daughter. But that day the tears had no end. She lay down, hugged Chrissie's tombstone, and began to cry harder—now not only for Chrissie but, finally, for all the others, all the other losses.

She cried for her sons, for the unrecoverable years, for the wreckage of their lives. She cried for the two lost daughters she never knew. She cried for her father—whoever, whatever he was. She cried for her husband, for the young, vanished, hopeful times they had shared. She cried even for her poor old mother and the sisters she had blotted from her life twenty years ago. But most of all she cried for herself, for the life she dreamed and never lived.

Soon our time was up. We stood, walked to the door, shook hands, and parted. I watched her go down the stairs. She saw me watching, turned, and said, "Don't you worry about me. I'll be all right. Remember"—and she held out a silver chain she wore around her neck—"I was a latchkey kid."

## Epilogue

I saw Penny once more, a year later, when I returned from my sabbatical. To my relief, she was much improved. Though she had reassured me that she would be all right, I had been greatly concerned about her. Never have I had a patient who was willing to uncover such painful material in such a short time. Nor one who sobbed more noisily. (My secretary, whose office is immediately next to mine, habitually took prolonged coffee breaks during Penny's therapy hour.)

In our first session Penny had said to me, "Just get me started. I'll take care of the rest." In effect, that was what happened. During the year following our therapy, Penny did not consult the therapist I had suggested to her but had continued to make progress on her own.

At our follow-up session it was apparent that her grief, which had been so gridlocked, had become more fluid. Penny was still a haunted woman, but her demons now dwelled in the present rather than the past. She suffered now, not because she had forgotten the events surrounding Chrissie's death, but because of the way she had neglected her two sons.

In fact, her behavior with her sons was the most tangible evidence of change. Both her sons had returned home; and although the mother-son conflict still raged, its character had altered. Penny and her sons had ceased to fight about cemetery plot payments and birthday parties for Chrissie, but argued about Brent's borrowing the pickup and Jim's inability to hold on to a job.

Furthermore, Penny had continued to detach herself from Chrissie. Her cemetery visits were briefer and less frequent; she had given away most of Chrissie's clothes and toys and turned her room over to Brent; she removed Chrissie's last will and testament from the refrigerator, stopped phoning Chrissie's friends and stopped imagining the events Chrissie would have experienced had she lived—for example, her senior prom or her application to college.

Penny was a survivor. I think I had known that from the beginning. I recalled our first meeting and how determined I had been not to get trapped into offering her therapy. Yet Penny had gotten what she had set out to get: therapy, free of charge, from a Stanford professor. How had that happened? Did things just work out that way? Or had I been expertly maneuvered?

Or, perhaps, it was I who had done the maneuvering? It really didn't matter. I, too, had profited from our relationship. I had wanted to learn about bereavement, and Penny had, in only twelve hours, taken me, layer by layer, to the very nucleus of grief.

First, we explored guilt, a state of mind few survivors escape. Penny felt guilty for her amnesia, for not having talked more about death with her daughter. Other survivors feel guilty for other things, for not having done enough, for not having sought medical help sooner, for not having cared more, nursed better. One patient of mine, a particularly attentive wife, hardly left her husband's side for weeks during his final hospitalization, but tormented herself for years because he had died during the few minutes she had gone out to buy a newspaper.

The sentiment that one "should have done something more" reflects, it seems to me, an underlying wish to control the uncontrollable. After all, if one is guilty about not having done something that one should have done, then it follows that there is something that *could* have been done—a comforting thought that decoys us from our patent helplessness in the face of death. Encased in an elaborate illusion of unlimited power and progress, each of us subscribes, at least until one's midlife crisis, to the belief that existence consists of an eternal, upward spiral of achievement, dependent on will alone.

This comforting illusion may be shattered by some urgent, irreversible experience, often referred to by philosophers as a "boundary experience." Of all possible boundary experiences, none—as in the story of Carlos ("If Rape Were Legal . . . ")—more potently confronts us with finiteness and contingency (and none is more able to effect immediate dramatic personal change) than the imminence of our own death.

Another compelling boundary experience is the death of a significant other—a beloved husband or wife or friend—which shatters the illusion of our own invulnerability. For most people, the greatest loss to bear is the death of a child. Then life seems to be attacking on all fronts: parents feel guilty and frightened at their own inability to act; they are angry at the impotence and apparent insensitivity of medical caregivers; they may rail at the injustice of God or of the universe (many ultimately come to understand that what has seemed injustice is in reality cosmic indifference). Bereaved parents are also, by analogy, confronted with their own death: they have not been able to protect a defenseless child, and as night follows day they comprehend the bit-ter truth that they, in their turn, will not be protected. "And therefore," as John Donne wrote, "never send to know for whom the bell tolls; it tolls for thee."

Penny's fear of her own death, while not explicitly emerging in our therapy, manifested itself indirectly. For example, she was greatly con-cerned about "time running out"—too little time left to get an educa-tion, to take a vacation, to leave behind some tangible legacy; and too little time for us to finish our work together. Furthermore, she had showed, early in therapy, considerable evidence of death anxiety in dreams. In two dreams she faced death through drowning: in the first, she clung to insubstantial floating planks while the level of water rose inexorably toward her mouth; in the other, she clasped the floating rem-nants of her house and called for help from a doctor dressed in white who, instead of rescuing her from the water, stamped on her fingers.

In working with these dreams, I did not address her concerns about death. Twelve hours of therapy is far too brief a time to identify, to ex-press, and to do useful work with death anxiety. Instead, I used the dream material to explore themes that had already emerged in our work. Such pragmatic use of dreams is commonplace in therapy. Dreams, like symptoms, have no single explanation: they are overde-termined and contain many levels of meaning. No one ever exhaus-tively analyzes a dream; instead, most therapists approach dreams expediently by examining the dream themes that will accelerate the immediate work of therapy.

Hence I focused on the themes of losing her house and the wash-ing away of the foundations of her life. I also used the dreams to work upon our own relationship. Diving into deep water not uncommonly symbolizes the act of diving into the depths of one's unconscious. And, of course, I was the doctor clad in white who refused to help her and, instead, stamped upon her fingers. In the ensuing discussion, Penny explored, for the first time, her desire for support and guidance from me and her resentment about my efforts to regard her as a re-search subject rather than as a patient.

I used a rational approach to her guilt and her tenacious clinging to the memory of her daughter: I confronted her with the incongruity between her reincarnation beliefs and her behavior. While often such an appeal to reason is ineffective, Penny was fundamentally a well-integrated and resourceful person who was responsive to persuasive rhetoric.

In the next stage of therapy, we explored the idea that "one must learn to live with the living before one can learn to live with the dead." By now I have forgotten whether those were Penny's words or mine or a colleague's, but I am certain it was she who made me aware of the importance of this concept.

In many ways her sons were the real victims of this tragedy—as is often true of the siblings of children who die. Sometimes, as in Penny's family, the surviving children suffer because so much of the parents' energy is bound up with the dead child, who is both memorialized and idealized. Some surviving children are filled with resentment toward their dead sibling for such claims upon the parents' time and energy; often the resentment exists side by side with their own grief and their own understanding of the parents' dilemma. Such a combination is a perfect formula for guilt in the surviving child and to a perceived sense of worthlessness and badness.

Another possible scenario, which fortunately did not happen with Penny, is for the parents to bear immediately another, replacement, child. Often circumstances favor such a course, but sometimes more problems are generated than solved. For one thing, it can damage relationships with surviving children. In addition, the replacement child suffers, too, especially if the parents' grief remains unresolved. Growing up bearing the parents' hopes that one will fulfill the unrealized goals of their life is hard enough, but the additional burden of housing a dead sibling's spirit may overwhelm the delicate process of identity formation.

Still another common scenario is for parents to overprotect the surviving children. I learned, at follow-up, that Penny was falling prey to this dynamic: she had grown fearful about her sons' driving, was reluctant to lend them her pickup, and adamantly refused to allow either of them to buy a motorcycle. Furthermore, she insisted that they have unnecessarily frequent medical checkups to screen for cancer.

In our discussion of her sons, I felt I had to tread carefully and to content myself with helping her to appreciate from their perspective the consequences of Chrissie's death. I did not want Penny's guilt, so recently pried loose, to "discover" her great neglect of her boys and attach itself to this new object. Eventually, months later, she did develop guilt about her relationship with her sons, but by that time she was better able to tolerate it and to ameliorate it by changing her behavior.

The fate of Penny's marriage is, unfortunately, all too common in families that have lost a child. Research has shown that contrary to the expectation that the tragedy of a child's death might bind a family together, many bereaved parents report increased marital discord. The sequence of events in Penny's marriage is prototypical: husband and wife grieve in different—in fact, diametrically opposed—fashions; husband and wife are often unable to understand and to support each other; and the mourning of each spouse actively interferes with the mourning of the other, causing friction, alienation, and eventual separation.

Therapy has much to offer grieving parents. Couples treatment may illuminate the sources of marital tension and help each partner to recognize and to respect the other's mode of grief. Individual therapy may help to alter dysfunctional mourning. Wary though I am always of generalizations, in this instance male-female stereotypes often hold true. Many women, like Penny, need to move past the repetitive expression of their loss and to plunge back into engagement with the living, with projects, with all the things that may supply meaning for their own lives. Men usually must be taught to experience and share (rather than to suppress and evade) their sadness.

In her next stage of grief work, Penny allowed her two dreams—the soaring train and evolution, and the wedding and the search for a changing room—to guide her to the exceptionally important discovery that her grief for Chrissie was mingled with grief for herself and for her own unrealized desires and potential.

The ending of our relationship led Penny to discover one final layer of grief. She dreaded the end of therapy for several reasons: naturally she would miss my professional guidance, and she would miss me personally—after all, she had never before been willing to trust and to accept help from a man. But beyond that, the sheer act of ending evoked vivid memories of all the other painful losses she had endured but never allowed herself to feel and to mourn.

The fact that much of Penny's therapeutic change was self-generated and self-directed contains an important lesson for therapists, a consoling thought a teacher shared with me early in my training: "Remember, you can't do all the work. Be content to help a patient realize what must be done and then trust his or her own desire for growth and change."

# 4

❧❧❧

# Fat Lady

*The world's finest tennis players train five hours a day to eliminate weaknesses* in their game. Zen masters endlessly aspire to quiescence of the mind, the ballerina to consummate balance; and the priest forever examines his conscience. Every profession has within it a realm of possibility wherein the practitioner may seek perfection. For the psychotherapist that realm, that inexhaustible curriculum of self-improvement from which one never graduates, is referred to in the trade as countertransference. Where *transference* refers to feelings that the patient erroneously attaches ("transfers") to the therapist but that in fact originated out of earlier relationships, *countertransference* is the reverse—similar irrational feelings the therapist has toward the patient. Sometimes countertransference is dramatic and makes deep therapy impossible: imagine a Jew treating a Nazi, or a woman who has once been sexually assaulted treating a rapist. But, in milder form, countertransference insinuates itself into every course of psychotherapy.

The day Betty entered my office, the instant I saw her steering her ponderous two-hundred-fifty-pound, five-foot-two-inch frame toward my trim, high-tech office chair, I knew that a great trial of countertransference was in store for me.

I have always been repelled by fat women. I find them repulsive: their absurd sidewise waddle, their absence of body contour— breasts, laps, buttocks, shoulders, jawlines, cheekbones, *everything*, everything I like to see in a woman, obscured in an avalanche of flesh.

And I hate their clothes—the shapeless, baggy dresses or, worse, the stiff elephantine blue jeans. How dare they impose that body on the rest of us?

The origins of these sorry feelings? I had never thought to inquire. So deep do they run that I never considered them prejudice. But were an explanation demanded of me, I suppose I could point to the family of fat, controlling women, including—featuring—my mother, who peopled my early life. Obesity, endemic in my family, was a part of what I had to leave behind when I, a driven, ambitious, first-generation American-born, decided to shake forever from my feet the dust of the Russian shtetl.

I can take other guesses. I have always admired, perhaps more than many men, the woman's body. No, not just admired: I have elevated, idealized, ecstacized it to a level and a goal that exceeds all reason. Do I resent the fat woman for her desecration of my desire, for bloating and profaning each lovely feature that I cherish? For stripping away my sweet illusion and revealing its base of flesh—flesh on the rampage?

I grew up in racially segregated Washington, D.C., the only son of the only white family in the midst of a black neighborhood. In the streets, the black attacked me for my whiteness, and in school, the white attacked me for my Jewishness. But there was always fatness, the fat kids, the big asses, the butts of jokes, those last chosen for athletic teams, those unable to run the circle of the athletic track. I needed someone to hate, too. Maybe this is where it began.

Of course, I am not alone in my bias. Cultural reinforcement is everywhere. Who ever has a kind word for the fat lady? But my contempt surpasses all cultural norms. Early in my career, I worked in a maximum security prison where the *least* heinous offense committed by any of my patients was a simple, single murder. Yet I had little difficulty accepting those patients, attempting to understand them, and finding ways to be supportive.

But when I see a fat lady eat, I move down a couple of rungs on the ladder of human understanding. I want to tear the food away. "Stop stuffing yourself! Haven't you had enough, for Chrissakes?" I'd like to wire her jaws shut!

Poor Betty—thank God, thank God—knew none of this as she innocently continued her course toward my chair, slowly lowered her body, arranged her folds and, with her feet not quite reaching the floor, looked up at me expectantly.

Now why, thought I, do her feet not reach the ground? She's not that short. She sat high in the chair, as though she were sitting in her own lap. Could it be that her thighs and buttocks are so inflated that her feet have to go farther to reach the floor? I quickly swept this conundrum from my mind—after all, this person had come to seek help from me. A moment later, I found myself thinking of the little fat woman cartoon figure in the movie *Mary Poppins*—the one who sings "Supercalifragilisticexpialidocious"—for that was who Betty reminded me of. With an effort I swept that away as well. And so it went: the entire hour with her was an exercise of my sweeping from my mind one derogatory thought after another in order to offer her my full attention. I fantasized Mickey Mouse, the sorcerer's apprentice in *Fantasia*, sweeping away my distracting thoughts until I had to sweep away that image, too, in order to attend to Betty.

As usual, I began to orient myself with demographic questions. Betty informed me that she was twenty-seven and single, that she worked in public relations for a large New York–based retail chain which, three months ago, had transferred her to California for eighteen months to assist in the opening of a new franchise.

She had grown up, an only child, on a small, poor ranch in Texas where her mother has lived alone since her father's death fifteen years ago. Betty was a good student, attended the state university, went to work for a department store in Texas, and after two years was transferred to the central office in New York. Always overweight, she became markedly obese in late adolescence. Aside from two or three brief periods when she lost forty or fifty pounds on crash diets, she had hovered between two hundred and two hundred fifty since she was twenty-one.

I got down to business and asked my standard opening question: "What ails?"

"Everything," Betty replied. Nothing was going right in her life. In fact, she said, she had no life. She worked sixty hours a week, had no friends, no social life, no activities in California. Her life, such as it was, she said, was in New York, but to request a transfer now would doom her career, which was already in jeopardy because of her unpopularity with co-workers. Her company had originally trained her, along with eight other novices, in a three-month intensive course. Betty was preoccupied that she was neither performing nor progressing through promotions as well as her eight classmates. She lived in a furnished suburban apartment doing nothing, she said, but working and eating and chalking off the days till her eighteen months were up.

A psychiatrist in New York, Dr. Farber, whom she saw for approximately four months, had treated her with antidepressant medication. Though she continued to take it, it had not helped her: she was deeply depressed, cried every evening, wished she were dead, slept fitfully, and always awoke by four or five a.m. She moped around the house and on Sundays, her day off, never dressed and spent the day eating sweets in front of the television set. The week before, she had phoned Dr. Farber, who gave her my name and suggested she call for a consultation.

"Tell me more about what you're struggling with in your life," I asked.

"My eating is out of control," Betty said, chuckling, and added, "You could say my eating is always out of control, but now it is *really* out of control. I've gained around twenty pounds in the past three months, and I can't get into most of my clothes."

That surprised me, her clothes seemed so formless, so infinitely expandable, that I couldn't imagine them being outdistanced.

"Other reasons why you decided to come in just now?"

"I saw a medical doctor last week for headaches, and he told me that my blood pressure is dangerously high, around 220 over 110, and that I've got to begin to lose weight. He seemed upset. I don't know how seriously to take him—everyone in California is such a health nut. He wears jeans and running shoes in his office."

She uttered all these things in a gay chatty tone, as though she were talking about someone else, or as though she and I were college sophomores swapping stories in a dorm some rainy Sunday afternoon. She tried to poke me into joining the fun. She told jokes. She had a gift for imitating accents and mimicked her laid-back Marin County physician, her Chinese customers, and her Midwestern boss. She must have laughed twenty times during the session, her high spirits apparently in no way dampened by my stern refusal to be coerced into laughing with her.

I always take very seriously the business of entering into a treatment contract with a patient. Once I accept someone for treatment, I commit myself to stand by that person: to spend all the time and all the energy that proves necessary for the patient's improvement; and most of all, to relate to the patient in an intimate, authentic manner.

But could I relate to Betty? It was an effort for me to locate her face, so layered and swathed in flesh as it was. Her silly commentary was equally offputting. By the end of our first hour, I felt irritated and bored. Could I be intimate with her? I could scarcely think of a single person with whom I *less* wished to be intimate. But this was *my* problem, not Betty's. It was time, after twenty-five years of practice, for me to change. Betty represented the ultimate countertransference challenge—and, for that very reason, I offered then and there to be her therapist.

Surely no one can be critical of a therapist striving to improve his technique. But what, I wondered uneasily, about the rights of the patient? Is there not a difference between a therapist scrubbing away unseemly countertransference stains and a dancer or a Zen master striving for perfection in each of those disciplines? It is one thing to improve one's backhand service return but quite another to sharpen one's skills at the expense of some fragile, troubled person.

These thoughts all occurred to me but I found them dismissible. It was true that Betty offered an opportunity to improve my personal skills as a therapist. It was, however, also true that my future patients would benefit from whatever growth I could attain. Besides, human service professionals have always practiced on the living patient. There is no alternative. How could medical education, to take one example, survive without student clinical clerkships? Furthermore, I have always found that responsible neophyte therapists who convey their sense of curiosity and enthusiasm often form excellent therapeutic relationships and can be as effective as a seasoned professional.

It's the relationship that heals, the relationship that heals, the relationship that heals—my professional rosary. I say that often to students. And say other things as well, about the way to relate to a patient—positive unconditional regard, nonjudgmental acceptance, authentic engagement, empathic understanding. How was I going to be able to heal Betty through our relationship? How authentic, empathic, or accepting could I be? How honest? How would I respond when she asked about my feelings toward her? It was my hope that I would change as Betty and I progressed in her (our) therapy. For the time being, it seemed to me that Betty's social interactions were so primitive and superficial that no penetrating therapist-patient relationship analysis would be necessary.

I had secretly hoped that her appearance would be offset in some way by her interpersonal characteristics—that is, by the sheer vivacity or mental agility I have found in a few fat women—but that, alas, was not to be. The better I knew her, the less interesting she seemed.

During the first few sessions, Betty described, in endless detail, problems she encountered at work with customers, co-workers, and bosses. She often, despite my inner groans, described some particularly banal conversation by playing several of the roles—I've always hated that. She described, again in tedious detail, all the attractive men at work and the minute, pathetic machinations she'd go through to exchange a few sentences with them. She resisted every effort on my part to dip beneath the surface.

Not only was our initial, tentative "cocktail chatter" indefinitely prolonged, but I had a strong sense that, even when we got past this stage, we would remain fused to the surface of things—that as long as Betty and I met, we were doomed to talk about pounds, diets, petty work grievances, and the reasons she did not join an aerobics class. Good Lord, what had I gotten myself into?

Every one of my notes of these early sessions contains phrases such as: "Another boring session"; "Looked at the clock about every three minutes today"; "The most boring patient I have ever seen"; "Almost fell asleep today—had to sit up in my chair to stay awake"; "Almost fell off my chair today."

While I was considering shifting to a hard, uncomfortable chair, it suddenly occurred to me that when I was in therapy with Rollo May, he used to sit in a straight-backed wooden chair. He said he had a bad back, but I knew him well for many years afterward and never heard him mention back trouble. Could it be that he found *me*——?

Betty mentioned that she hadn't liked Dr. Farber because he often fell asleep during their hour. Now I knew why! When I spoke to Dr. Farber on the phone, he did not mention his naps, of course, but he did volunteer that Betty had not been able to learn how to use therapy. It was not hard to understand why he had started her on medication; we psychiatrists so often resort to that when we cannot get anything going in therapy.

Where to start? How to start? I struggled to find some handhold. It was pointless to begin by addressing her weight. Betty made it clear immediately that she hoped therapy would help her get to the point where she could seriously consider weight reduction, but she was a long way from that at this time. "When I'm this depressed, eating is the only thing that keeps me going."

But when I focused on her depression, she presented a persuasive case that depression was an appropriate response to her life situation. Who wouldn't feel depressed holed up in a small furnished apartment in an impersonal California suburb for eighteen months, torn away from one's real life—one's home, social activities, friends?

So I then attempted to help her work on her life situation, but I could make little headway. She had plenty of daunting explanations.

She didn't make friends easily, she pointed out: no obese woman does. (On that point I needed no persuasion.) People in California had their own tight cliques and did not welcome strangers. Her only social contacts were at work, where most of her co-workers resented her supervisory role. Besides, like all Californians, they were jocks—into surfing and skydiving. Could I see her doing that? I swept away a fantasy of her slowly sinking on a surfboard and acknowledged she had a point—those did not seem to be her sports.

What other options were there? she asked. The singles world is impossible for obese people. To prove that point, she described a desperation date she had had the month before—her only date in years. She answered an ad in the personal section of *The Bay Guardian,* a local newspaper. Although most of the ads placed by men explicitly specified a "slim" woman, one did not. She called and arranged to go out to dinner with a man named George, who asked her to wear a rose in her hair and to meet him in the bar of a local restaurant.

His face fell, she reported, when he first caught sight of her, but, to his everlasting credit, he acknowledged that he was indeed George and then behaved like a gentleman throughout dinner. Though Betty never again heard from George, she often thought about him. On several other such attempts in the past, she had been stood up by men who probably spotted her from afar and left without speaking to her.

In some desperation, I stretched for ways to be helpful to Betty. Perhaps (in an effort to conceal my negative feelings) I tried too hard, and I made the beginner's mistake of suggesting other options. Had she considered the Sierra Club? No, she lacked the stamina for hiking. Or Overeaters Anonymous, which might provide some social network? No, she hated groups. Other suggestions met a similar fate. There had to be some other way.

The first step in all therapeutic change is responsibility assumption. If one feels in no way responsible for one's predicament, then how can one change it? That is precisely the situation with Betty: she completely externalized the problem. It was not *her* doing: it was the work transfer, or the sterile California culture, or the absence of cultural events, or the jock social scene, or society's miserable attitude toward obese people. Despite my best efforts, Betty denied any personal contribution to her unhappy life situation.

Oh yes, she could, on an intellectual level, agree that, if she stopped eating and lost weight, the world might treat her differently. But that was too far removed from her, too long term, and her eating seemed too much out of her control. Besides she marshaled other responsibility-absolving arguments: the genetic component (there was considerable obesity on both sides of her family); and the new research demonstrating physiological abnormalities in the obese, ranging from lower basal metabolic rates to the present, programmed, relatively uninfluencible body weight. No, that would not work. Ultimately I would have to help her assume responsibility for her appearance—but saw no leverage for achieving that at this time. I had to start with something more immediate. I knew a way.

The psychotherapist's single most valuable practical tool is the "process" focus. Think of *process* as opposed to *content*. In a conversation, the content consists of the actual words uttered, the substantive issues discussed; the process, however, is *how* the content is expressed and especially what this mode of expression reveals about the relationship between the participating individuals.

What I had to do was to get away from the content—to stop, for example, attempting to provide simplistic solutions to Betty—and to focus on process—on how we were relating to each other. And there was one outstanding characteristic of our relationship—*boredom*. And that is precisely where countertransference complicates things: I had to be clear about how much of the boredom was *my* problem, about how bored I would be with *any* fat woman.

So I proceeded cautiously—too cautiously. My negative feelings slowed me down. I was too afraid of making my aversion visible. I would never have waited so long with a patient I liked more. I spurred myself to get moving. If I were going to be helpful to Betty, I had to sort out, to trust, and to act upon my feelings.

The truth was that this was indeed a boring woman, and I needed to confront her with that in some acceptable way. She could deny responsibility for anything else—the absence of friends in her current life, the tough singles scene, the horrors of suburbia—but I was *not* going to let her deny responsibility for boring me.

I dared not utter the word *boring*—far too vague and too hurtful. I needed to be precise and constructive. I asked myself what, exactly, was boring about Betty, and identified two obvious characteristics. First of all, she never revealed anything intimate about herself. Second, there was her damned giggling, her forced gaiety, her reluctance to be appropriately serious.

It would be difficult to make her aware of these characteristics without hurting her. I decided upon a general strategy: my basic position would be that I wanted to get closer to her but that her behavioral traits got in the way. I thought it would be difficult for her to take offense with any criticism of her behavior when framed in that context. She could only be pleased at my wanting to know her better. I decided to start with her lack of self-revelation and, toward the end of a particularly soporific session, took the plunge.

"Betty, I'll explain later why I'm asking you this, but I'd like you to try something new today. Would you give yourself a score from one to ten on how much revealing about yourself you've done during our hour together today? Consider ten to be the most significant revealing you can imagine and one to be the type of revealing you might do, let's say, with strangers in a line at the movies."

A mistake. Betty spent several minutes explaining why she wouldn't go to the movies alone. She imagined people pitied her for having no friends. She sensed their dread that she might crowd them by sitting next to them. She saw the curiosity, the bemusement in their faces as they watched to see whether she could squeeze into a single narrow movie seat. When she began to digress further—extending the discussion to airline seats and how seated passengers' faces grew white with fear when she started down the aisle searching for her seat—I interrupted her, repeated my request, and defined "one" as "casual conversation at work."

Betty responded by giving herself a "ten." I was astonished (I had expected a "two" or "three") and told her so. She defended her rating on the basis that she had told me things she had never shared before: that, for example, she had once stolen a magazine from a drugstore and was fearful about going alone to a restaurant or to the movies.

We repeated that same scenario several times. Betty insisted she was taking huge risks, yet, as I said to her, "Betty, you rate yourself 'ten,' yet it didn't *feel* that way to me. It didn't feel that you were taking a real risk with me."

"I have never told anybody else these things. Not Dr. Farber, for example."

"How do you feel telling me these things?"

"I feel fine doing it."

"Can you use other words than *fine*? It must be scary or liberating to say these things for the first time!"

"I feel O.K. doing it. I know you're listening professionally. It's O.K. I feel O.K. I don't know what you want."

"How can you be so sure I'm listening professionally? You have no doubts?"

Careful, careful! I couldn't promise more honesty than I was willing to give. There was no way that she could deal with my revelation of negative feelings. Betty denied any doubts—and at this point told me about Dr. Farber's falling asleep on her and added that I seemed much more interested than he.

What *did* I want from her? From *her* standpoint she was revealing much. I had to be sure I really knew. What was there about her revealing that left me unmoved? It struck me that she was always revealing something that occurred elsewhere—another time, another place. She was incapable, or unwilling, to reveal herself in the immediate present that we two were sharing. Hence, her evasive response of "O.K." or "Fine" whenever I asked about her here-and-now feelings.

That was the first important discovery I made about Betty: she was desperately isolated, and she survived this isolation only by virtue of the sustaining myth that her intimate life was being lived elsewhere. Her friends, her circle of acquaintances, were not here, but elsewhere, in New York, in Texas, in the past. In fact, everything of importance was elsewhere. It was at this time that I first began to suspect that for Betty there was no "here" there.

Another thing: if she was revealing more of herself to me than to anyone before, then what was the nature of her close relationships? Betty responded that she had a reputation for being easy to talk to. She and I, she said, were in the same business: she was everyone's therapist. She added that she had a lot of friends, but no one knew *her*. Her trademark was that she listened well and was entertaining. She hated the thought, but the stereotype was true: she was the jolly fat woman.

This led naturally into the other primary reason I found Betty so boring: she was acting in bad faith with me—in our face-to-face talks she was never real, she was all pretense and false gaiety.

"I'm really interested in what you said about being, or rather pretending to be, jolly. I think you are determined, absolutely committed, to be jolly with me."

"Hmmm, interesting theory, Dr. Watson."

"You've done this since our first meeting. You tell me about a life that is full of despair, but you do it in a bouncy 'aren't-we-having-a-good-time?' way."

"That's the way I am."

"When you stay jolly like that, I lose sight of how much pain you're having."

"That's better than wallowing in it."

"But you come here for help. Why is it so necessary for you to entertain me?"

Betty flushed. She seemed staggered by my confrontation and retreated by sinking into her body. Wiping her brow with a tiny handkerchief, she stalled for time.

"Zee suspect takes zee fifth."

"Betty, I'm going to be persistent today. What would happen if you stopped trying to entertain me?"

"I don't see anything wrong with having some fun. Why take everything so . . . so . . . I don't know—— You're always so serious. Besides, this is me, this is the way I am. I'm not sure I know what you're talking about. What do you mean by my entertaining you?"

"Betty, this is important, the most important stuff we've gotten into so far. But you're right. First, you've got to know exactly what I mean. Would it be O.K. with you if, from now on in our future sessions, I interrupt and point out when you're entertaining me—the moment it occurs?"

Betty agreed—she could hardly refuse me; and I now had at my disposal an enormously liberating device. I was now permitted to interrupt her instantaneously (reminding her, of course, of our new agreement) whenever she giggled, adopted a silly accent, or attempted to amuse me or to make light of things in any distracting way.

Within three or four sessions, her "entertaining" behavior disappeared as she, for the first time, began to speak of her life with the seriousness it deserved. She reflected that she had to be entertaining to keep others interested in her. I commented that, in this office, the opposite was true: the more she tried to entertain me, the more distant and less interested I felt.

But Betty said she didn't know how else to be: I was asking her to dump her entire social repertoire. Reveal herself? If she were to reveal herself, what would she show? There was nothing there inside. She was empty. (The word *empty* was to arise more and more frequently as therapy proceeded. Psychological "emptiness" is a common concept in the treatment of those with eating disorders.)

I supported her as much as possible at this point. *Now*, I pointed out to Betty, she was taking risks. *Now* she was up to eight or nine on the revealing scale. Could she feel the difference? She got the point quickly. She said she felt frightened, like jumping out of a plane without a parachute.

I was less bored now. I looked at the clock less frequently and once in a while checked the time during Betty's hour not, as before, to count the number of minutes I had yet to endure, but to see whether sufficient time remained to open up a new issue.

Nor was it necessary to sweep from my mind derogatory thoughts about her appearance. I no longer noticed her body and, instead, looked into her eyes. In fact, I noted with surprise the first stirrings of empathy within me. When Betty told me about going to a western bar where two rednecks sidled up behind her and mocked her by mooing like a cow, I felt outraged for her and told her so.

My new feelings toward Betty caused me to recall, and to be ashamed of, my initial response to her. I cringed when I reflected on all the other obese women whom I had related to in an intolerant fashion.

These changes all signified that we were making progress: we were successfully addressing Betty's isolation and her hunger for closeness. I hoped to show her that another person could know her fully and still care for her.

Betty now felt definitely engaged in therapy. She thought about our discussions between sessions, had long imaginary conversations with me during the week, looked forward to our meetings, and felt angry and disappointed when business travel caused her to miss meetings.

But at the same time she became unaccountably more distressed and reported more sadness and more anxiety. I pounced at the opportunity to understand this development. Whenever the patient begins to develop symptoms in respect to the relationship with the therapist, therapy has really begun, and inquiry into these symptoms will open the path to the central issues.

Her anxiety had to do with her fear of getting too dependent or addicted to therapy. Our sessions had become the most important thing in her life. She didn't know what would happen to her if she didn't have her weekly "fix." It seemed to me she was still resisting closeness by referring to a "fix" rather than to me, and I gradually confronted her on that point.

"Betty, what's the danger in letting me matter to you?"

"I'm not sure. It feels scary, like I'll need you too much. I'm not sure you'll be there for me. I'm going to have to leave California in a year, remember."

"A year's a long time. So you avoid me now because you won't always have me?"

"I know it doesn't make sense. But I do the same thing with California. I like New York and I don't want to like California. I'm afraid that, if I form friends here and start to like it, I might not want to leave. The other thing is that I start to feel, 'Why bother?' I'm here for such a short time. Who wants temporary friendships?"

"The problem with that attitude is you end up with an unpeopled life. Maybe that's part of the reason you feel empty inside. One way or another, every relationship must end. There's no such thing as a lifetime guarantee. It's like refusing to enjoy watching the sun rise because you hate to see it set."

"It sounds crazy when you put it like that, but that's what I do. When I meet a new person whom I like, I start right away to imagine what it will be like to say goodbye to them."

I knew this was an important issue, and that we would return to it. Otto Rank described this life stance with a wonderful phrase: "Refusing the loan of life in order to avoid the debt of death."

Betty now entered into a depression which was short-lived and had a curious, paradoxical twist. She was enlivened by the closeness and the openness of our interaction; but, rather than allow herself the enjoyment of that feeling, she was saddened by the realization that her life heretofore had been so devoid of intimacy.

I was reminded of another patient I had treated the year before, a forty-four-year-old excessively responsible, conscientious physician. One evening in the midst of a marital dispute, she uncharacteristically drank too much, went out of control, threw plates against the wall, and narrowly missed her husband with a lemon pie. When I saw her two days later, she seemed guilty and depressed. In an effort to console her, I tried to suggest that losing control is not always a catastrophe. But she interrupted and told me I had misunderstood: she felt no guilt but was instead overcome with regret that she had waited until she was forty-four to relinquish her control and let some real feelings out.

Despite her two hundred and fifty pounds, Betty and I had rarely discussed her eating and her weight. She had often talked about epic (and invariably unproductive) struggles she had had with her mother and with other friends who tried to help her control her eating. I was determined to avoid that role; instead, I placed my faith in the assumption that, if I could help remove the obstacles that lay in her path, Betty would, on her own, take the initiative to care for her body.

So far, by addressing her isolation, I had already cleared away major obstacles: Betty's depression had lifted; and, having established a social life for herself, she no longer regarded food as her sole source of satisfaction. But it was not until she stumbled upon an extraordinary revelation about the dangers of losing weight that she could make the decision to begin her diet. It came about in this way.

When she had been in therapy for a few months, I decided that her progress would be accelerated if she worked in a therapy group as well as in individual therapy. For one thing, I was certain it would be wise to establish a supportive community to help sustain her in the difficult diet days yet to come. Furthermore, a therapy group would provide Betty an opportunity to explore the interpersonal issues we had opened up in our therapy—the concealment, the need to entertain, the feeling she had nothing to offer. Though Betty was very frightened and initially resisted my suggestion, she gamely agreed and entered a therapy group led by two psychiatric residents.

One of her first group meetings happened to be a highly unusual session in which Carlos, also in individual therapy with me (see "If Rape Were Legal . . . "), informed the group of his incurable cancer. Betty's father had died of cancer when she was twelve, and since then she had been terrified of the disease. In college she had initially elected a premedical curriculum but gave it up for fear of being in contact with cancer patients.

Over the next few weeks, the contact with Carlos generated so much anxiety in Betty that I had to see her in several emergency sessions and had difficulty persuading her to continue in the group. She developed distressing physical symptoms—including headaches (her father died of brain cancer), backaches, and shortness of breath—and was tormented with the obsessive thought that she, too, had cancer. Since she was phobic about seeing doctors (because of her shame about her body, she rarely permitted a physical exam and had never had a pelvic exam), it was hard to reassure her about her health.

Witnessing Carlos's alarming weight loss reminded Betty of how, over a twelve-month period, she had watched her father shrink from an obese man to a skeleton wrapped in great folds of spare skin. Though she acknowledged that it was an irrational thought, Betty realized that since her father's death she had believed that weight loss would make her susceptible to cancer.

She had strong feelings about hair loss as well. When she first joined the group, Carlos (who had lost his hair as a result of chemotherapy) was wearing a toupee, but the day he informed the group about his cancer, he came bald to the meeting. Betty was horrified, and visions of her father's baldness—he had been shaven for his brain surgery—returned to her. She remembered also how frightened she had been when, on previous strenuous diets, she herself had suffered considerable hair loss.

These disturbing feelings had vastly compounded Betty's weight problems. Not only did food represent her sole form of gratification, not only was it a method of assuaging her feeling of emptiness, not only did thinness evoke the pain of her father's death, but she felt, unconsciously, that losing weight would result in *her* death.

Gradually Betty's acute anxiety subsided. She had never before talked openly about these issues: perhaps the sheer catharsis helped; perhaps it was useful for her to recognize the magical nature of her thinking; perhaps some of her horrifying thoughts were simply desensitized by talking about them in the daylight in a calm, rational manner.

During this time, Carlos was particularly helpful. Betty's parents had, until the very end, denied the seriousness of her father's illness. Such massive denial always plays havoc with the survivors, and Betty had neither been prepared for his death nor had the opportunity to say goodbye. But Carlos modeled a very different approach to his fate: he was courageous, rational, and open with his feelings about his illness and his approaching death. Furthermore, he was especially kind to Betty—perhaps it was that he knew she was my patient, perhaps that she came along when he was in a generous ("everybody has got a heart") state of mind, perhaps simply that he always had a fondness for fat women (which, I am embarassed to say, I had always considered further proof of his perversity).

Betty must have felt that the obstructions to losing weight had been sufficiently removed because she gave unmistakable evidence that a major campaign was about to be launched. I was astonished by the scope and complexity of the preparatory arrangements.

First, she enrolled in an eating-disorder program at the clinic where I worked and completed their demanding protocol, which included a complex physical workup and a battery of psychological tests. She then cleared her apartment of food—every can, every package, every bottle. She made plans for alternative social activities: she pointed out to me that eliminating lunches and dinners puts a crimp into one's social calendar. To my surprise, she joined a square-dancing group (this lady's got guts, I thought) and a weekly bowling league—her father had often taken her bowling when she was a child, she explained. She bought a used stationary bicycle and set it up in front of her TV set. She then said her goodbyes to old friends—her last Granny Goose Hawaiian-style potato chip, her last Mrs. Fields chocolate chip cookie, and, toughest of all, her last honey-glazed doughnut.

There was considerable internal preparation as well, which Betty found difficult to describe other than to say she was "gathering inner resolve" and waiting for the right moment to commence the diet. I grew impatient and amused myself with a vision of an enormous Japanese sumo wrestler pacing, posturing, and grunting himself into readiness.

Suddenly she was off! She went on a liquid Optifast diet, ate no solid food, bicycled forty minutes every morning, walked three miles every afternoon, and bowled and square-danced once a week. Her fatty casing began to disintegrate. She began to shed bulk. Large folds of overhanging flesh broke off and were washed away. Soon the pounds flowed off in rivulets—two, three, four, sometimes five pounds a week.

Betty started each hour with a progress report: ten pounds lost, then twenty, twenty-five, thirty. She was down to two hundred forty pounds, then two hundred thirty, and two hundred twenty. It seemed astonishingly fast and easy. I was delighted for her and commended her strongly each week on her efforts. But in those first weeks I was also aware of a cruel voice within me, a voice saying, "Good God, if she's losing it that fast, think of how much food she must have been putting away!"

The weeks passed, the campaign continued. After three months, she weighed in at two hundred ten. Then two hundred, a fifty-pound loss! Then one hundred ninety. The opposition stiffened. Sometimes she came into my office in tears after a week without food and no compensating weight loss. Every pound put up a fight, but Betty stayed on the diet.

Those were ghastly months. She hated everything. Her life was a torment—the disgusting liquid food, the stationary bicycle, the hunger pangs, the diabolic McDonald's hamburger ads on television, and the smells, the ubiquitous smells: popcorn in the movies, pizza in the bowling alley, croissants in the shopping center, crab at Fisherman's Wharf. Was there nowhere in the world an odor-free place?

Every day was a bad day. Nothing in her life gave her pleasure. Others in the eating-disorder clinic's weight-reduction group gave up—but Betty hung tough. My respect for her grew.

I like to eat, too. Often I look forward all day to a special meal; and, when the craving strikes, no obstacle can block my way to the dim sum restaurant or the gelato stand. But as Betty's ordeal continued, I began to feel guilty eating—as though I were acting in bad faith toward her. Whenever I sat down to eat pizza or pasta al pesto or enchiladas con salsa verde or German-chocolate-cake ice cream, or any other special treat I knew Betty liked, I thought of her. I shuddered when I thought of her dining, can opener in hand, on Optifast liquid. Sometimes I passed up seconds in her honor.

It happened that, during this period, I passed the upper weight limit I allow myself, and went on a three-week diet. Since my diets consist primarily of eliminating ice cream and French fries, I could hardly say to Betty that I was joining hands with her in a sympathy fast. Nonetheless, during these three weeks I felt her deprivation more keenly. I was moved now when she told me how she cried herself to sleep. I ached for her when she described the starving child within her howling, "Feed me! Feed me!"

One hundred eighty. One hundred seventy. An eighty-pound weight loss! Betty's mood now fluctuated wildly, and I grew increasingly concerned for her. She had occasional brief periods of pride and exhilaration (especially when she went shopping for slimmer clothing), but mainly she experienced such deep despondency that it was all she could do to get herself to work each morning.

At times she grew irritable and raised several old grievances with me. Had I referred her to a therapy group as a way of dumping her or, at least, sharing the load and getting her partly off my hands? Why had I not asked her more about her eating habits? After all, eating was her life. Love her, love her eating. (Careful, careful, she's getting close.) Why had I not disagreed with her when she listed the reasons that medical school was not possible for her (her age, lack of stamina, laziness, having taken few of the prerequisite courses, and lack of funds)? She viewed, she told me now, my suggestion about a possible career in nursing as a put-down, and accused me of saying, "The girl's not smart enough for medical school—so let her be a nurse!"

At times, she was petulant and regressed. Once, for example, when I inquired about why she had become inactive in her therapy group, she simply glared and refused to answer. When I pressed her to say exactly what was on her mind, she said in a singsong child's voice, "If I can't have a cookie, I won't do anything for you."

During one of her depressed periods, she had a vivid dream.

*I was in a place like Mecca where people go to commit suicide legally. I was with a close friend but I don't remember who. She was going to commit suicide by jumping down a deep tunnel. I promised her I'd retrieve her body but, later, I realized that to do this I'd have to crawl down this terrible tunnel with all sorts of dead and decaying bodies around and I didn't think I could do it.*

In associating to this dream Betty said that, earlier the day of the dream, she had been thinking that she had shed a whole body: she had lost eighty pounds, and there was a woman in her office who weighed only eighty pounds. At the time she had imagined granting an autopsy and holding a funeral for the "body" she had shed. This macabre thought, Betty suspected, was echoed in the dream image of retrieving her friend's dead body from the tunnel.

The imagery and depth of the dream brought home to me how far she had come. It was hard to remember the giggling, superficial woman of a few months before. Betty had my full attention for every minute of every session now. Who could have imagined that, out of that woman whose vacuous chatter had so bored me and her previous psychiatrist, this thoughtful, spontaneous, and sensitive person could have emerged?

One hundred sixty-five. Another kind of emergence was taking place. One day in my office I looked over at Betty and noticed, for the first time, that she had a lap. I looked again. Had it always been there? Maybe I was paying more attention to her now. I didn't think so: her body contour, from chin to toes, had always been smoothly globular. A couple of weeks later, I saw definite signs of a breast, two breasts. A week later, a jawline, then a chin, an elbow. It was all there—there had been a person, a handsome woman, buried in there all the time.

Others, especially men, had noticed the change, and now touched and poked her during conversations. A man at the office walked her out to her car. Her hairdresser, gratuitously, gave her a scalp massage. She was certain her boss was eyeing her breasts.

One day Betty announced, "one hundred fifty-nine," and added that this was "virgin territory"—that is, she hadn't weighed in the one hundred fifties since high school. Though my response—asking whether she worried about entering "nonvirgin territory"—was a sorry joke, it nonetheless initiated an important discussion about sex.

Though she had an active sexual fantasy life, she had never had any physical contact with a man—not a hug, not a kiss, not even a lascivious grab. She had always craved sex and was angry that society's attitude toward the obese sentenced her to sexual frustration. Only now, when she was approaching a weight when sexual invitations might materialize, only now when her dreams teemed with menacing male figures (a masked doctor plunging a large hypodermic needle into her abdomen, a leering man peeling the scab off a large abdominal wound), did she recognize that she was very frightened of sex.

These discussions released a flood of painful memories about a lifetime of rejection by males. She had never been asked on a date and never attended a school dance or party. She played the confidante role very well and had helped many friends plan their weddings. They were just about all married off now, and she could no longer conceal from herself that she would forever play the role of the unchosen observer.

We soon moved from sex into the deeper waters of her basic sexual identity. Betty had heard that her father had really wanted a son and been silently disappointed when she was born. One night she had two dreams about a lost twin brother. In one dream she and he wore identification badges and kept switching them with each other. She finished him off in another dream: he squeezed into a crowded elevator into which she couldn't fit (because of her size). Then the elevator crashed, killing all the passengers, and she was left sifting through his remains.

In another dream, her father gave her a horse called "She's a Lady." She had always wanted a horse from him, and in the dream not only was that childhood wish fulfilled but her father officially christened her a lady.

Our discussions about sexual practice and her sexual identity generated so much anxiety and such an agonizing sense of emptiness that, on several occasions, she binged on cookies and doughnuts. By now Betty was permitted some solid food—one diet TV dinner a day—but found this more difficult to follow than the liquid-only diet.

Looming ahead was an important symbolic marker—the loss of the one-hundredth pound. This specific goal, never to be attained, had powerful sexual connotations. For one thing Carlos had, months before, only half jokingly told Betty he was going to take her to Hawaii for a weekend when she had lost a hundred pounds. Furthermore, as part of her pre-diet mental preparation, Betty had vowed herself that when she lost a hundred pounds she was going to contact George, the man whose personal ad she had answered, to surprise him with her new body and reward his gentlemanly behavior with her sexual favors.

In an effort to reduce her anxiety, I urged moderation and suggested she approach sex with less drastic steps: for example, by spending time talking to men; by educating herself about such topics as sexual anatomy, sexual mechanics, and masturbation. I recommended reading material and urged her to visit a female gynecologist and to explore these issues with her girlfriends and her therapy group.

Throughout this period of rapid weight loss, another extraordinary phenomenon was taking place. Betty experienced emotional flashbacks and would spend much of a therapy hour tearfully discussing startlingly vivid memories, such as the day she left Texas to move to New York, or her college graduation, or her anger at her mother for being too timid and fearful to attend her high school graduation.

At first it seemed that these flashbacks, as well as the accompanying extreme mood swings, were chaotic, random occurrences; but after several weeks, Betty realized that they were following a coherent pattern: as she lost weight she *re-experienced the major traumatic or unresolved events of her life that had occurred when she was at a particular weight*. Thus her descent from two hundred fifty pounds set her spinning backward in time through the emotionally charged events of her life: leaving Texas for New York (210 pounds), her college graduation (190 pounds), her decision to drop the pre-med curriculum (and to give up the dream of discovering the cure for the cancer that killed her father) (180 pounds), her loneliness at her high school graduation—her envy of other daughters and fathers, her inability to get a date for the senior prom (170 pounds), her junior high graduation and how much she missed her father at that graduation (155 pounds). What a wonderful proof of the unconscious realm! Betty's body had remembered what her mind had long forgotten.

Memories of her father permeated these flashbacks. The closer we looked, the more apparent it was that everything led back to him, to his death, and to the one hundred fifty pounds Betty weighed at that time. The closer she approached that weight, the more depressed she grew and the more her mind swarmed with feelings and recollections of her father.

Soon we spent entire sessions talking about her father. The time had come to unearth everything. I plunged her into reminiscence and encouraged her to express everything she could remember about his illness, his dying, his appearance in the hospital the last time she saw him, the details of his funeral, the clothes she wore, the minister's speech, the people who attended.

Betty and I had talked about her father before but never with such intensity and depth. She felt her loss as never before and, over a two-week period, wept almost continuously. We met thrice weekly during this time, and I attempted to help her understand the source of her tears. In part she cried because of her loss, but in large part because she considered her father's life to have been such a tragedy: he never obtained the education he wanted (or that she wanted for him), and he died just before he retired and never enjoyed the years of leisure for which he had longed. Yet, as I pointed out to her, her description of his life's activities—his large extended family, his wide social circle, his daily bull sessions with friends, his love of the land, his youth in the navy, his afternoons fishing—was a picture of a full life in which her father was immersed in a community of people who knew and loved him.

When I urged her to compare his life with her own, she realized that some of her grief was misplaced: it was her own life, not her father's, that was tragically unfulfilled. How much of her grief, then, was for all her unrealized hopes? This question was particularly painful for Betty who, by that time, had visited a gynecologist and been told that she had an endocrine disorder that would make it impossible for her to have children.

I felt cruel during these weeks because of the pain our therapy was uncovering. Every session was an ordeal, and Betty often left my office badly shaken. She began to have acute panic attacks and many disturbing dreams, and, as she put it, she died at least three times a night. She could not remember the dreams except for two recurrent ones that had begun in adolescence, shortly after her father's death. In one dream, she lay paralyzed in a small closet which was being bricked up. In the other, she was lying in a hospital bed with a candle, which represented her soul, burning at the head of the bed. She knew that when the flame went out she would die, and she felt helpless as she watched it get smaller and smaller.

Discussing her father's death obviously evoked fears of her own death. I asked Betty to talk about her first experiences and early conceptions of death. Living on a ranch, she was no stranger to death. She watched her mother kill chickens and heard the squeal of hogs being slaughtered. Betty was extremely unsettled by her grandfather's death when she was nine. According to her mother (Betty told me she had no recollection of this), she was reassured by her parents that only old people die, but then she pestered them for weeks by chanting she didn't want to grow old and by repeatedly asking her parents how old they were. But it was not until shortly after her father died that Betty grasped the truth about the inevitability of her own death. She remembered the precise moment.

"It was a couple days after the funeral, I was still taking off from school. The teacher said I should return when I felt ready. I could have gone back earlier, but it didn't seem right to go back so soon. I was worried that people wouldn't think I was sad enough. I was walking in the fields behind the house. It was cold out—I could see my breath, and it was hard to walk because the earth was clumped and the plow ridges were frozen. I was thinking of my father lying beneath the ground and how cold he must have been, and I suddenly heard a voice from above saying to me, 'You're next!'"

Betty stopped and looked at me. "You think I'm crazy?"

"No, I told you before, you don't have the knack for it."

She smiled. "I've never told that story to anyone. In fact I'd forgotten it, forgotten it for years until this week."

"I feel good you're willing to trust me with it. It sounds important. Say some more about being 'next.'"

"It's like my father was no longer there to protect me. In a way he stood between me and the grave. Without him there, I was next in line." Betty hunched up her shoulders and shuddered. "Can you believe I still feel spooky when I think about this?"

"Your mother? Where was she in all this?"

"Like I've told you before—way, way in the background. She cooked and she fed me—she was real good at that—but she was weak—I was the one protecting her. Can you believe a Texan who can't drive? I started driving at twelve when my father got sick, because she was afraid to learn."

"So there was no one shielding you?"

"That's when I started having nightmares. That dream about the candle—I must have had it twenty times."

"That dream makes me think of what you said before about your fear of losing weight, about having to stay heavy to avoid dying of cancer like your father. If the candle flame stays fat, you live."

"Maybe, but sounds farfetched."

Another good example, I thought, of the pointlessness of the therapist rushing in with an interpretation, even a good one like this. Patients, like everyone else, profit most from a truth they, themselves, discover.

Betty continued, "And somewhere in that year I got the idea I was going to die before I was thirty. You know, I think I still believe that."

These discussions undermined her denial of death. Betty began to feel unsafe. She was always on guard against injury—when driving, bicycling, crossing the street. She became preoccupied with the capriciousness of death. "It could come at any instant," she said, "when I least expect it." For years her father had saved money and planned a family trip to Europe only to develop a brain tumor shortly before the departure date. She, I, anyone, can be struck down at any time. How does anyone, how do *I*, cope with that thought?

Now committed to being entirely "present" with Betty, I tried not to flinch from any of her questions. I told her of my own difficulties in coming to terms with death; that, though the fact of death cannot be altered, one's attitude toward it can be vastly influenced. From both my personal and my professional experience, I had come to believe that the fear of death is always greatest in those who feel that they have not lived their life fully. A good working formula is: the more unlived life, or unrealized potential, the greater one's death anxiety.

My hunch was, I told Betty, that when she entered more fully into life, she would lose her terror of death—some, not all of it. (We are all stuck with some anxiousness about death. It's the price of admission to self-awareness.)

At other times Betty expressed anger at my forcing her to think about morbid topics. "Why think about death? We can't do anything about it!" I tried to help her understand that, though the *fact* of death destroys us, the *idea* of death can save us. In other words, our awareness of death can throw a different perspective on life and incite us to rearrange our priorities. Carlos had learned that lesson—it was what he meant on his deathbed when he talked about his life having been saved.

It seemed to me that an important lesson Betty could learn from an awareness of death was that life had to be lived *now*; it could not be indefinitely postponed. It was not difficult to lay out before her the ways she avoided life: her reluctance to engage others (because she dreaded separation); her overeating and obesity, which had resulted in her being left out of so much life; her avoidance of the present moment by slipping quickly into the past or the future. It was also not difficult to argue that it was within her power to change these patterns—in fact she had already begun: consider how she was engaging me that very day!

I encouraged her to plunge into her grief; I wanted her to explore and express every facet of it. Again and again, I asked the same question: "Who, what, are you grieving for?"

Betty responded, "I think I'm grieving for love. My daddy was the only man who ever held me in his arms. He was the only man, the only person, who told me he loved me. I'm not sure that will come my way again."

I knew we were entering an area where once I would never have dared to go. It was hard to remember that less than a year before it had been difficult for me even to look at Betty. Today I felt positively tender toward her. I stretched to find a way to respond, but still it was less than I wanted to give.

"Betty, being loved is not sheer chance or fate. You can influence it—more than you think. You are much more available for love now than you were a few months ago. I can see, I can feel the difference. You look better, you relate better, you are so much more approachable and available now."

Betty was more open with her positive feelings toward me and shared long daydreams in which she became a physician or a psychologist and she and I worked together side by side on a research project. Her wish that I could have been her father led us into one final aspect of her grief that had always caused her much torment. Alongside her love for her father, she also had negative feelings: she felt ashamed of him, of his appearance (he was extremely obese), of his lack of ambition and education, of his ignorance of social amenities. As she said this, Betty broke down and sobbed. It was so hard to talk about this, she said, because she was so ashamed of being ashamed of her own father.

As I searched for a reply, I remembered something my first analyst, Olive Smith, said to me over thirty years before. (I remember it well, I think, because it was the only remotely personal—and the most helpful—thing she said in my six hundred hours with her.) I had been badly shaken by having expressed some monstrous feelings about my mother, and Olive Smith leaned over the couch and said gently, "That just seems to be the way we're built."

I cherished those words; and now, thirty years later, I passed along the gift and said them to Betty. The decades had eroded none of their restorative powers: she exhaled deeply, calmed herself, and sat back in her chair. I added that I knew personally how difficult it is for highly educated adults to relate to uneducated blue-collar parents.

Betty's year-and-a-half assignment in California was now drawing to a close. She did not want to stop therapy and asked her company to extend her time in California. When that failed, she considered searching for a job in California but ultimately decided to return to New York.

What a time to stop—in the midst of work on important issues and with Betty still camped outside the one-hundred-fifty-pound road-block! At first I thought that the timing could not have been worse. Yet, in a more reflective moment, I realized that Betty may have plunged so deeply into therapy *because* of, not despite, our limited time frame. There is a long tradition in psychotherapy going back to Carl Rogers and, before him, to Otto Rank, which understood that a pre-set termination date often increases the efficiency of therapy. Had Betty not known that her time in therapy was limited, she might, for example, have taken far longer to achieve the inner resolve she needed to begin her weight loss.

Besides, it was by no means clear that we could have gone much further. In our last months of therapy, Betty seemed interested more in resolving the issues we had already opened than in uncovering new ones. When I recommended that she continue therapy in New York and offered her the name of a suitable therapist, she was noncommital, stating that she wasn't sure whether she would continue, that maybe she had done enough.

There were other signs as well that Betty might go no further. Though not bingeing, she was no longer dieting. We agreed to concentrate on maintaining her new weight of one hundred sixty and, to that end, Betty bought a whole new wardrobe.

A dream illuminated this juncture in therapy:

> I dreamed that the painters were supposed to paint the outside trim of my house. They were soon all over the house. There was a man at every window with a spray gun. I got dressed quickly and tried to stop them. They were painting the whole outside of the house. There were wisps of smoke coming up all over the house from between the floorboards. I saw a painter with a stocking over his face spraying inside the house. I told him I just wanted the trim painted. He said he had orders to paint everything, inside and out. "What is the smoke?" I asked. He said it was bacteria and added they had been in the kitchen culturing deadly bacteria. I got scared and kept saying over and over, "I only wanted the trim painted."

At the onset of therapy, Betty had indeed wanted only the trim painted but had been drawn inexorably into reconstructive work on the deep interior of the house. Moreover, the painter-therapist had sprayed death—her father's death, her own death—into her house. Now she was saying she had gone far enough; it was time to stop.

As we neared our final session, I felt a mounting relief and exhilaration—as though I had gotten away with something. One of the axioms of psychotherapy is that the important feelings one has for another *always* get communicated through one channel or another—if not verbally, then nonverbally. For as long as I can remember, I have taught my students that if something big in a relationship is not being talked about (by either patient or therapist), then nothing else of importance will be discussed either.

Yet I had started therapy with intense negative feelings about Betty—feelings I had never discussed with her and that she had never recognized. Nevertheless, without doubt, we had discussed important issues. Without doubt, we had made progress in therapy. Had I disproven the catechism? Are there no "absolutes" in psychotherapy?

Our final three hours were devoted to work on Betty's distress at our impending separation. What she had feared at the very onset of treatment had come to pass: she had allowed herself to feel deeply about me and was now going to lose me. What was the point of having trusted me at all? It was as she had said at first: "No involvement, no separation."

I was not dismayed by the re-emergence of these old feelings. First, as termination approaches, patients are bound to regress temporarily. (*There* is an absolute.) Second, issues are never resolved once and for all in therapy. Instead, therapist and patient inevitably return again and again to adjust and to reinforce the learning—indeed, for this very reaso, psychotherapy has often been dubbed "cyclotherapy."

I attempted to address Betty's despair, and her belief that once she left me all our work would come to naught, by reminding her that her growth resided neither in me nor in any outside object, but was a part of her, a part she would take with her. If, for example, she was able to trust and to reveal herself to me more than to anyone previously, then she contained within herself that experience as well as the ability to do it again. To drive my point home, I attempted, in our final session, to use myself as an example.

"It's the same with me, Betty. I'll miss our meetings. But I'm changed as a result of knowing you—"

She had been crying, her eyes downcast, but at my words she stopped sobbing and looked toward me, expectantly.

"And, even though we won't meet again, I'll still retain that change."

"What change?"

"Well, as I mentioned to you, I hadn't had much professional experience with . . . er . . . with the problem of obesity——" I noted Betty's eyes drop with disappointment and silently berated myself for being so impersonal.

"Well, what I mean is that I hadn't worked before with heavy patients, and I've gotten a new appreciation for the problems of——" I could see from her expression that she was sinking even deeper into disappointment. "What I mean is that my attitude about obesity has changed a lot. When we started I personally didn't feel comfortable with obese people——"

In unusually feisty terms, Betty interrupted me. "Ho! ho! ho! 'Didn't feel comfortable'—that's putting it mildly. Do you know that for the first six months you hardly ever looked at me? And in a whole year and a half you've never—not once—touched me? Not even for a handshake!"

My heart sank. My God, she's right! I *have* never touched her. I simply hadn't realized it. And I guess I didn't look at her very often, either. I hadn't expected her to notice!

I stammered, "You know, psychiatrists don't ordinarily touch their——"

"Let me interrupt you before you tell any more fibs and your nose gets longer and longer like Pinocchio." Betty seemed amused at my squirming. "I'll give you a hint. Remember, I'm in the same group with Carlos and we often chat after the group about you."

Uh-oh, I knew I was cornered now. I hadn't anticipated this. Carlos, with his incurable cancer, was so isolated and felt so shunned that I had decided to support him by going out of my way to touch him. I shook his hand before and after each hour and usually put my hand on his shoulder as he left the office. Once, when he learned about the spread of his cancer to his brain, I held him in my arms while he wept.

I didn't know what to say. I couldn't point out to Betty that Carlos was a special case, that he needed it. God knows she had needed it, too. I felt myself flushing. I saw I had no choice but to own up.

"Well, you're pointing out one of my blind spots! It is true—or, rather, was true—that, when we first began to meet, I was put off by your body."

"I know. I know. It wasn't too subtle."

"Tell me, Betty, knowing this—seeing that I didn't look at you or was uncomfortable with you—why did you stay? Why didn't you stop

seeing me and find someone else? Plenty of other shrinks around."
(Nothing like a question to get off the hot seat!)

"Well, I can think of at least two reasons. First, remember that I'm used to it. It's not like I expect anything more. Everyone treats me that way. People hate my looks. No one *ever* touches me. That's why I was surprised, remember, when my hairdresser massaged my scalp. And, even though you wouldn't look at me, you at least seemed interested in what I had to say—no, no, that's not right—you were interested in what I *could* or *might* say if I stopped being so jolly. Actually, that was helpful. Also, you didn't fall asleep. That was an improvement on Dr. Farber."

"You said there were two reasons."

"The second reason is that I could understand how you felt. You and I are very much alike—in one way, at least. Remember when you were pushing me to go to Overeaters Anonymous? To meet other obese people—make some friends, get some dates?"

"Yeah, I remember. You said you hated groups."

"Well, that's true. I do hate groups. But it wasn't the whole truth. The *real* reason is that *I* can't stand fat people. They turn my stomach. I don't want to be seen with them. So how can I get down on you for feeling the same way?"

We were both on the edge of our chairs when the clock said we had to finish. Our exchange had taken my breath away, and I hated to end. I didn't want to stop seeing Betty. I wanted to keep on talking to her, to keep on knowing her.

We got up to leave, and I offered her my hand, both hands.

"Oh no! Oh no, I want a hug! That's the only way you can redeem yourself."

When we embraced, I was surprised to find that I could get my arms all the way around her.

# 5

❦

# "I Never Thought
It Would Happen to Me"

*I greeted Elva in my waiting room, and together we walked the short distance to* my office. Something had happened. She was different today, her gait labored, discouraged, dispirited. For the last few weeks there had been a bounce in her steps, but today she once again resembled the forlorn, plodding woman I had first met eight months ago. I remember her first words then: "I think I need help. Life doesn't seem worth living. My husband's been dead for a year now, but things aren't getting any better. Maybe I'm a slow learner."

But she hadn't proved to be a slow learner. In fact, therapy had progressed remarkably well—maybe it had been going too easily. What could have set her back like this?

Sitting down, Elva sighed and said, "I never thought it would happen to me."

She had been robbed. From her description it seemed an ordinary purse snatching. The thief, no doubt, spotted her in a Monterey seaside restaurant and saw her pay the check in cash for three friends—elderly widows all. He must have followed her into the parking lot and, his footsteps muffled by the roaring of the waves, sprinted up and, without breaking stride, ripped her purse away and leaped into his nearby car.

Elva, despite her swollen legs, hustled back into the restaurant to call for help, but of course it was too late. A few hours later, the police found her empty purse dangling on a roadside bush.

Three hundred dollars meant a lot to her, and for a few days Elva was preoccupied by the money she had lost. That concern gradually evaporated and in its place was left a bitter residue—a residue expressed by the phrase "I never thought it would happen to me." Along with her purse and her three hundred dollars, an illusion was snatched away from Elva—the illusion of personal specialness. She had always lived in the privileged circle, outside the unpleasantness, the nasty inconveniences visited on ordinary people—those swarming masses of the tabloids and newscasts who are forever being robbed or maimed.

The robbery changed everything. Gone was the coziness, the softness in her life; gone was the safety. Her home had always beckoned her with its cushions, gardens, comforters, and deep carpets. Now she saw locks, doors, burglar alarms, and telephones. She had always walked her dog every morning at six. The morning stillness now seemed menacing. She and her dog stopped from time to time and listened for danger.

None of this is remarkable. Elva had been traumatized and now-suffered from commonplace post-traumatic stress. After an accident or an assault, most people tend to feel unsafe, to have a reduced startle threshold, and to be hypervigilant. Eventually time erodes the memory of the event, and victims gradually return to their prior, trusting state.

But for Elva it was more than a simple assault. Her world view was fractured. She had often claimed, "As long as a person has eyes, ears, and a mouth, I can cultivate their friendship." But no longer. She had lost her belief in benevolence, in her personal invulnerability. She felt stripped, ordinary, unprotected. The true impact of that robbery was to shatter illusion and to confirm, in brutal fashion, her husband's death.

Of course, she knew that Albert was dead. Dead and in his grave for over a year and a half. She had taken the ritualized widow walk—through the cancer diagnosis; the awful, toxic, gut-wrenching chemotherapy; their last visit together to Carmel; their last drive down El Camino Real; the hospital bed at home; the funeral; the paperwork; the ever-dwindling dinner invitations; the widow and widower's clubs; the long, lonely nights. The whole dreadful catastrophe.

Yet, despite all this, Elva had retained her feeling of Albert's continued existence and thereby of her persisting safety and specialness. She had continued to live "as if"—as if the world were safe, as if Albert were there, back in the workshop next to the garage.

Mind you, I do not speak of delusion. Rationally, Elva knew Albert was gone, but still she lived her routine, everyday life behind a veil of illusion which numbed the pain and softened the glare of the knowing. Over forty years ago, she had made a contract with life whose explicit genesis and terms had been eroded by time but whose basic nature was clear: Albert would take care of Elva forever. Upon this unconscious premise, Elva had built her entire assumptive world—a world featuring safety and benevolent paternalism.

Albert was a fixer. He had been a roofer, an auto mechanic, a general handyman, a contractor; he could fix anything. Attracted by a newspaper or magazine photograph of a piece of furniture or some gadget, he would proceed to replicate it in his workshop. I, who have always been hopelessly inept in a workshop, listened in fascination. Forty-one years of living with a fixer is powerfully comforting. It was not hard to understand why Elva clung to the feeling that Albert was still there, out back in the workshop looking out for her, fixing things. How could she give it up? Why should she? That memory, reinforced by forty-one years of experience, had spun a cocoon around Elva that shielded her from reality—that is, until her purse was snatched.

Upon first meeting Elva eight months before, I could find little to love in her. She was a stubby, unattractive woman, part gnome, part sprite, and each of those parts ill tempered. I was transfixed by her facial plasticity: she winked, grimaced, and popped her eyes either singly or in duet. Her brow seemed alive with great washboard furrows. Her tongue, always visible, changed radically in size as it darted in and out or circled her moist, rubbery lips. I remember amusing myself by imagining introducing her to patients on long-term tranquilizer medication who had developed tardive dyskinesia (a drug-induced abnormality of facial musculature). The patients would, within seconds, become deeply offended because they would believe Elva to be mocking them.

But what I really disliked about Elva was her anger. She dripped with rage and, in our first few hours together, had something vicious to say about everyone she knew—save, of course, Albert. She hated the friends who no longer invited her. She hated those who did not put her at ease. Inclusion or exclusion, it was all the same to her: she found something to hate in everyone. She hated the doctors who had told her that Albert was doomed. She hated even more those who offered false hope.

Those hours were hard for me. I had spent too many hours in my youth silently hating my mother's vicious tongue. I remember the games of imagination I played as a child trying to invent the existence of someone she did not hate: A kindly aunt? A grandfather who told her stories? An older playmate who defended her? But I never found anyone. Save, of course, my father, and he was really part of her, her mouthpiece, her animus, her creation who (according to Asimov's first law of robotics) could not turn against his maker—despite my prayers that he would once—just once, please, Dad—pop her.

All I could do with Elva was to hold on, hear her out, somehow endure the hour, and use all my ingenuity to find something supportive to say—usually some vapid comment about how hard it must be for her to carry around that much anger. At times I, almost mischievously, inquired about others of her family circle. Surely there must be someone who warranted respect. But no one was spared. Her son? She said his elevator "didn't go to the top floor." He was "absent": even when he was there, he was "absent." And her daughter-in-law? In Elva's words, a "GAP"—gentile American princess. When driving home, her son would call his wife on his automobile telephone to say he wanted dinner right away. No problem. She could do it. Nine minutes, Elva reminded me, was all the time required for the GAP to cook dinner— to "nuke" a slim gourmet TV dinner in the microwave.

Everyone had a nickname. Her granddaughter, "Sleeping Beauty" (she whispered with an enormous wink and a nod), had two bathrooms—two, mind you. Her housekeeper, whom she had hired to attenuate her loneliness, was "Looney Tunes," and so dumb that she tried to hide her smoking by exhaling the smoke down the flushing toilet. Her pretentious bridge partner was "Dame May Whitey" (and Dame May Whitey was spry-minded compared with the rest, with all the Alzheimer zombies and burned-out drunks who, according to Elva, constituted the bridge-playing population of San Francisco).

But somehow, despite her rancor and my dislike of her and the evocation of my mother, we got through these sessions. I endured my irritation, got a little closer, resolved my countertransference by disentangling my mother from Elva, and slowly, very slowly, began to warm to her.

I think the turning point came one day when she plopped herself in my chair with a "Whew! I'm tired." In response to my raised eyebrows, she explained she had just played eighteen holes of golf with her twenty-year-old nephew. (Elva was sixty, four foot eleven, and at least one hundred sixty pounds.)

"How'd you do?" I inquired cheerily, keeping up my side of the conversation.

Elva bent forward, holding her hand to her mouth as though to exclude someone in the room, showed me a remarkable number of enormous teeth, and said, "I whomped the shit out of him!"

It struck me as wonderfully funny and I started to laugh, and laughed until my eyes filled with tears. Elva liked my laughing. She told me later it was the first spontaneous act from Herr Doctor Professor (so that was *my* nickname!), and she laughed with me. After that we got along famously. I began to appreciate Elva—her marvelous sense of humor, her intelligence, her drollness. She had led a rich, eventful life. We were similar in many ways. Like me, she had made the big generational jump. My parents arrived in the United States in their twenties, penniless immigrants from Russia. Her parents had been poor Irish immigrants, and she had straddled the gap between the Irish tenements of South Boston and the duplicate bridge tournaments of Nob Hill in San Francisco.

At the beginning of therapy, an hour with Elva meant hard work. I trudged when I went to fetch her from the waiting room. But after a couple of months, all that changed. I looked forward to our time together. None of our hours passed without a good laugh. My secretary said she always could tell by my smile that I had seen Elva that day.

We met weekly for several months, and therapy proceeded well, as it usually does when therapist and patient enjoy each other. We talked about her widowhood, her changed social role, her fear of being alone, her sadness at never being physically touched. But, above all, we talked about her anger—about how it had driven away her family and her friends. Gradually she let it go; she grew softer and more gentle. Her tales of Looney Tunes, Sleeping Beauty, Dame May Whitey, and the Alzheimer bridge brigade grew less bitter. Rapprochements occurred; as her anger receded, family and friends reappeared in her life. She had been doing so well that, just before the time of the purse snatching, I had been considering raising the question of termination.

But when she was robbed, she felt as though she were starting all over again. Most of all, the robbery illuminated her ordinariness, her "I never thought it would happen to me" reflecting the loss of belief in her personal specialness. Of course, she was still special in that she had special qualities and gifts, that she had a unique life history, that no one who had ever lived was just like her. That's the rational side of specialness. But we (some more than others) also have an irrational sense of specialness. It is one of our chief methods of denying death, and the part of our mind whose task it is to mollify death terror generates the irrational belief that we are invulnerable—that unpleasant things like aging and death may be the lot of others but not our lot, that we exist beyond law, beyond human and biological destiny.

Although Elva responded to the purse snatching in ways that *seemed* irrational (for example, proclaiming that she wasn't fit to live on earth, being afraid to leave her house), it was clear that she was *really* suffering from the stripping away of irrationality. That sense of specialness, of being charmed, of being the exception, of being eternally protected— all those self-deceptions that had served her so well suddenly lost their persuasiveness. She saw through her own illusions, and what illusion had shielded now lay before her, bare and terrible.

Her grief wound was now fully exposed. This was the time, I thought, to open it wide, to debride it, and to allow it to heal straight and true.

"When you say you never thought it would happen to you, I know just what you mean," I said. "It's so hard for me, too, to accept that all these afflictions—aging, loss, death—are going to happen to me, too."

Elva nodded, her tightened brow showing that she was surprised at my saying anything personal about myself.

"You must feel that if Albert were alive, this would never have happened to you." I ignored her flip response that if Albert were alive she wouldn't have been taking three old hens to lunch. "So the robbery brings home the fact that he's really gone."

Her eyes filled with tears, but I felt I had the right, the mandate, to continue. "You knew that before, I know. But part of you didn't. Now you really know that he's dead. He's not in the yard. He's not out back in the workshop. He's not anywhere. Except in your memories."

Elva was really crying now, and her stubby frame heaved with sobs for several minutes. She had never done that before with me. I sat there and wondered, "Now what do I do?" But my instincts luckily led me to what proved to be an inspired gambit. My eyes lit upon her purse—that same ripped-off, much-abused purse; and I said, "Bad luck is one thing, but aren't you asking for it carrying around something that large?" Elva, plucky as ever, did not fail to call attention to my overstuffed pockets and the clutter on the table next to my chair. She pronounced the purse "medium-sized."

"Any larger," I responded, "and you'd need a luggage carrier to move it around."

"Besides," she said, ignoring my jibe, "I need everything in it."

"You've got to be joking! Let's see!"

Getting into the spirit of it, Elva hoisted her purse onto my table, opened its jaws wide, and began to empty it. The first items fetched forth were three empty doggie bags.

"Need two extra ones in case of an emergency?" I asked.

Elva chuckled and continued to disembowel the purse. Together we inspected and discussed each item. Elva conceded that three packets of Kleenex and twelve pens (plus three pencil stubs) were indeed superfluous, but held firm about two bottles of cologne and three hairbrushes, and dismissed, with an imperious flick of her hand, my challenge to her large flashlight, bulky notepads, and huge sheaf of photographs.

We quarreled over everything. The roll of fifty dimes. Three bags of candies (low-calorie, of course). She giggled at my question: "Do you believe, Elva, that the more of these you eat, the thinner you will become?" A plastic sack of old orange peels ("You never know, Elva, when these will come in handy"). A bunch of knitting needles ("Six needles in search of a sweater," I thought). A bag of sourdough starter. Half of a paperback Stephen King novel (Elva threw away sections of pages as she read them: "They weren't worth keeping," she explained). A small stapler ("Elva, this is crazy!"). Three pairs of sunglasses. And, tucked away into the innermost corners, assorted coins, paper clips, nail clippers, pieces of emery board, and some substance that looked suspiciously like lint.

When the great bag had finally yielded all, Elva and I stared in wonderment at the contents set out in rows on my table. We were sorry the bag was empty and that the emptying was over. She turned and smiled, and we looked tenderly at each other. It was an extraordinarily intimate moment. In a way no patient had ever done before, she showed me everything. And I had accepted everything and asked for even more. I followed her into her every nook and crevice, awed that one old woman's purse could serve as a vehicle for both isolation and intimacy: the absolute isolation that is integral to existence and the intimacy that dispels the dread, if not the fact, of isolation.

That was a transforming hour. Our time of intimacy—call it love, call it love making—was redemptive. In that one hour, Elva moved from a position of forsakenness to one of trust. She came alive and was persuaded, once more, of her capacity for intimacy.

I think it was the best hour of therapy I ever gave.

# 6

## "Do Not Go Gentle"

*I didn't know how to respond. Never before had a patient asked me to be the* keeper of love letters. Dave presented his reasons straightforwardly. Sixty-nine-year-old men have been known to die suddenly. In that event, his wife would find the letters and be pained by reading them. There was no one else he could ask to keep them, no friend he had dared tell of this affair. His lover, Soraya? Thirty years dead. She had died while giving birth. Not his child, Dave was quick to add. God knows what had happened to his letters to her!"

"What do you want me to do with them?" I asked.

"Nothing. Do nothing at all. Just keep them."

"When was the last time you read them?"

"I haven't read them for at least twenty years."

"They seem like such a hot potato," I ventured. "Why keep them at all?"

Dave looked at me incredulously. I think a shiver of doubt went through him. Was I really that stupid? Had he made a mistake in thinking I was sensitive enough to help him? After a few seconds, he said, "I'll never destroy those letters."

These words had an edge to them, the first signs of strain in the relationship we had been forming over the past six months. My comment had been a blunder, and I retreated to a more conciliatory, open-ended line of questioning. "Dave, tell me some more about the letters and what they mean to you."

Dave began to talk about Soraya, and in a few minutes the tension had gone and his self-assured easy jauntiness returned. He had met her while he was managing a branch of an American company in Beirut. She was the most beautiful woman he had ever conquered. *Conquer* was his word. Dave always surprised me with such statements, part ingenuousness, part cynicism. How could he say *conquer?* Was he even less self-aware than I had thought? Or, was it possible that he was far ahead of me and mocked himself—and me, too—with subtle irony?

He had loved Soraya—or, at least, she was the only lover (and they had been legion) to whom he had ever said, "I love you." He and Soraya had a deliciously clandestine affair for four years. (Not delicious *and* clandestine but *deliciously clandestine,* for secrecy—and I shall say more about this shortly—was the axis of Dave's personality around which all else rotated. He was aroused by, compelled by, secrecy, and often courted it at great personal expense. Many relationships, especially those with his three ex-wives and his current wife, had been twisted and torn by his unwillingness to be open or straight about anything.)

After four years Dave's company transferred him to another part of the world, and for the next six years until her death, Dave and Soraya saw each other only four times. But they corresponded almost daily. He had kept Soraya's letters (numbering in the hundreds) well hidden. Sometimes he put them in a file cabinet in quirky categories (under *G* for guilty, or *D* for depression—that is, to be read when deeply depressed).

Once, for three years, he had stored them in a safe deposit box. I wondered, but did not ask, about the relationship between his wife and the key to that safe deposit box. Knowing his penchant for secrecy and intrigue, I could imagine what would happen: he would accidentally let his wife see the key and then devise an obviously false cover story to churn her curiosity; then, as she grew anxious and inquisitive, he would proceed to despise her for snooping and for constricting him by her unseemly suspiciousness. Dave had frequently enacted that type of scenario.

"Now I'm getting more and more nervous about Soraya's letters, and I wondered if you'd keep them. It's just that simple."

We both looked at his large briefcase bulging with words of love from Soraya—the long-dead, dear Soraya whose brain and mind had vanished, whose scattered DNA molecules had drained back into the basin of earth, and who, for thirty years, had not thought of Dave or anything else.

I wondered whether Dave could step back and become witness to himself. To see how ludicrous, how pathetic, how idolatrous he was—an old man, stumbling toward death, comforted only by a clutch of letters, a marching banner proclaiming that he had loved and been loved once, thirty years before. Would it help Dave to see that image? Could I help him assume the "witness to himself" posture without his feeling that I was demeaning both him and the letters?

To my mind, "good" therapy (which I equate with deep, or penetrating, therapy, not with efficient or even, I am pained to say, helpful therapy) conducted with a "good" patient is at bottom a truth-seeking venture. My quarry when I was a novitiate was the truth of the past, to trace all of a life's coordinates and, thereby, to locate and to explain a person's current life, pathology, motivation, and actions.

I used to be so sure. What arrogance! And *now* what kind of truth was I stalking? I think my quarry is illusion. I war against magic. I believe that, though illusion often cheers and comforts, it ultimately and invariably weakens and constricts the spirit.

But there is timing and judgment. Never take away anything if you have nothing better to offer. Beware of stripping a patient who can't bear the chill of reality. And don't exhaust yourself by jousting with religious magic: you're no match for it. The thirst for religion is too strong, its roots too deep, its cultural reinforcement too powerful.

Yet I am not without faith, my Hail Mary being the Socratic incantation, "The unexamined life is not worth living." But that was not Dave's faith. So I curbed my curiosity. Dave scarcely wondered about the ultimate meaning of his clutch of letters and now, tight and brittle, he would not be receptive to such an inquiry. Nor would it be helpful—now or probably ever.

Besides, my questions had a hollow ring. I saw much of myself in Dave, and there are limits to my hypocrisy. I, too, had my sack of letters from a long-lost love. I, too, had them cutely hidden away (in my system, under B for *Bleak House*, my favorite Dickens novel, to be read when life was at its bleakest). I, too, had never reread the letters. Whenever I tried, they brought pain, not comfort. They had lain there untouched for fifteen years, and I, too, could not destroy them.

Were I my own patient (or my own therapist), I would say, "Imagine the letters gone, destroyed or lost. What would you feel? Plunge into that feeling, explore it." But I could not. Often I thought of burning them, but that thought always evoked an inexpressible ache. My great interest in Dave, my surge of curiosity and fascination, I knew whence it came: I was asking Dave to do my work for me. Or *our* work for *us*.

From the outset I had felt drawn to Dave. At our first session six months before, I had asked him, after a few pleasantries, "What ails?"

He responded, "I can't get it up any more!"

I was astonished. I remember looking at him—his tall, lean, athletic body, his full head of glistening black hair, and his lively elfish eyes belying his sixty-nine years—and thinking, "*Chapeau!*" "Hats off!" My father had his first coronary at forty-eight. I hoped that when I was sixty-nine I'd be sufficiently alive and vital to worry about "getting it up."

Dave and I both had a proclivity to sexualize much in our environment. I contained it better than he, and had long since learned to prevent it from dominating my life. I also did not share Dave's passion for secrecy, and have many friends, including my wife, with whom I share everything.

Back to the letters. What should I do? Should I keep Dave's letters? Well, why not? After all, was it not an auspicious sign that he was willing to trust me? He had never been able to confide much in anyone and certainly not in a male. Although impotence had been his explicit reason for choosing to see me, I felt that the real task of therapy was to improve the way he related to others. A trusting, confiding relationship is a prerequisite for any therapy and, in Dave's, might be instrumental in changing his pathological need for secrecy. Keeping the letters would forge a bond of trust between us.

Perhaps the letters might give me additional leverage. I had never felt that Dave was securely lodged in therapy even though we had worked well with his impotence. My tactic had been to focus on the marital discord, and to suggest that impotence was to be expected in a relationship with so much anger and mutual suspicion. Dave, who had been recently married (for the fourth time), described his current marriage in the same way he described his previous marriages: he felt he was in prison and his wife was a prison guard who listened to his phone conversations and read his mail and personal papers. I had helped him realize that, to the extent that he was in prison, it was a prison of his own construction. *Of course*, his wife tried to obtain information about him. *Of course*, she was curious about his actions and correspondence. But it was he who had whetted her curiosity by refusing to share even innocent crumbs of information about his life.

Dave had responded well to this approach and made impressive attempts to share with his wife more of his life and internal experience. His action broke the vicious circle, his wife softened, his own anger diminished, and his sexual performance improved.

I had turned, now, in treatment to a consideration of unconscious motivation. What payoff did Dave get from a belief that he was imprisoned by a woman? What fueled his passion for secrecy? What had prevented him from forming even one intimate nonsexualized relationship with either man or woman? What had happened to his cravings for closeness? Could these cravings, even now at sixty-nine, be excavated, reanimated, and realized?

But these seemed more my project than Dave's. I suspected that, in part, he agreed to examine unconscious motivations simply to humor me. He liked to talk to me, but I believe that the primary attraction was the opportunity to reminisce, to keep alive the halcyon days of sexual triumph. My connection with him felt tentative. I always felt that if I probed too far, ranged too close to his anxiety, he would simply disappear—fail to show up for his next appointment, and I would never be able to contact him again.

If I kept the letters, they could act as a guy line: he couldn't simply float away and disappear. At the very least, he would have to be up front about terminating: he'd have to face me and request the letters back.

Besides, I felt I *had* to accept the letters. Dave was so hypersensitive. How could I reject the letters without his feeling I was rejecting him? He was also highly judgmental. A mistake would be fatal: he rarely gave people a second chance.

Yet I was uncomfortable with Dave's request. I began to think of good reasons *not* to accept his letters. I would be making a pact with his shadow—an alliance with pathology. There was something conspiratorial about the request. We'd be relating together as two bad little boys. Could I build a solid therapeutic relationship on such insubstantial foundations?

My idea that keeping the letters would make it harder for Dave to terminate therapy was, I realized quickly, nonsense. I dismissed this angle as being just that—an angle, one of my dumb, harebrained, manipulative ploys that always backfire. Angles or gimmicks were not going to help Dave relate to others directly and authentically: I had to model straightforward, honest behavior.

Besides, if he wanted to stop therapy, he'd find a way to get the letters back. I recall a patient I saw twenty years ago whose therapy was pockmarked with duplicity. She was a multiple personality whose two personae (whom I shall call Blush and Brazen) waged a deceitful war against each other. The person I treated was Blush, a constricted, prudish young thing; while Brazen, whom I rarely encountered, referred to herself as a "sexual supermarket" and dated the king of California pornography. Blush often "awoke" surprised to find that Brazen had emptied her bank account and bought sexy gowns, red lace underwear, and airline tickets for jaunts to Tijuana and Las Vegas. One day Blush was alarmed to find an around-the-world airline ticket on her dresser, and thought that she could prevent the trip by locking up all of Brazen's sexy clothing in my office. Somewhat bemused and willing to try anything once, I agreed and stored her clothes under my desk. A week later, I arrived at work one morning to find my door broken open, my office rifled, and the clothes gone. Gone also was my patient. I never saw Blush (or Brazen) again.

Suppose Dave did die on me? However good his health, he *was* sixty-nine. People *do* die at sixty-nine. What would I do with the letters then? Besides, where in the hell would I store them? Those letters must weigh ten pounds. I imagined, for a moment, interring them together with mine. They might, if discovered, provide me some cover.

But the really major problem with keeping the letters had to do with group therapy. Several weeks before, I had suggested to Dave that he enter a therapy group, and over the past three sessions we had discussed this at great length. His penchant for concealment, his sexualization of all transactions with women, his fear and distrust of all men—all of these traits, it seemed to me, were excellent issues to work on in group therapy. Reluctantly he had agreed to begin my therapy group, and our session that day was to be our last individual meeting.

Dave's request for me to keep the letters had to be seen in this context. First, it was entirely possible that the imminent transfer to the group was the factor behind his request. No doubt he regretted losing his exclusive relationship with me and resented the idea of sharing me with the group members. Asking me to keep the letters might, thus, be a way of perpetuating our special, and private, relationship.

I tried very, very delicately to express that idea, in order not to provoke Dave's exquisite sensitivity. I was careful not to demean the letters by suggesting he was using them as a means to an end. I was also careful to avoid sounding as though I were minutely scrutinizing our relationship: this was a time to nurture its growth.

Dave, being a person who needed extensive time in therapy simply to learn how to use it, scoffed at my interpretation instead of considering whether there was any truth in it. He insisted that he had asked me to keep the letters at this time for one reason only: his wife was now doing a major housecleaning and working her way steadily and surely toward his study, where the letters lay hidden.

I didn't buy his reply, but the moment called for patience, not confrontation. I let it go. I was even more concerned that keeping the letters might ultimately sabotage his work in the therapy group. Group therapy for Dave was, I knew, a high-gain but high-risk venture, and I wanted to facilitate his entry into it.

The benefits might be great. The group could offer Dave a safe community in which he could identify his interpersonal problems and experiment with new behavior. For example, he might reveal more of himself, get closer to other men, relate to women as human beings rather than as sexual organs. Dave unconsciously believed that each of these acts would result in some calamitous event: the group was the ideal arena to disconfirm these assumptions.

Of the many risks, I feared one particular scenario. I imagined that Dave would not only refuse to share important (or trivial) information about himself but do so in a coy or provocative way. The other group members would proceed to request and then demand more. Dave would respond by sharing less. The group would be angered and accuse him of playing games with them. Dave would feel hurt and trapped. His suspicions and fears of the group members would be confirmed, and he would drop out of the group, more isolated and discouraged than when he began.

It seemed to me that if I were to keep the letters, I would be colluding, in a countertherapeutic way, with his penchant for secrecy. Even before starting the group, he would have entered into a conspiracy with me that excluded the other members.

Weighing all these considerations, I finally chose my response.

"I understand why the letters are important to you, Dave, and I also feel good that I'm the one you're willing to entrust with them. However, it's my experience that group therapy works best if everyone in the group, and that includes the group leader, is as open as possible. I really want the group to be helpful to you, and I think it best that we do it this way: I'll be glad to store the letters in a safe, locked place for as long as you wish, provided that you agree to tell the group about our bargain."

Dave looked startled. He hadn't anticipated this. Would he take the leap? He cogitated for a couple of minutes. "I don't know. I'll have to think about it. I'll get back to you." He left my office, his briefcase and homeless letters in tow.

Dave never did get back to me about the letters—at least not in any way I could anticipate. But he did join the group and attended the first several meetings faithfully. In fact, I was astounded at his enthusiasm: by the fourth meeting, he told us that the group was the high point of his week, and he found himself counting the days till the next session. The reason behind the enthusiasm was, alas, not the lure of self-discovery but the quartet of attractive women members. He focused solely upon them and, we learned later, tried to arrange to meet socially with two of them outside the group.

As I had anticipated, Dave kept himself well concealed in the group and, in fact, received reinforcement for his behavior from another secretive member, a beautiful and proud woman who, like him, looked decades younger than her years. At one meeting, she and Dave were asked to state their ages. Both refused, offering the ingenious dodge that they didn't want to be age-typed. Long ago (when genitals were referred to as "privates"), therapy groups were reluctant to talk about sex. In the last two decades, however, groups talk about sex with some ease, and money has become the private subject. In thousands of group meetings, whose members supposedly bare all, I have yet to hear group members disclose their incomes.

But in Dave's group, the burning secret was age. Dave teased and joked about it but adamantly refused to state his age: he would not jeopardize his chances of scoring with one of the women in the group. In one meeting when one of the women members pressed him to tell his age, Dave offered an exchange: his secret, his age, for her home telephone number.

I grew concerned with the amount of resistance in the group. Not only was Dave not seriously working in therapy, but his bantering and flirtatiousness had shifted the entire discourse of the therapy group to a superficial level.

At one meeting, however, the tone turned deeply serious. One woman announced that her boyfriend had just learned he had cancer. She was convinced he was going to die soon, though the doctors claimed that his prognosis was not hopeless despite his debilitated physical condition and his advanced age (he was sixty-three).

I flinched for Dave: that man at the "advanced" age of sixty-three was still six years younger than he. But he didn't bat an eye and, in fact, began to speak in a far more honest fashion.

"Maybe that's something I ought to be talking about in the group. I am very phobic about illness and death. I refuse to see a doctor—a *real* doctor"—gesturing mischievously at me. "My last physical exam was over fifteen years ago."

Another group member: "You look like you're in great shape, Dave, whatever your age."

"Thank you. I work at it. Between swimming, tennis, and walking, I exercise a minimum of two hours a day. Theresa, I feel for you and your boyfriend, but I don't know how to help. I do a lot of thinking about aging and death, but my thoughts are too morbid to talk about. To be honest, I don't even like to visit sick people or listen to talk about illness. The Doc"—again, gesturing at me—"always says I keep things light in the group—maybe that's why!"

"What's why?" I asked.

"Well, if I start being serious here, I'll start talking about how much I hate about growing older, how much I fear death. Some day I'll tell you about my nightmares—maybe."

"You're not the only one who has these fears, Dave. Maybe it would be helpful to find out everyone's in the same boat."

"No, you're alone in your own boat. That's the most terrible part about dying—you have to do it alone."

Another member: "Even so, even though you're alone in your boat, it's always comforting to see the lights of the other boats bobbing nearby."

As we ended this meeting, I was exceedingly hopeful. It felt like a breakthrough session. Dave was talking about something important, he was moved, he had become real, and the other members responded in kind.

At the next meeting, Dave related a powerful dream he had had the night after the previous session. The dream (recorded verbatim by a student observer):

*Death is all around me. I can smell death. I have a packet with an envelope stuffed inside of it, and the envelope contains some thing that is immune to death or decay or deterioration. I'm keeping it secret. I go to pick it up and feel it, and suddenly I see that the envelope is empty. I feel very distressed about that and notice that it's been slit open. Later I find what I assume was in the envelope on the street, and it is a dirty old shoe with the sole coming off.*

The dream floored me. I had often thought about his love letters and had wondered if I would ever get a chance again to explore their meaning with Dave.

Much as I love to do group therapy, the format has one important drawback for me: it often does not permit the exploration of deeper existential issues. Time and again in a group, I gaze longingly at a beautiful trail that would lead me deep into the interior of a person, but must content myself with the practical (and more helpful) task of clearing away the interpersonal underbrush. Yet I couldn't deny myself this dream; it was the *via regia* into the heart of the forest. Rarely have I ever heard of a dream that so transparently laid out the answer to an unconscious mystery.

Neither Dave nor the group knew what to make of the dream. They floundered for a few minutes, and then I supplied some direction by casually asking Dave whether he had any associations to the dream image of an envelope which he was keeping secret.

I knew I was taking a risk. It would be an error, probably a fatal error, either to force Dave into untimely revealing or for me to reveal information he had entrusted to me in our individual work before he started the group. I thought my question was within the margins of safety: I stayed concretely with the dream material, and Dave could easily demur by failing to have pertinent associations.

He gamely proceeded, but not without his usual coyness. He stated that perhaps the dream referred to some letters he had been keeping secret—letters of a "certain relationship." The other members, their curiosity aroused, questioned him until Dave related a few things about his old love affair with Soraya and the problem of finding a suitable resting place for the letters. He did not say that the affair was thirty years over. Nor did he mention his negotiations with me and my offer to keep the letters for him if he agreed to share all with the group.

The group focused upon the issue of secrecy—not the issue that now most fascinated me, though nonetheless a relevant therapeutic issue. Members wondered about Dave's hiddenness; some could understand his wish to keep the letters secret from his wife, but none could understand his excesses of secrecy. For example, why did Dave refuse to tell his wife that he was in therapy? No one bought his lame excuse that if she knew he was in therapy, she'd be very threatened because she'd think he was there to complain about her, and also she'd make his life miserable by grilling him each week about what he had said in the group.

If he were, indeed, concerned about his wife's peace of mind, they pointed out, look how much more irritating it must be for her not to know where he went each week. Look at all the limp excuses he gave her for leaving the house each week to attend the group (he was retired and had no ongoing business outside the house). And look at the machinations he went through to conceal his therapy-bill payment each month. All this cloak and dagger! What for? Even insurance forms had to be sent to his secret post office box number. The members complained, too, of Dave's secretiveness in the group. They felt distanced by his reluctance to trust them. Why did he have to say "letters of a certain relationship" earlier in the meeting?

They confronted him directly: "C'mon, Dave, how much extra would it cost to come out and say 'love letters'?"

The group members, bless their hearts, were doing just what they should have been doing. They chose that part of the dream—the theme of secrecy—that was most relevant to the way Dave related to them, and they whacked away at it beautifully. Though Dave seemed a little anxious, he was refreshingly engaged—no game playing today.

But I got greedy. That dream was pure gold, and I wanted to mine it. "Does anyone have any hunches about the rest of the dream?" I asked. "About, for example, the smell of death and the fact that the envelope contains something that 'is immune to death, decay, or deterioration'?"

The group was silent for a few moments, and then Dave turned to me and said, "What do *you* think, Doc? I'd really be interested in hearing."

I felt caught. I really couldn't answer without revealing some of the material Dave had shared with me in our individual session. He hadn't, for example, told the group that Soraya had been dead for thirty years, that he was sixty-nine and felt near death, that he had asked me to be the keeper of the letters. Yet, if I revealed these things, Dave would feel betrayed and probably leave therapy. Was I walking into a trap? The only possible way out was to be entirely honest.

I said, "Dave, it's really hard for me to respond to your question. I can't tell you my thoughts about the dream without revealing information you shared with me before you entered the group. I know you're very concerned about your privacy, and I don't want to betray your trust. So what do I do?"

I leaned back, pleased with myself. Excellent technique! Just what I tell my students. If you're caught in a dilemma, or have two strong conflicting feelings, then the best thing you can do is to share the dilemma or share both feelings with the patient.

Dave said, "Shoot! Go ahead. I'm paying you for your opinion. I have nothing to hide. Anything I've said to you is an open book. I didn't mention our discussion about the letters because I didn't want to compromise you. My request to you and your counteroffer were both a bit wacky."

Now that I had Dave's permission, I proceeded to give the group members, who were by now mystified by our exchange, the relevant background: the great importance of the letters to Dave, Soraya's death thirty years ago, Dave's dilemma about where to store the letters, his request that I store them, and my offer, which he had so far declined, to keep them only if he agreed to inform the group about the entire transaction. I was careful to respect Dave's privacy by not revealing his age or any extraneous material.

Then I turned to the dream. I thought the dream answered the question why the letters were loaded for Dave. And, of course, why my letters were loaded for me. But of my letters I did not speak: there are limits to my courage. Of course, I have my rationalizations. The patients are here for *their* therapy, not mine. Time is valuable in a group—eight patients and only ninety minutes—and is not well spent by the patients listening to the therapist's problems. Patients need to have faith that their therapists face and resolve their personal problems.

But these are indeed rationalizations. The real issue was want of courage. I have erred consistently on the side of too little, rather than too much, self-disclosure; but whenever I have shared a great deal of myself, patients have invariably profited from knowing that I, like them, must struggle with the problems of being human.

The dream, I continued, was a dream about death. It began with: "Death is all around me. I can smell death." And the central image was the envelope, an envelope that contained something immune to death and deterioration. What could be clearer? The love letters were an amulet, an instrument of death denial. They warded off aging and kept Dave's passion frozen in time. To be truly loved, to be remembered, to be fused with another forever, is to be imperishable and to be sheltered from the aloneness at the heart of existence.

As the dream continued Dave saw that the envelope had been slit open and was empty. Why slit open and empty? Perhaps he felt that the letters would lose their power if he shared them with others? There was something patently and privately irrational about the letters' ability to ward off aging and death—a dark magic that evaporates when examined under the cold light of rationality.

A group member asked, "What about the dirty old shoe with the sole coming off?"

I didn't know, but before I could make any response at all, another member said, "That stands for death. The shoe is losing its *soul*, spelled S-O-U-L."

Of course—*soul*, not *sole!* That's beautiful! Why hadn't I thought of that? I had grasped the first half: I knew that the dirty old shoe represented Dave. On a couple of occasions (for example, that time he asked a woman member forty years younger for her phone number), the group had come close, I thought, to calling Dave a "dirty old man." I winced for him and was glad that the epithet had not been uttered aloud. But in the group discussion, Dave took it upon himself.

"My God! A dirty old man whose soul is about to leave him. That's me all right!" He chuckled at his own creation. A lover of words (he spoke several languages), he marveled at the transposition of *soul* and *sole*.

Despite Dave's jocularity, it was apparent he was dealing with very painful material. One of the members asked him to share some more about feeling like a dirty old man. Another asked about what it felt like to reveal the existence of the letters to the group. Would that change his attitude about them? Another reminded him that everyone faced the prospect of aging and decline, and urged him to share more about this cluster of feelings.

But Dave had closed down. He had done all the work he was to do that day. "I've gotten my money's worth today. I need some time to digest all this. I've taken up seventy-five percent of the meeting already, and I know that others want some time today."

Reluctantly, we left Dave and turned to other matters in the group. We did not know, then, that it was to be a permanent farewell. Dave never returned to another group meeting. (Nor, it turned out, was he willing to resume individual therapy with me or anyone else.)

Everyone, no one more than I, did a great deal of self-questioning. What had we done to drive Dave away? Had we stripped away too much? Had we tried too quickly to make a foolish old man wise? Had I betrayed him? Had I stepped into a trap? Would it have been better not to have spoken of the letters and to have let the dream go? (The dream interpretative work was successful, but the patient died.)

Perhaps we might have forestalled his departure, but I doubt it. By this time I was certain that Dave's caginess, his avoidance and denial, would have ultimately led to the same result. I had strongly suspected from the beginning that he would likely drop out of the group. (The fact that I was a better prophet than therapist, however, gave me little solace.)

More than anything, I felt sorrow. Sorrow for Dave, for his isolation, for his clinging to illusion, for his want of courage, for his unwillingness to face the naked, harsh facts of life.

And then I slipped into a reverie about my own letters. What would happen if (I smiled at my "if") I died and they were found? Maybe I *should* give them to Mort or Jay or Pete to store for me. Why do I keep troubling myself about those letters? Why not relieve myself of all this aggravation and burn them? Why not now? Right now! But it hurts to think about it. A stab right through my sternum. But why? Why so much pain about old yellowing letters? I'm going to have to work on this—someday.

# 7

## Two Smiles

*Some patients are easy. They appear in my office poised for change, and the* therapy runs itself. Sometimes so little effort is required of me that I invent work, posing a question or offering an interpretation simply to reassure myself, and the patient, that I am a necessary character in this transaction.

Marie was not one of the easy ones. Every session with her demanded great effort. When she first came to see me three years ago, her husband had already been dead for four years, but she remained frozen in grief. Her facial expression was frozen, as well as her imagination, her body, her sexuality—the whole flow of her life. For a long time she had remained lifeless in therapy, and I had to do the job of two people. Even now, long after her depression had lifted, there remained a stiffness in our work and a coldness and remoteness in our relationship that I had never been able to alter.

Today was a therapy holiday. Marie was to be interviewed by a consultant, and I was to enjoy the luxury of sharing an hour with her and yet being "off duty." For weeks I had urged her to see a hypnotherapist in consultation. Though she resisted almost any new experience and was particularly fearful of hypnosis, she finally consented with the condition that I remain present during the entire session. I didn't mind; in fact, I liked the idea of sitting back and letting the consultant, Mike C., a friend and colleague, do the work.

Furthermore, being an observer would provide me an unusual opportunity to reevaluate Marie. For after three years it was possible that my view of her had become fixed and narrow. Perhaps she had changed significantly and I had not taken note of it. Perhaps others would evaluate her very differently from the way I would. It was time to try to see her again through fresh eyes.

Marie was of Spanish descent and had emigrated from Mexico City eighteen years before. Her husband, whom she had met while a student at the university in Mexico, had been a surgeon and was killed in an automobile accident one evening while rushing to the hospital on an emergency call. An exceptionally handsome woman, Marie was tall, statuesque, with a boldly chiseled nose and long black hair swirled in a knot at the back of her head. How old? One might guess twenty-five: perhaps, without her makeup, thirty. It was impossible to think that she was forty.

Marie was a forbidding presence and most people felt daunted and distanced by her beauty and hauteur. I, on the other hand, was strongly drawn toward her. I was moved by her, I wanted to comfort her, I imagined embracing her and feeling her body unfreeze in my arms. I had often wondered about the strength of my attraction. Marie reminded me of a beautiful aunt who wore her hair the same way and played a major role in my adolescent sexual fantasies. Perhaps that was it. Perhaps it was simply that I was flattered to be the sole confidant and protector of this regal woman.

She concealed her depression well. No one could have guessed that she felt her life was over; that she was desperately lonely; that she wept every night; that in the seven years since her husband died, she had not once had a relationship, even a personal conversation, with a man.

For the first four years of her bereavement, Marie made herself totally inaccessible to men. Over the past two years, as her depression lessened, she had arrived at the conclusion that her only possible salvation was to develop a new romantic relationship, but she was so proud and intimidating that men regarded her as unapproachable. For several months I had attempted to challenge her belief that life, real life, can only be lived if one is loved by a man. I had tried to help her broaden her horizons, to develop new interests, to value relationships with women. But her belief was deeply held. I eventually decided it was unassailable, and turned my attention to helping her learn how to meet and engage men.

But all our work had come to a halt four weeks before when Marie was thrown from a cable car in San Francisco and fractured her jaw, suffering extensive facial and dental damage and deep lacerations in her face and neck. After being hospitalized for a week, she began treatment with an oral surgeon to repair her teeth. Marie had a low threshold for pain, especially dental pain, and dreaded her frequent visits to the oral surgeon. Moreover, she had damaged a facial nerve and suffered from severe and relentless pain on one side of her face. Medication had been of no value and it was to relieve the pain that I had suggested a hypnotic consultation.

Under ordinary conditions Marie could be a difficult patient, but after her accident she was astonishingly resistive and caustic.

"Hypnosis works for stupid people or people with weak wills. Is that why you're suggesting it for me?"

"Marie, how can I persuade you that hypnosis has nothing to do with will power or intelligence? The ability to be hypnotized is simply a trait someone is born with. What's the risk? You tell me that the pain is unbearable—there's a good possibility a one-hour consultation will offer some relief."

"It may sound simple to you, but I don't want to be made a fool of. I've seen hypnosis on TV—the victims look like idiots. They think they're swimming when they're on a dry stage, or that they're rowing a boat when sitting in a chair. Someone's tongue was stuck out and she couldn't get it back in."

"If I thought that sort of thing would happen to me, I'd feel as concerned as you. But there's all the difference in the world between TV hypnosis and medical hypnosis. I've told you precisely what you can expect. The main thing is that no one is going to control you. Instead, you'll learn to put yourself in a state of mind where you can control your pain. It sounds like you're still having trouble trusting me and other doctors."

"If doctors were trustworthy, they would have thought of calling the neurosurgeon in time and my husband would still be alive!"

"There's so much going on here today, so many issues—your pain, your concerns (and misconceptions) about hypnosis, your fears of appearing foolish, your anger and distrust of doctors, including me—I don't know which to attend to first. Do you feel the same way? Where do you think we should start today?"

"You're the doctor, not me."

And so therapy had proceeded. Marie was brittle, irritable, and despite her avowed gratitude to me, often sarcastic or provocative. She never stayed focused on any issue but quickly moved on to other grievances. Occasionally she caught herself and apologized for being bitchy, but invariably, a few minutes later, was once again irritable and self-pitying. I knew that the most important thing I could do for her, especially in this time of crisis, was to maintain our relationship and not allow her to drive me away. Thus far I had persevered, but my patience was not unlimited, and I felt relieved to share the burden with Mike.

I also wanted support from a colleague. That was my ulterior motive in the consultation. I wanted another to bear witness to what I had been going through with Marie, someone to say to me, "She's tough. You've done a helluva good job with her." That needy part of me did not act in Marie's best interests. I did not want Mike to have a smooth and easy consultation: I wanted him to struggle as I had to struggle. Yes, I admit it, a part of me was rooting for Marie to give Mike a hard time: "Come on, Marie, do your stuff!"

But, to my amazement, the session proceeded well. Marie was a good hypnotic subject, and Mike skillfully induced her and taught her how to put herself into a trance. He then addressed her pain by using an anesthetic technique. He suggested that she imagine herself in the dentist's chair getting an injection of novocaine.

"Think of your jaw and cheek growing more and more numb. Now your cheek is very numb, indeed. Touch it with your hand and see how numb it is. Think of your hand as a storehouse of numbness. It becomes numb when it touches your numb cheek, and it can transfer that numbness to any other part of your body."

From there it was an easy step for Marie to transfer her numbness to all the painful areas of her face and neck. Excellent. I could see the look of relief on her face.

Then Mike discussed pain with her. First, he described the function of pain: how it served as a warning to inform her just how much she could move her jaw and how hard she could chew. This was necessary, functional pain in contrast to the unnecessary pain stemming from irritated, bruised nerves which served no useful purpose.

Marie's first step, Mike suggested, was to learn more about her pain: to differentiate between functional and unnecessary pain. The best way to do that was to begin to ask the right questions and to discuss her pain in depth with her oral surgeon. He was the one who knew the most about what was happening in her face and mouth.

Mike's statement was wonderfully lucid and delivered with just the proper mixture of professionalism and paternalism. Marie and he locked gazes for a moment. Then she smiled and nodded. He understood that she had received and registered the message.

Mike, obviously pleased with Marie's response, turned to his final task. She was a heavy smoker and one of her motives in agreeing to the consultation with him was to enlist his help in stopping. Mike, an expert in this field, began a well-practiced, polished presentation. He emphasized three major points: that she wanted to live, that she needed her body to live, and that cigarettes were a poison to her body.

To illustrate, Mike suggested, "Think of your dog or, if you don't have one now, imagine a much-loved dog. Now imagine cans of dog food with labels marked 'poison.' You wouldn't feed your dog poisoned dog food, would you?"

Once again, Marie and Mike locked gazes; and, once again, Marie smiled and nodded. Though Mike knew that his patient had grasped the concept, he nonetheless pressed the point home: "Then why not treat your body as well as you would treat your dog?"

In the remaining time, he reinforced his instructions on self-hypnosis and taught her how to respond to cigarette craving with auto-hypnosis and increased awareness (hyperception, as he put it) of the fact that she needed her body to live and that she was poisoning it.

It was an excellent consultation. Mike had done a superb job: he had established a good rapport with Marie and had effectively achieved all of his consultation goals. Marie left the office obviously pleased with him and with the work they had done.

Afterward, I mused about the hour we three had shared. Although the consultation satisfied me professionally, I had not gotten the personal support and appreciation I had been seeking. Of course, Mike had no idea of what I really wanted from him. I could hardly admit my immature needs to a colleague much my junior. Furthermore, he could not have guessed how difficult a patient Marie had been and what a herculean job I had done with her—with him, she had played, perhaps from sheer perversity, the model patient.

Of course, all these sentiments remained hidden from Mike and Marie. Then I wondered about the two of *them*—their unfilled wishes, their hidden reflections and opinions about the consultation. Suppose, a year from now, Mike and Marie and I each wrote recollections of our time together. To what extent would we agree? I suspect each of us would barely be able to recognize the hour from the other's account. But why a year? Suppose we were able to write it a week from now? Or this very moment? Would we be able to recapture and record the real, the definitive, history of this hour?

This is no trivial question. On the basis of data patients choose to provide about events taking place long before, therapists routinely believe they can reconstruct a life: that they can discover the crucial events of the early developmental years, the real nature of the relationship with each parent, the relationship between the parents, between the siblings, the family system, the inner experience accompanying the frights and bruises of early life, the texture of childhood and adolescent friendships.

Yet, can therapists or historians or biographers reconstruct a life with any degree of accuracy if the reality of even a single hour cannot be captured? Years ago I conducted an experiment in which a patient and I each wrote our own view of each of our therapy hours. Later when we compared them, it was at times difficult to believe that we described the same hour. Even our views of what was helpful varied. My elegant interpretations? She never even heard them! Instead she remembered, and treasured, casual, personal, supportive comments I had made.*

At such times one longs for an umpire of reality or some official sharp-imaged snapshot of the hour. How disquieting to realize that reality is illusion, at best a democratization of perception based on participant consensus.

If I were to write my summary of that hour, I would stucture it around two particularly "real" moments: the two times Marie and Mike locked gazes and she smiled and nodded. The first smile followed Mike's recommendation that Marie discuss her pain in detail with her oral surgeon; the second when he drove home the point that she would not feed poisoned food to her dog.

Later I had a long talk with Mike about the hour. Professionally, he regarded it as a successful consultation. Marie was a good hypnotic subject, and he had achieved each of his consultation goals. Furthermore, it had been a good personal experience after a bad week, in which he had hospitalized two patients and had a run-in with the department chairman. It was gratifying to him that I had seen him performing so competently and efficiently. He was younger than I and had always respected my work. My good opinion of him meant a great deal. How ironic that he should have gotten from me what I had wanted from him.

I asked him about the two smiles. He remembered them well and was convinced that they signified impact and connection. The smiles,

---

*These differing visions were later published as *Every Day Gets a Little Closer: A Twice-Told Therapy* (New York: Basic Books, 1974).

appearing at points of power in his presentation, signified that Marie had understood and was affected by his message.

Yet, as a result of my long relationship with Marie, I interpreted those smiles very differently. Consider the first, when Mike suggested that Marie seek more information from her oral surgeon, Dr. Z. What a story there was behind Marie's relationship with him!

She had first met him twenty years before when they were college classmates in Mexico City. At that time he had tried energetically, but unsuccessfully, to court her. She had lost touch with him until her husband's automobile accident. Dr. Z., who had also come to the United States, worked at the hospital where her husband was brought after his accident, and was a major source of medical information and support to Marie during the two weeks her husband had lain in terminal coma with a fatal head injury.

Almost immediately after her husband's death, Dr. Z., despite his wife and five children, renewed his courtship and began to make sexual overtures to Marie. She rebuffed him angrily, but he was not deterred. On the telephone, in church, even in the courtroom (she sued the hospital for negligence in her husband's death), he winked and leered. Marie regarded his behavior as odious and gradually became harsher in her refusals. Dr. Z. desisted only when she told him that she was disgusted by him, that he was the last man in the world with whom she would have an affair, and that she would inform his wife, a formidable woman, if he continued to harass her.

When Marie fell from the cable car, she struck her head and was unconscious for about an hour. Awaking to extraordinary pain, she felt desperately alone: she had no close friends, and her two daughters were vacationing in Europe. When the emergency room nurse asked her for the name of her doctor, she moaned, "Call Dr. Z." By general consensus he was the most talented and experienced oral surgeon in the area, and Marie felt that too much was at stake to gamble with an unknown surgeon.

Dr. Z. contained his feelings during his initial major surgical procedures (apparently he had done an excellent job), but they came

pouring out during the postoperative course. He was sarcastic, author-
itarian, and, I believe, sadistic. Having persuaded himself that Marie
was hysterically overreacting, he refused to prescribe adequate med-
ications for pain relief or sedation. He frightened her by making off-
hand statements about dangerous complications or residual facial
distortions and threatened to leave the case if she continued to complain so much. When I spoke to Dr. Z. about the need for pain relief,
he grew belligerent and reminded me he knew a lot more than I did
about surgical pain. Perhaps, he suggested, I was tired of talking treatments and wanted to switch specialties. I was reduced to prescribing
Marie sedation *sub rosa.*

I listened for many long hours as Marie complained about her pain
and about Dr. Z. (whom she was convinced would treat her better if
she would even now, with her mouth and face throbbing with pain, accept his sexual advances). Her dental sessions in his office were hu-
miliating: whenever his assistant left the room, he would make sexually
suggestive comments and manage frequently to brush his hands across
her breasts.

Finding no way to be helpful to Marie in her situation with Dr. Z.,
I strongly urged that she change doctors. At the very least, I urged
that she obtain a consultation with another oral surgeon, and supplied
her with names of excellent consultants. She hated what was happening, and she hated Dr. Z., but my every suggestion was met by "but"
or "yes, but." She was a "yes, but-er" (also referred to in the trade as a
"help-rejecting complainer") of considerable prowess. Her major "buts"
were that since Dr. Z. had started the job, he—and only he—really
knew what was going on in her mouth. She was terrified of having a
permanent facial or oral deformity. (Always greatly concerned about
her physical appearance, she was even more so now that she was entering the singles world.) Nothing—not anger, pride, or hostile brush-
ing of her breasts—took precedence over her functional and cosmetic
recovery.

There was one additional and important consideration. Because the
cable car had lurched, causing her to fall as she was leaving it, she had

initiated a lawsuit against the city. As a result of her injury Marie had lost her job, and her financial situation was precarious. She was counting on a sizable financial settlement, and she feared antagonizing Dr. Z., whose strong testimony about the extent of her injury and suffering would be essential in winning the suit.

And so Marie and Dr. Z. were locked in a complex dance, whose steps included a spurned surgeon, a million-dollar lawsuit, a broken jaw, several fractured teeth, and brushed breasts. It was into this extraordinary tangle that Mike—of course, knowing none of this—had dropped his innocent, rational suggestion that Marie seek her doctor's help in understanding her pain. And then it was that Marie smiled.

The second time she smiled was in response to Mike's equally ingenuous question, "Would you feed your dog poisoned dog food?"

There was a story, too, behind that smile. Nine years before, Marie and Charles, her husband, had obtained a dog, an ungainly dachshund named Elmer. Though Elmer was really Charles's dog, and though Marie had an aversion to dogs, she had gradually grown affectionate toward Elmer, who for years had slept in her bed.

Elmer grew old, crochety, and arthritic and, after Charles's death, had commanded so much of Marie's attention that he may have done her a service. Enforced busyness is often the friend of the bereaved and Elmer provided blessed distraction in the early stages of mourning. (In our culture the busyness may be supplied by the funeral arrangements and the paperwork of medical insurance and estate settlement.)

After approximately one year of psychotherapy, Marie's depression lifted, and she turned her attention to rebuilding her life. She was convinced that she could attain happiness only through coupling. Everything else was prelude; other types of friendship, all other experiences were simply ways of marking time until her life began anew with a man.

But Elmer loomed as a major barrier between Marie and her new life. She was determined to find a man; however, Elmer apparently thought he was sufficient man for her household. He howled and nipped at strangers, especially men. He became perversely incontinent:

he refused to urinate outdoors but, waiting till he had gained entry to the house, drenched the living room carpet. No training or punishment was effective. If Marie left him outside, he howled so incessantly that neighbors, even several doors away, phoned her to plead or demand that she do something. If she punished him in any manner, Elmer retaliated by hosing down carpets in other rooms.

Elmer's odor permeated the house. It hit the visitor at the front door and no amount of air, shampoo, deodorizing, or perfume could cleanse Marie's home. Too ashamed to invite any visitor inside, she tried at first to repay invitations by entertaining in restaurants. Gradually she despaired of ever having a true social life.

I am not a lover of dogs, but this one seemed worse than most. I met Elmer once when Marie brought him to my office—an ill-mannered creature that growled and noisily licked his genitals during the entire hour. Perhaps it was there and then that I resolved that Elmer would have to go. I refused to allow him to ruin Marie's life. Or mine.

But there were formidable obstacles. It was not that Marie could not be decisive. There had been another odor polluter in the house, a tenant who, according to Marie, dieted on decomposed fish. In that situation, Marie had acted with alacrity. She followed my advice to have a direct confrontation; and when the tenant refused to alter her cooking habits, Marie scarcely hesitated to ask the woman to move.

But Marie felt trapped with Elmer. He had been Charles's dog, and a bit of Charles still lived through Elmer. Marie and I endlessly discussed her options. The veterinarian's extensive and expensive incontinence diagnostic work-up was of little value. Visits to a pet psychologist and trainer were equally fruitless. Slowly and sadly she realized (abetted, of course, by me) that she and Elmer had to part company. She called all her friends to ask if they wanted Elmer, but no one was fool enough to adopt that dog. She advertised in the newspaper, but even the inducement of free dog food failed to generate a prospect.

The inevitable decision loomed. Her daughters, her friends, her veterinarian, all urged her to have Elmer put to sleep. And, of course, behind the scenes, I was subtly guiding her toward that decision. Finally, Marie agreed. She gave the thumbs-down signal and one gray morning took Elmer on his final visit to the veterinarian.

Concurrently, a problem on another front had developed. Marie's father, who lived in Mexico, had grown so frail that she contemplated inviting him to come to live with her. This seemed to me to be a poor solution for Marie since she so feared and disliked her father that she had had little communication with him for years. In fact, the wish to escape from his tyranny had been a major force in her decision, eighteen years before, to emigrate to the United States. The notion of inviting him to come live with her was spurred by guilt rather than concern or love. Pointing this out to Marie, I also questioned the advisability of yanking an eighty-year-old, non-English-speaking man out of his culture. She ultimately concurred and arranged residential care for her father in Mexico.

Marie's view of psychiatry? She had often joked with her friends, "Go see a psychiatrist. They're wonderful. First, they tell you to evict your tenant. Next, they have you put your father in a nursing home. Finally, they make you kill your dog!"

And she had smiled when Mike leaned over to her and asked gently, "You wouldn't feed your dog poisoned dog food, would you?"

So, from my perspective, Marie's two smiles had not signified moments of concurrence with Mike but were instead smiles of irony, smiles that said, "If you only knew . . . " When Mike asked her to have a talk with her oral surgeon, I imagined that she must have been thinking, "Have a long talk with Dr. Z.! That's rich! I'll talk all right! When I am healed and my lawsuit settled, I'll talk to his wife and everybody I know. I'll blow the whistle on that bastard so loud his ears will never stop ringing."

And certainly the smile about poisoned dog food was equally ironic. She must have been thinking, "Oh, I wouldn't feed him poisoned dog food—not unless he got a little old and bothersome. Then I'd knock him off—fast!"

When, in our next individual session, we discussed the consultation, I asked her about the two smiles. She remembered each of them very well. "When Dr. C. advised me to have a long talk with Dr. Z. about my pain, I suddenly became very ashamed. I began to wonder if you had told him everything about me and Dr. Z. I liked Dr. C. very much. He's very attractive, he's the kind of man I'd like to have in my life."

"And the smile, Marie?"

"Well, obviously I was embarrassed. Would Dr. C. think I was a slut? If I really think about it (which I don't), I guess it boils down to an exchange of goods—I humor Dr. Z. and let him have his disgusting little feels in exchange for his help in my lawsuit."

"So the smile said———?"

"My smile said——— Why are you so interested in my smile?"

"Go on."

"I guess my smile said, 'Please, Dr. C., go on to something else. Don't ask me any more questions about Dr. Z. I hope you don't know about what's going on between us."

The second smile? The second smile was not, as I had thought, an ironic signal about the care of her dog but something else entirely.

"I felt funny when Dr. C. kept talking about the dog and the poison. I knew you hadn't told him about Elmer—otherwise, he wouldn't have picked a dog to illustrate his talk."

"And———?"

"Well, it's hard to say all this. But, even though I don't show it very much—I'm not good at saying thank you—I really appreciate what you've done for me these last months. I wouldn't have made it without you. I've told you my psychiatrist joke (my friends love it)—first, your tenant, then your father, then they make you kill your dog!"

"So?"

"So, I think maybe you overstepped your role as a doctor—I told you it would be hard to talk about this. I thought psychiatrists weren't supposed to give direct advice. Maybe you let your personal feelings about dogs and fathers get out of hand!"

"And the smile said——?"

"God, you're persistent! The smile said, 'Yes, yes, Dr. C., I get the point. Now quickly, let's pass on to another subject. Don't question me more about my dog. I don't want to make Dr. Yalom look bad.'"

I had mixed feelings about her response. Was she right? Had I let my own feelings get in the way? The more I thought about it, the more I was convinced it didn't fit. I had always had warm feelings toward my father and would have welcomed the opportunity to invite him to live in my home. And dogs? It is true I was unsympathetic to Elmer, but I knew about my lack of interest in dogs and had been carefully monitoring myself. Every person who knew about the situation had advised her to get rid of Elmer. Yes, I was certain I had acted with her best interests in mind. Hence, I was uncomfortable with accepting Marie's protection of my professionalism. It felt conspiratorial—as though I acknowledged that I had something to hide. I was also aware, however, that she had expressed gratitude to me, and *that* felt good.

Our discussion about the smiles opened up such rich material for therapy that I put aside my musings about differing views of reality and helped Marie explore her self-contempt for the way she had compromised herself with Dr. Z. She also examined her feelings toward me with more honesty than before: her fears of dependency, her gratitude, her anger.

The hypnosis helped her to tolerate the pain until, after three months, her fractured jaw had healed, her dental work had been completed, and the facial pain had subsided. Her depression improved, and her anger lessened; yet, despite these developments, I was never able to transform Marie in the way I had wished. She remained proud, somewhat judgmental, and resistive to new ideas. We continued to meet, but there seemed less and less to talk about; and finally, several months later, we agreed that our work had come to an end. Marie came in to see me for some minor crisis every few months for the next four years; and, after that, our lives never crossed.

The lawsuit dragged on for three years, and she settled for a disappointingly small sum. By that time, her anger toward Dr. Z. had rusted away, and she forgot about her resolution to raise her voice against him. Ultimately she married a sweet, elderly man. I'm not certain whether she was ever truly happy again. But she never smoked another cigarette.

## Epilogue

Marie's consultation hour is a testament to the limits of knowing. Though she, Mike, and I shared an hour, each of us had a vastly different, and unpredictable, experience. The hour was a triptych, each panel reflecting the perspective, the hues, the concerns, of its creator. Perhaps if I had given Mike more information about Marie, his panel would have resembled mine more closely. But of my hundred hours with her, what should I have shared? My irritation? My impatience? My self-pity for being stuck with Marie? My pleasure with her progress? My sexual arousal? My intellectual curiosity? My desire to change Marie's vision, to teach her to look within, to dream, to fantasize, to extend her horizons?

Yet had I spent hours with Mike and shared all this information, still I would not have adequately conveyed my experience of Marie. My impressions of her, my pleasure, my impatience are not precisely like any others I have known. I reach out for words, metaphors, analogies, but they never really work; they are at best feeble approximations of the rich images that once coursed through my mind.

A series of distorting prisms block the knowing of the other. Before the invention of the stethoscope, a physician listened to the sounds of life with an ear pressed against a patient's rib cage. Imagine two minds pressed tight together and, like paramecia exchanging micronuclei, directly transferring thought images: that would be union nonpareil.

Perhaps in some millennium, such union will come to pass—the ultimate antidote for isolation, the ultimate scourge of privacy. For now, there exist formidable barriers to such mind coupling.

First, there is the barrier between image and language. Mind thinks in images but, to communicate with another, must transform image into thought and then thought into language. That march, from image to thought to language, is treacherous. Casualties occur: the rich, fleecy texture of image, its extraordinary plasticity and flexibility, its private nostalgic emotional hues—all are lost when image is crammed into language.

Great artists attempt to communicate image directly through suggestion, through metaphor, through linguistic feats intended to evoke some similar image in the reader. But ultimately they realize the inadequacy of their tools for the task. Listen to Flaubert's lament, in *Madame Bovary*:

> Whereas the truth is that fullness of soul can sometimes over flow in utter vapidity of language, for none of us can ever express the exact measure of his needs or his thoughts or his sorrows; and human speech is like a cracked kettle on which we tap crude rhythms for bears to dance to, while we long to make music that will melt the stars.

Another reason we can never fully know another is that we are selective about what we choose to disclose. Marie sought Mike's assistance for impersonal goals, to control pain and stop smoking, and so chose to reveal to him little of herself. Consequently, he mistook the meaning of her smiles. I knew more about Marie and about her smiles. But I, too, mistook their meaning: what I knew of her was but a small fragment of what she would and could tell me of herself.

Once I worked in a group with a patient who, during two years of therapy, rarely addressed me directly. One day Jay surprised me and the other members by announcing ("confessing" was his word) that everything he had ever said in the group—his feedback to others, his self-revelations, all his angry and caring words—everything, had really been said for my benefit. Jay recapitulated, in the group, his life experiences in his family, where he yearned for his father's love but had never—could never—ask for it. In the group, he had participated in many dramas but always against the horizon of what he might get from me. Though he pretended to speak to other members of the group, he spoke *through* them to me as he continuously sought my approval and support.

In that instant of confession, my entire construct of Jay exploded. I thought I had known him well a week, a month, six months before. But I had never known the real, the secret Jay; and, after his confession, I had to reconstruct my image of him and assign new meanings to past experiences. But this new Jay, this changeling, how long would he stay? How long before new secrets would accrue? How long before he revealed this new layer? I knew that, stretching out into the future, there would be an infinite number of Jays. Never could I catch up with the "real" one.

A third barrier to the full knowing of another lies not in the one who shares but in the other, the knower, who must reverse the sharer's sequence and translate language back into image—the script the mind can read. It is wildly improbable that the receiver's image will match the sender's original mental image.

Translation error is compounded by bias error. We distort others by forcing them into our own preferred ideas and gestalts, a process Proust beautifully describes:

> We pack the physical outline of the creature we see with all the ideas we already formed about him, and in the complete picture of him which we compose in our minds, those ideas have certainly the principal place. In the end they come to fill out so completely the curve of his cheeks, to follow so exactly the line of his nose, they blend so harmoniously in the sound of his voice that these seem to be no more than a transparent envelope, so that each time we see the face or hear the voice it is our own ideas of him which we recognize and to which we listen.

"Each time we see the face . . . it is our own *ideas* of him which we recognize"—these words provide a key to understanding many miscarried relationships. Dan, one of my patients, attended a meditation retreat where he engaged in treposa, a meditation procedure in which two people hold hands for several minutes, lock gazes, meditate deeply upon one another, and then repeat the process with new partners. After many such interactions, Dan could clearly discriminate between partners: with some he felt little connection, while with others he felt a strong bond, one so powerful, so compelling that he was convinced he had entered into a spiritual linkage with another kindred soul.

Whenever Dan discussed such experiences, I had to constrain my skepticism and rationalism: "Spiritual linkage, indeed! What we have here, Dan, is an autistic relationship. You don't know this person. In a Proustian way, you've packed this creature full of the attributes you so desire. You've fallen in love with your own creation."

Of course, I never explicitly expressed these sentiments. I don't think Dan would have wanted to work with someone so skeptical. Yet I am sure I aired my views in many indirect ways: a quizzical look, the timing of comments or inquiries, my fascination with some topics and indifference to others.

Dan picked up these innuendos and, in his own defense, cited Nietzsche who said somewhere that when you first meet someone, you know all about him; on subsequent meetings, you blind yourself to your own wisdom. Nietzsche carries a lot of weight with me, and that citation gave me pause. Perhaps on a first meeting, guards *are* down; perhaps one has not yet determined what persona to don. Maybe first impressions *are* more accurate than second or third impressions. But that is a far distance from spiritually communing with the other. Besides, though Nietzsche was a seer in many domains, he was no guide to interpersonal relationships—has there ever lived a lonelier, more isolated man?

Was Dan right? Had he, through some mystical channel, discovered something vital and real about the other person? Or had he simply packed his own ideas and desires into some human profile—a profile he found attractive only because it ignited cozy, loving, nurturing associations?

We could never test the treposa situation because such meditation retreats usually follow the rule of "noble silence": no speech whatsoever is permitted. But on several occasions he encountered a woman socially, locked gazes, and experienced a spiritual melding with her. With rare exceptions he learned that the spiritual union was a mirage. The woman was usually baffled or frightened by his assumption that there was some deep bond between them. Often it took Dan a long time to see this. Sometimes I felt cruel as I confronted him with my view of reality.

"Dan, this intense closeness you feel toward Diane—maybe she did allude to the possibility of a relationship some time in the future, but look at the facts. She doesn't return your calls, she's been living with a man and now that's breaking up, she's making arrangements to move in with someone else. Listen to what she's telling you."

Occasionally the woman into whose eyes Dan was gazing experienced the same deep spiritual linkage, and they were drawn together into love—but a love that invariably passed quickly. Sometimes it simply waned painfully away; sometimes it turned into violent jealous accusations. Often Dan, his lover, or both, ended up depressed. Whatever the route the passing of love took, the final outcome was the same; neither got what they wanted from the other.

I am persuaded that, in these infatuating first meetings, Dan and the woman mistook what they each saw in the other. They each saw the reflection of their own beseeching, wounded gaze and mistook it for desire and fullness. They were each fledglings with broken wings who sought to fly by clasping another broken-winged bird. People who feel empty never heal by merging with another incomplete person. On the contrary, two broken-winged birds coupled into one make for clumsy flight. No amount of patience will help it fly; and, ultimately, each must be pried from the other, and wounds separately splinted.

The unknowability of the other inheres not only in the problems I have described—the deep structures of image and language, the individual's intentional and unintentional decision to conceal, the observer's scotomata—but also in the vast richness and intricacy of each individual being. While vast research programs seek to decipher electrical and biochemical activity of the brain, each person's flow of

experience is so complex that it will forever outdistance new eaves-
dropping technology.

Julian Barnes has, in *Flaubert's Parrot*, illustrated in a beautiful and
whimsical manner a person's inexhaustible complexity. The author sets
out to discover the real Flaubert, the flesh-and-blood man behind the
public image. Frustrated by direct traditional methods of biography,
Barnes attempted to catch Flaubert's essence off-guard by using indirect means: discussing, for example, his interest in trains, the animals
for which he felt an affinity, or the number of different methods (and
colors) he used to describe Emma Bovary's eyes.

Barnes, of course, never captured the quintessence of the man,
Flaubert, and ultimately set a more modest task for himself. On visits
to the two Flaubert museums—one at Flaubert's childhood home and
the other at the house where he lived as an adult—Barnes sees in each
a stuffed parrot that each museum claims to be the model Flaubert
used for Lulu, the parrot prominent in his "A Simple Soul." This situation stirs Barnes's investigative reflexes: by God, though he can't locate Flaubert, he will at least determine which was the real parrot and
which the imposter.

The physical appearance of the two parrots is of no help: they re-
semble one another closely; and both, moreover, satisfy Flaubert's published description of Lulu. Then, at one museum, the aged guardian
offers proof his parrot is the real one. His parrot's perch has a stamp
on it—"Museum of Rouen"; and he then shows Barnes a photocopy of
a receipt indicating that Flaubert, over a hundred years ago, had rented
(and later returned) the municipal museum's parrot. Elated at being
close to a solution, the author hurries to the other museum only to
discover that the competing parrot has the identical stamp on its perch.
Later he spoke to the oldest living member of the Société des Amis
de Flaubert who told him the true story of the parrots. When the two
museums were under construction (long after Flaubert's death), each
of the curators went, separately, to the municipal museum with a copy
of the receipt in hand, and asked for Flaubert's parrot for his museum.
Each curator was escorted into a large stuffed-animal room containing

at least fifty virtually identical stuffed parrots! "Take your choice," each was told.

The impossibility of discovering the authentic parrot puts an end to Barnes's belief that the "real" Flaubert, or the "real" anyone, can be ensnared. But many people never discover the folly of such a search and continue to believe that, given enough information, they can define and explain a person. Controversy has always existed among psychiatrists and psychologists about the validity of personality diagnosis. Some believe in the merits of the enterprise and devote their careers to ever greater nosological precision. Others, and among them I include myself, marvel that anyone can take diagnosis seriously, that it can ever be considered more than a simple cluster of symptoms and behavioral traits. Nonetheless, we find ourselves under ever-increasing pressure (from hospitals, insurance companies, governmental agencies) to sum up a person with a diagnostic phrase and a numerical category.

Even the most liberal system of psychiatric nomenclature does violence to the being of another. If we relate to people believing that we can categorize them, we will neither identify nor nurture the parts, the vital parts, of the other that transcend category. The enabling relationship always assumes that the other is never fully knowable. If I were forced to assign an official diagnostic label to Marie, I would follow the formula prescribed in the current psychiatric diagnostic and statistical manual and arrive at a precise and official-sounding six-part diagnosis. Yet I know that it would have little to do with the flesh-and-blood Marie, the Marie who always surprised me and outdistanced my grasp, the Marie of the two smiles.

# 8

౾౾

# Three Unopened Letters

"*The first one came on a Monday. The day started out like any other day.*
I spent the morning working on a paper, and around noontime I
strolled down to the end of my driveway to collect the mail—I usually
read the mail as I eat lunch. For some reason, I'm not sure why, I had a
premonition that this day was not going to be an ordinary day. I got to
the mailbox and——and——"

Saul could go no further. His voice cracked. He put his head down
and tried to collect himself. I had never seen him look worse. His face
was lined with despair, causing him to look far older than his sixty-
three years; his puffy, hangdog eyes were reddened; his blotchy skin
glistened with perspiration.

After a few minutes he tried to continue. "In the mail I saw that it
had come . . . I . . . I can't go on, I don't know what to do——"

In the three or four minutes Saul had been in my office, he had
worked himself into a state of deep agitation. He began to breathe rapidly, taking short, staccato, shallow breaths. He put his head between
his knees and held his breath, but without avail. Then he rose from his
chair and paced about in my office, gulping air in great draughts. Much
more hyperventilation and I knew Saul would pass out. I wished I had
a brown paper bag for him to breathe into but, lacking that old folk
remedy (as good as any other for counteracting hyperventilation), I
tried to talk him down.

"Saul, nothing's going to happen to you. You've come to see me for
help, and this is just what I'm trained to do. We'll be able to work this

out together. Here's what I want you to do. Start by lying here on the couch and concentrating on your breathing. First breathe deep and fast; then we'll gradually slow it down. I want you to focus on one thing, nothing else. You hear me? Just keep noticing that the air entering your nostrils always feels cooler than the air leaving your nostrils. Meditate on that. Soon you'll notice that, as you breathe more slowly, your exhaling air will feel even warmer."

My suggestion was more effective than I anticipated. Within minutes Saul relaxed, his breathing slowed, his look of panic disappeared.

"Now that you're looking better, Saul, let's go back to work. Remember, I need to be filled in—I haven't seen you in three years. Exactly what's happened to you? Tell me everything. I want to hear every detail."

Details are wonderful. They are informative, they are calming, and they penetrate the anxiety of isolation: the patient feels that, once you have the details, you have entered into his life.

Saul chose not to give me any background but continued with his description of recent events, continuing his story where he had left off.

"I picked up my mail and walked back to the house, flipping through the usual batch of junk—advertisements, charity requests. Then I saw it—an oversized, brown, formal envelope from the Stockholm Research Institute. It had finally come! For weeks I've dreaded getting that letter, and now that it had finally come, I could not open it." He paused.

"What happened then? Don't skip anything."

"I think I just collapsed in a kitchen chair and sat there. Then I folded the letter and jammed it into my rear trouser pocket. I began making lunch." Another pause.

"Keep going. Don't leave out anything."

"I boiled two eggs and made egg salad. It's funny but egg salad sandwiches have always been soothing. I only eat them when I'm upset— no lettuce, no tomato, no chopped celery or onion. Just mashed egg, salt, pepper, mayonnaise served on very fluffy white bread."

"Did it work? Did the sandwiches soothe you?"

"I had a hard time getting to them. First, I was distracted by the envelope—its jagged edges were gouging my ass. I took the letter out of my pocket and started playing around with it. You know—holding it up to the light, feeling its weight, trying to guess how many pages it had. Not that it would make any difference. I knew that its message would be brief—and brutal."

In spite of my curiosity, I decided to let Saul tell the story in his own way, and at his own pace.

"Keep going."

"Well, I ate the sandwiches. I even ate them the way I used to when I was a kid—by sucking out the egg salad filling. But they didn't help. I needed something stronger. This letter was too devastating. Finally, I stowed it away in a drawer in my study."

"Still unopened?"

"Yes, unopened. And still unopened. Why open it? I know what's in it. To read the exact words would only tear open the wound even more."

I didn't know what Saul was talking about. I didn't even know about his connection to the Stockholm Institute. By now I was itching with curiosity, yet took a perverse pleasure in not scratching. My children have always kidded me about the way I rip open a present as soon as it is handed me. Surely my patience that day was a sign of having arrived at some degree of maturity. What's the rush? Saul would fill me in soon enough.

"The second letter arrived eight days later. The envelope was identical to the first. I put it, also unopened, on top of the first one in the same desk drawer. But hiding them didn't accomplish anything. I couldn't stop thinking about them, yet I couldn't bear to think of them. If only I had never gone to the Stockholm Institute!" He sighed.

"Keep going."

"I spent a lot of the last couple of weeks lost in daydreams. You sure you want to hear all this?"

"I'm sure. Tell me about the daydreams."

"Well, sometimes I thought about being on trial. I'd appear before the members of the institute—they'd be wigged and robed. I would be brilliant. I would refuse counsel and dazzle everyone by the way I answered every charge. Soon it would be clear that I had nothing to conceal. The judges would be thrown into disarray. One by one they would break ranks and rush to be the first to congratulate me and ask my forgiveness. That's one kind of daydream. It made me feel better for a few minutes. The others weren't as good, very morbid."

"Tell me about them."

"Sometimes I'd feel this tightness in my chest and think I was having a coronary, a silent coronary. Those are the symptoms—no pain, just difficulty breathing and thoracic tightness. I'd try to feel my pulse but could never find the damned thing when I wanted it. When I finally got a beat, I'd start to wonder whether it was coming from my radial artery or from the tiny arterioles in my fingers squeezing my wrist.

"I'd get a pulse of about twenty-six in fifteen seconds. Twenty-six times four is one hundred and four a minute. Then I'd wonder whether one hundred and four was good or bad? I didn't know whether a silent coronary was accompanied by a fast or a slow pulse. Björn Borg's pulse is fifty, I've heard.

"Then I'd daydream about slicing that artery, relieving the pressure, and letting the blood out. At one hundred and four beats a minute, how long would it take to enter darkness? Then I'd think about speeding up my pulse to let the blood out faster. I could exercise on my stationary bicycle! In a couple of minutes, I could get my pulse up to one hundred twenty.

"Sometimes I'd imagine the blood filling a paper cup. I could hear each spurt splatter against the waxed walls of the cup. Perhaps one hundred spurts would fill a cup—that's only fifty seconds. Then I'd think about how to slice my wrists. The knife in the kitchen? The small sharp one with the black handle? Or a razor blade? But there are no more slicing razor blades—just those safe injectable ones. I had never before noticed the passing of the razor blade. I thought that's the way I, too, will pass. Without a ripple. Maybe someone will think of me in some freak moment just as I think of the extinct single-edged razor blade.

"Yet the blade is not extinct. Thanks to my thoughts, it still lives. You know, there is no one alive now who was grown-up when I was a child. So I, as a child, am dead. Some day soon, perhaps in forty years, there will be no one alive who has *ever* known me. That's when I will be *truly* dead—when I exist in no one's memory. I thought a lot about how someone very old is the last living individual to have known some person or cluster of people. When that old person dies, the whole cluster dies, too, vanishes from living memory. I wonder who that person will be for me. Whose death will make me truly dead?"

For the past few minutes Saul had been speaking with closed eyes. He opened them suddenly and checked with me: "You asked for this. You want me to go on? This is pretty morbid stuff."

"Everything, Saul. I want to know exactly what you've been going through."

"One of the worst things was that I had no one to talk to, nowhere to turn, no confidant, no trusted friend with whom I could dare talk about this stuff."

"How about me?"

"I don't know if you remember, but it took me fifteen years to make the decision to see you the first time. I just couldn't bear the disgrace now of coming back to see you. We had done so well together, I couldn't deal with the shame of coming back defeated."

I understood what Saul meant. We had worked together very productively for a year and a half. Three years ago, as we ended therapy, Saul and I had taken great pride in the changes he had made. Our termination session was a high-spirited graduation—it lacked only a brass band accompanying his triumphant march out into the world.

"So I tried to deal with it on my own. I knew what those letters meant: they were my final judgment, my personal apocalypse. I think I've been staying just ahead of them for sixty-three years. Now, maybe because I've slowed down—my age, my weight, my emphysema—they've overtaken me. I've always had ways to delay the judgment. You remember them?"

I nodded. "Some of them."

"I'd offer profuse apologies, prostrate myself, spread innuendoes that I had advanced cancer (that has never failed). And always, if nothing else worked, there was always the cash payoff. I figure that fifty thousand dollars will cure this whole Stockholm Institute catastrophe."

"What changed your mind? Why did you decide to call me?"

"It was the third letter. It arrived about ten days after the second. It put an end to everything, to all my planning, to any hope of escape. I guess it put an end, too, to my pride. Within minutes of getting it, I was on the phone with your secretary."

The rest I knew. My secretary had told about his call: "Any time the doctor can see me. I know how busy he is. Yes, a week from Tuesday would be fine—no emergency."

When my secretary told me about his second call a few hours later ("I hate to bother the doctor, but I wonder if he could fit me in, even for a few minutes, just a *little* earlier"), I recognized Saul's signal of great desperation and called him back to arrange for an immediate consultation.

He then proceeded to summarize the events of his life since we had last met. Shortly after termination of therapy, about three years ago, Saul, an accomplished neurobiologist, had received a distinguished award—a six-month fellowship at the Stockholm Research Institute in Sweden. The terms of the award were generous: a fifty-thousand-dollar stipend, no strings attached, and he was free to pursue his own research and to do as little or as much teaching and collaborative work as he chose.

When he arrived at the Stockholm Institute, he was greeted by Dr. K., a renowned cellular biologist. Dr. K. was a great presence: speaking in an impeccable Oxonian dialect, he refused to be bowed by seven and a half decades and employed every one of his seventy-six inches in the construction of one of the world's great postures. Poor Saul strained chin and neck to reach five foot six. Though others regarded as endearing his antiquated Brooklynese, Saul cringed at the sound of his own voice. While Dr. K. had never won a Nobel Prize (though had been, it was well known, runner-up on two occasions), he was unquestionably made of the stuff from which laureates come. For thirty years Saul had admired him from afar and now, in his presence, could barely summon the nerve to look into the great man's eyes.

When Saul was seven his parents had died in an automobile accident, and he had been raised by an aunt and uncle. Since then the leitmotif in his life had been a ceaseless search for home, affection, and approval. Failure had always inflicted terrible wounds, which healed slowly and deeply intensified his feeling of insignificance and loneliness; success offered stupendous but evanescent exhilaration.

But the moment Saul arrived at the Stockholm Research Institute, the moment he was greeted by Dr. K., he felt strangely convinced that his goal was within his grasp, that there was hope for some final peace. The moment he shook Dr. K.'s powerful hand, Saul had a vision, redemptive and beatific, of the two of them, he and Dr. K., working side by side as full collaborators.

Within hours and with insufficient planning, Saul put forward a proposal that he and Dr. K. collaborate on a review of the world literature on muscle cell differentiation. Saul suggested they offer a creative synthesis and identify the most promising directions for future research. Dr. K. listened, gave cautious assent, and agreed to meet twice weekly with Saul, who would do the library research. Saul threw himself passionately into the hastily conceived project and treasured his consultation hours with Dr. K., in which they reviewed Saul's progress and sought meaningful patterns in the disparate basic research literature.

Saul so basked in the glow of the collaborative relationship that he failed to notice that the library research was not productive. Consequently, he was shocked when, two months later, Dr. K. expressed his disappointment about the work and recommended it be abandoned. Never in his life had Saul failed to complete a project, and his first reaction was to suggest he continue on it alone. Dr. K. responded, "I can't prevent you, of course, but I consider it ill advised. At any rate, I wish to dissociate myself from the work."

Saul hastily concluded that another publication (lengthening his bibliography from 261 to 262 entries) would be far less nourishing than some continued collaboration with the great doctor and, after a few days' consideration, suggested another project. Once again, Saul proposed to do 95 percent of the work. Once again, Dr. K. gave guarded assent. In his remaining months at the Stockholm Institute, Saul worked like a demon. Having already overscheduled himself with teaching and consultation commitments to younger colleagues, he was forced to work much of the night preparing for his sessions with Dr. K.

At the end of his six months, the project was still unfinished, but Saul assured Dr. K. he would complete it and see it published in a leading journal. Saul had in mind one edited by a former student who often solicited articles from him. Three months later, Saul completed the article and, after obtaining Dr. K.'s approval, submitted it to the journal, only to be informed, after eleven months, that the editor was gravely ill with a chronic disease and that the publishers had regretfully decided not to continue publication of the journal and were therefore returning all submitted articles.

Saul, by now growing alarmed, immediately dispatched the article to another journal. Six months later, he received a rejection note—his first in twenty-five years—which explained, with deference considering the stature of the authors, why the journal could not publish the article: in the previous eighteen months, three other competent reviews of the same literature had been published, and, furthermore, preliminary research reports published in the last few months did not support the conclusions Saul and Dr. K. had reached about promising directions in the field. However, the journal would be delighted to reconsider the article if it were updated, the basic accent altered, the conclusions and recommendations reformulated.

Saul did not know what to do. He could not, would not, face the shame of telling Dr. K. that now, eighteen months later, their article was not yet accepted for publication. Dr. K. had, Saul was certain, never had an article rejected—not until he had teamed up with this short, pushy, New York fraud. Review articles, Saul knew, age quickly, especially in fast-moving fields like cellular biology. He had also had enough experience on editorial boards to know that the journal editors were merely being polite: the article was beyond salvage unless he and Dr. K. put in massive amounts of time revising it. Furthermore, it would be difficult to complete a revision by international mail: face-to-face collaboration was necessary. Dr. K. had work of far higher priority, and Saul was certain that he would prefer simply to wash his hands of this whole pestilence.

And that was the impasse: for any decision to be made, Saul had to tell Dr. K. what had happened—and that Saul could not bring himself to do. So Saul, as he was wont to do in such situations, did nothing.

To make matters worse, he had written an important article on a related subject that was immediately accepted for publication. In that article he had credited Dr. K. for some of the ideas expressed and had cited their now unpublished article. The journal informed Saul that their new policy did not permit him to credit anyone without that person's written consent (to avoid spurious use of famous names). Nor, for the same reason, could it permit citations from unpublished papers without the written consent of the co-authors.

Saul was stuck. He could not—without mentioning the fate of their collaborative venture—write Dr. K. to obtain his permission to credit him. Again, Saul did nothing.

Several months later, his paper (with no mention of Dr. K. and no citation of their collaborative work) appeared as the lead article of an outstanding neurobiology journal.

"And that," Saul told me with a great sigh, "brings us up to now. I've been dreading the publication of this article. I knew that Dr. K. would read it. I knew what he would think and feel about me. I knew that, in his eyes and in the eyes of the entire Stockholm Institute community, I would be a fraud, a thief, worse than a thief. I waited to hear from him, and I received the first letter four weeks after publication— right on schedule—just time enough for the journal issue to reach

Scandinavia, for Dr. K. to read it, to pass judgment, to deliver sentence. Just time enough for his letter to reach me in California."

Saul stopped here. His eyes pleaded with me: "I can't go on. Take this all away. Take away this pain."

Though I had never seen Saul so abject, I was convinced that I would be able to render help quickly. Hence I assumed my efficient, task-oriented voice and wondered what plans he had made, what steps taken? He hesitated and then said that he had decided to return the fifty-thousand-dollar stipend to the Stockholm Institute! Knowing, from our previous work, that I disapproved of his penchant for buying his way out of difficult situations, Saul left me no time to respond but rushed ahead, saying that he had yet to decide upon the best method. He was considering a letter stating that he was returning the money because he had not used his fellowship time productively at the institute. Another possibility was to give a simple outright gift to the Stockholm Institute—a gift that would appear to be unrelated to anything else. Such a gift might be a deft move, he thought—an insurance policy to quell any possible censure of his behavior.

I could see Saul's discomfort as he revealed these plans to me. He knew I would disagree. He hated to displease anyone and wanted my approval almost as much as he wanted Dr. K.'s. I felt relieved that he had been willing to share so much with me—the only bright spot I saw in the session so far.

For a short time we both lapsed into silence. Saul was spent and leaned back, exhausted. I, too, sank back in my chair and took stock of the situation. This whole story was a comic nightmare—a tar baby saga in which, at every step, Saul's social ineptitude glued him more tightly to the impossible predicament.

But there was nothing funny about Saul's appearance. He looked awful. He always minimized his pain—always fearful of "bothering" me. If I multiplied every sign of stress by ten, I would have it: his willingness to pay fifty thousand dollars; his morbid, suicidal ruminations (he had made a serious suicide attempt five years before); his anorexia; his insomnia; his request to see me sooner. His blood pressure (he had told me earlier) had risen to one hundred ninety over one hundred twenty; and six years before, at a time of stress, he had had a severe, nearly fatal coronary.

So it was clear that I must not underestimate the gravity of the situation: Saul was *in extremis*, and I must offer some immediate help. His overwrought reaction was, I thought, totally irrational. God knows what was in those letters—probably some irrelevant announcement, a scientific meeting or a new journal. But I was certain of one thing: those letters, despite their timing, were *not* letters of censure from either Dr. K. or the Stockholm Institute; and, without doubt, as soon as he read them, his distress would evaporate.

Before proceeding, I considered alternatives: Was I being too hasty, too active? What about my countertransference? It was true I felt impatient with Saul. "This whole thing is ridiculous," some part of me wanted to say. "Go home and read those goddamn letters!" Perhaps I was annoyed that my previous therapy with him was showing signs of wear. Was my piqued vanity causing me to be impatient with Saul?

Though it is true that on that day I regarded him as foolish, in the main I always liked him very much. I had liked him from the moment I met him. One of the things he said at our first meeting endeared him to me: "I'm going to be fifty-nine soon, and some day I'd like to be able to stroll down Union Street and spend the afternoon window shopping."

I have always felt drawn to patients who struggle with the same issues I do. I know all about the longing to take a noonday stroll. How many times have I yearned for the luxury of a carefree Wednesday afternoon walk through San Francisco? Yet, like Saul, I have continued to work compulsively and to impose a professional schedule on myself that makes that stroll impossible. I knew we were both chased by the same man with a rifle.

The more I looked into myself, the surer I was that my positive feelings for Saul were still intact. Despite his offputting physical appearance, I felt very warm toward him, I imagined cradling him in my arms and found the idea agreeable. I was certain that I, even in my impatience, would act in Saul's best interests.

I also realized there are certain disadvantages in being too ener-getic. The overactive therapist often infantilizes the patient: he does not, in Martin Buber's term, guide or help the other to "unfold" but instead imposes himself upon the other. Nonetheless, I felt convinced that I could resolve this whole crisis in one or two sessions. In the light of that belief, the perils of overactivity seemed slender.

Also (as I was able to appreciate only later with a more objective view of myself), it was unfortunate for Saul that he had consulted me at a stage of my professional career when I was impatient and manage-rial, and insisted that patients promptly and fully confront their feelings about everything, including death (even if it killed them). Saul called me at approximately the same time that I was attempting to dynamite Thelma's love obsession (see "Love's Executioner"). It was also about the time that I was coercing Marvin into recognizing that his sexual preoccupation was in reality deflected death anxiety (see "In Search of the Dreamer"), and unwisely badgering Dave into understanding that his attachment to ancient love letters was a futile attempt to deny physical decline and aging ("Do Not Go Gentle").

And so, for better or worse, I decided to focus sharply upon the letters and to get them opened in one or, at the most, two sessions. During those years I often led therapy groups of hospitalized patients, whose hospital stay was generally brief. Since I had them for only a few sessions, I had become adept at helping patients quickly formulate an appropriate and realistic agenda for their therapeutic goals and con-centrate on fulfilling it efficiently. I drew on those techniques in my session with Saul.

"Saul, how do you think I can help today? What would you most like me to do?"

"I know I'll be all right in a few days. I'm just not thinking clearly. I should have written Dr. K. immediately. I'm working on a letter to him now which reviews, step by step, every detail of what's happened."

"Is it your plan to send that letter before opening the three letters?" I hated the thought of Saul ruining his career with some foolish action.

I could only imagine the perplexity on Dr. K.'s face when reading Saul's long letter defending himself against charges he, Dr. K., had never made.

"When I think about what to do, I often hear your voice asking rational questions. After all, what can the man do to me? Would someone like Dr. K. write a letter to the journal belittling me? He'd never stoop to that. He'd foul himself as much as me. Yes, I can hear the kind of questions you'd ask. But you've got to remember that I'm not thinking in a completely logical fashion."

There was a veiled but unmistakable rebuke in these words. Saul had always been ingratiating, and much of our previous therapy had focused upon the meaning and correction of that trait. So I was pleased with his being able to take a more forceful stand toward me. But I also felt chagrined at his having to remind me that people in distress don't necessarily think logically.

"O.K., then tell me about your illogical scenario."

Dammit! I thought, that hadn't come out right! There's some condescension in there that I don't feel at all. But before I had time to modify my response, Saul had dutifully proceeded to respond. Ordinarily in therapy I would make sure to return and analyze this short sequence, but that day was not the time for such subtleties.

"Maybe I'll give up science. A few years ago I had a severe headache and the neurologist sent me for X rays, saying undoubtedly it was a migraine but there was a slight chance it was a tumor. My reaction then was that my aunt was right: there *is* something basically wrong with me. I felt, when I was about eight, that she had lost confidence in me and wouldn't have minded if something bad had happened to me."

I knew from our work three years before that this aunt, the one who had brought him up after his parents' death, was a bitter, vindictive woman.

"If it were true," I asked, "that she thought so poorly of you, would she have put so much pressure on you to marry her daughter?"

"That only happened when her daughter reached thirty. No fate—not even having me for a son-in-law—was worse than having a spinster daughter."

Wake up! What am I doing? Saul did what I asked and shared his illogical scenario, and here I am, dumb enough to get lost in it. Stay focused!

"Saul, what kind of timetable are you on? Put yourself into the future. One month from now—will you have opened the three letters?"

"Yes, without question, they'll be open in one month."

Well, I thought, that was *something!* More than I had expected. I tried for more.

"Will you open the letters before you mail that letter to Dr. K.? As you say, I'm being rational, but one of us has to stay rational." Saul didn't crack a smile. Gone completely was his sense of humor. I had to stop bantering, I could no longer connect to him in that way. "It would seem rational to read them first."

"I'm not sure. I absolutely do not know. I do know that for the entire six months I was at the Stockholm Institute, I took off only three days. I worked Saturdays and Sundays. On several occasions I refused social invitations, some even from Dr. K., because I would not leave the library."

He's scrambling for diversions, I thought. He keeps tossing me enticing tidbits. Stay focused!

"What do you think, will you have opened the letters before you send back the fifty thousand dollars?"

"I'm not sure if I will or I won't."

There's a fair chance, I thought, that he's already sent that money and, if so, he's going to get caught in a tangle of lies with me that will really jeopardize our work. I've got to find out the truth.

"Saul, we've got to start out on the same trusting footing we had before. Please tell me, have you already sent that money?"

"Not yet. But I'll be honest with you—it makes a lot of sense and I probably will do it. I've got to sell some stocks first to raise that much cash."

"Well, here's what I think. It seems clear that the reason you've come to see me is to get help in opening those letters." I was being a little manipulative here—he hadn't quite said that. "We both know that eventually, certainly in the next month"—more manipulation: I wanted to transform Saul's rough guess into a firm commitment—"you'll open them. We both also know—and I'm speaking to the rational part of you—that it's unwise to take major irreversible steps before you open them. It seems the real questions are *when*—when will you open them?—and *how*—how can I best help?"

"I should just do it. But I'm not sure. I absolutely do not know."

"Is it that you want to bring them here and open them in my office?" Was I acting on Saul's behalf now or merely being voyeuristic (much like watching Al Capone's vault or the *Titanic*'s safe being opened on TV)?

"I could bring them in and open them here with you and have you take care of me if I collapse. But I don't want to. I want to go about it in an adult manner."

*Touché!* Hard to quarrel with that. Saul's assertiveness today was impressive. I had not anticipated such tenacity. I just wished it weren't in the service of defending this craziness about the letters. Saul was really digging in but, though I began to question my choice of a direct approach, I persisted.

"Or is it that you want me to visit you at home and help open them there?" I suspected I would have cause to regret this crude pressure, but I couldn't stop myself. "Or any other way? If you could plan our time together, what would be the best possible way for me to help?"

Saul didn't budge. "I absolutely do not know."

Since we had now run almost fifteen minutes over, and I had another patient, also in crisis, waiting, I reluctantly ended the session. I was left with such concern about Saul (and about my choice of strategy) that I wanted to see him again the next day. There was no time in my schedule, however, and we arranged another session in two days.

During my meeting with my next patient, it was hard to get my mind off Saul. I was astounded by the resistance he had put up. Time

202 ⁂ Love's Executioner

and again I had hit against a concrete wall. Not at all like the Saul I had known who had always been so pathologically accommodating that many people had exploited him. Two previous wives had obtained enormously generous and uncontested divorce settlements. (Saul felt so defenseless in the face of others' demands that he had chosen to remain single these last twenty years.) Students routinely extracted extravagant favors from him. He habitually undercharged for his professional consultative services (and was habitually underpaid).

In a sense, I, too, had exploited this trait in Saul (but for his own good, I told myself): to please me, he had begun to charge a fair price for his services and to refuse many requests he did not want to grant. The change in behavior (even though conceived out of a neurotic wish to gain and retain my love) initiated an adaptive spiral and begot many other salubrious changes. I tried the same approach with the letters, expecting that Saul, at my request, would open them immediately. But, obviously, I had miscalculated. Somewhere Saul had found the power to take a stand against me. I could have rejoiced in his new strength had not the cause it served been so self-destructive.

Saul did not show up for his next appointment. About thirty minutes before the hour, he called my secretary to inform me that he had thrown out his back and was unable to leave his bed. I called back immediately but reached only his answering machine. I left a message that he call me, but several hours passed with no word from him. I phoned again and left a message irresistible to patients: to call me because I had something very important to tell him.

When Saul called later that evening, I was alarmed by the somber and aloof timbre of his voice. I knew that he had not injured his back (he often avoided unpleasant confrontations by malingering), and he knew I knew it; but the crisp tone of his voice signaled unmistakably that I no longer had the right to comment on it. What to do? I was alarmed for Saul. I worried about rash decisions. I worried about suicide. No, I would not permit him to terminate. I would trap him into seeing me. I hated that role—but saw no other way.

"Saul, I believe I misjudged the amount of pain you were experiencing, and put too much pressure on you to open the letters. I've a better idea about how we should work. But, one thing for sure, this is not the time for us to miss sessions. I propose that, until you're well enough to travel, I visit you at home."

Saul demurred, of course, raising many objections, predictable objections: he wasn't my only patient, I was much too busy, he was already feeling better, it was no emergency, he should be able to travel to my office soon. But I was as tenacious as he and refused to be dissuaded. Finally, he agreed to receive me early the following morning.

On my way to Saul's house the next day, I felt cheerful. I was back in a nearly forgotten role. It had been a long time since I had made a home visit. I thought of my medical student days, of my home-visit clerkship in South Boston, of the faces of patients long gone, of the smells of the Irish tenements—the cabbage, the staleness, yesterday's beer, the bedpans, the aging flesh. I thought of one old regular patient on my rounds, a diabetic who had both legs amputated. He would quiz me with some new fact gleaned from the morning paper: "What vegetable has the highest sugar content? Onions! Didn't you know that? What are they teaching you in medical school nowadays?"

I was pondering whether onions really *do* have a lot of sugar when I arrived at Saul's home. The front door was ajar, as he had told me it would be. I hadn't asked who would leave it ajar if he were confined to bed. Since it was best that Saul lie to me as little as possible, I had asked few questions about his back or how he was being cared for. Knowing he had a married daughter living nearby, I had intimated, in passing, that I assumed she was looking after his needs.

Saul's bedroom was spartan—bare stucco walls and wooden floors, no decorative touches, no family pictures, no trace of an aesthetic sense (or of a woman's presence). He lay immobile, flat on his back. He expressed little curiosity about the new treatment plan I had mentioned on the phone. Indeed, he seemed so distant that I decided the first thing I had to do was tend to our relationship.

"Saul, on Tuesday I felt about the letters the way I believe a surgeon feels about a large, dangerous abscess." Saul had in the past been amenable to surgical analogies, being familiar with them from medical school (which he had attended before settling on a research career); moreover, his son was a surgeon.

"I was convinced the abscess had to be incised and drained and that what I needed to do was to persuade you to permit me to do it. Perhaps I was premature, perhaps the abscess hadn't pointed yet. Maybe we can try the psychiatric equivalent of heat and systemic antibiotics. For the time being, let's leave the opening of the letters out of our discussion; it's clear you'll open them when you're ready." I paused, resisting the temptation to make a reference to a month's time frame as though he had made a formal commitment; this was not the time for manipulation—Saul would see through any guile.

Instead of responding to me, Saul lay still, his eyes averted.

"Agreed?" I prompted.

A perfunctory nod.

I continued, "I've been thinking about you the last couple of days." Now I was reaching deep into my repertory of engaging devices! A comment stating that the therapist has been thinking about the patient outside of their scheduled hour has never, in my experience, failed to galvanize the latter's interest.

But not a flicker of interest in Saul's eyes. Now I was really worried but, again, decided not to comment on his withdrawal. Instead, I sought for a way to connect with him.

"We both agree that your reaction to Dr. K. has been excessive. It reminds me of the strong feeling you've often expressed of never belonging anywhere. I think of your aunt reminding you so often that you were lucky she agreed to take care of you rather than let you go into an orphanage."

"Did I ever tell you that she never adopted me?" Saul suddenly was back with me again. No, not really—we were now speaking together but in parallel, not face to face.

"When her two daughters were sick, the family doctor made a house call. When I was sick, she took me to the county hospital and shouted, 'This orphan needs medical attention!'"

I wondered whether Saul noticed that he had finally, at the age of sixty-three, gotten a doctor's house call.

"So you never really belonged anywhere, never were truly 'at home.' I think of what you told me about your bed in your aunt's house—that cot you'd unfold every night in the living room."

"The last to sleep, the first to rise. I couldn't open up my bed until everyone was out of the living room at night, and in the morning had to get up and fold it away before anyone was up and about."

I grew more aware of his bedroom, as stark as a second-class third-world hotel room, and thought, also, of a description I had read of Wittgenstein's bare, whitewashed cell at Cambridge. It was as though Saul still had no bedroom, no room he had made his own, that was unmistakably his.

"I wonder if Dr. K. and the Stockholm Institute don't represent a real haven. Finally you found where you belong, the home and perhaps the father you had always been seeking."

"Maybe you're right, Doctor." It didn't matter whether I was or not. Nor did it matter that Saul was being deferential. We were talking—that was the important thing. I felt calmer, we were coasting in familiar waters.

Saul continued, "A couple of weeks ago I saw a book in the bookstore about the 'imposter complex.' It fits me closely. I've always misrepresented myself, always felt like a fraud, always feared exposure."

This was routine stuff, we had been over this material many times, and I didn't bother to challenge his self-reproaches. There was no point. I had often done so in the past and he had a ready answer for everything. ("You've had a highly successful academic career." "At a second-rate university in a third-rate department." "Two hundred and sixty-three publications?" "I've been publishing for forty-two years, that's only six a year. Besides, most are less than three pages. I often wrote the same article five different ways. Also, that figure includes abstracts, book reviews, and chapters—almost no original stuff.")

Instead, I said (and could do so with the ring of authority since I was talking about myself as well as him), "That's what you meant when you said that these letters have been pursuing you all your life! No matter what you have accomplished, no matter that you've done enough for three men, you always fear imminent judgment and exposure. How can I detoxify this for you? How to help you see this is guilt without a crime?"

"My crime is misrepresentation. I've done nothing of substance in the field. I know this, Dr. K. knows it now, and if you knew something about neurobiology, you'd know it, too. No one is in a position to make a more accurate judgment of my work than me."

I immediately thought: Not "than *me*"; it's "than *I*." Your only real crime is using the wrong form of the first-person pronoun.

Then I noticed how critical I became whenever Saul got feisty. Fortunately I kept all this to myself—where I should as well have kept my next comment.

"Saul, if you're as bad as you say, if, as you insist, you lack all virtues and all discriminating mental faculties, why is it that you think your judgment, especially your judgment of yourself, is impeccable and beyond reproach?"

No response. In the past Saul's eyes would have smiled and met mine, but today he was clearly in no mood for wordplay.

I ended the session by establishing a contract. I agreed to help in any way I could, to see him through the crisis, to visit him at home for as long as necessary. I asked, in return, that he agree not to make any irreversible decisions. I explicitly extracted a promise from him not to injure himself, not (without prior consultation with me) to write Dr. K., and not to repay the fellowship money to the Stockholm Institute.

The no-suicide contract (a written or oral contract in which the patient promises to call the therapist when feeling dangerously self-destructive, and the therapist vows to terminate therapy if the patient violates the contract by a suicidal attempt) has always struck me as ludicrous ("If you kill yourself, I won't treat you ever again"). Yet it can be remarkably effective, and I felt much reassured by having established one with Saul. The home visits had their usefulness, too: though inconvenient for me, they put Saul in my debt and increased the power of the contract.

The next session, two days later, proceeded along similar lines. Saul was strongly motivated to send the fifty-thousand-dollar gift, and I continued firm in my opposition to that plan and explored the history of his penchant for buying his way out of problems.

He gave me a chilling description of his first contact with money. From the ages of ten to seventeen, he sold newspapers in Brooklyn. His uncle, a coarse, brusque man whom Saul had rarely mentioned, procured him a spot near a subway entrance and dropped him off every morning at five-thirty and retrieved him three hours later to deposit him at school—no matter that Saul was invariably late by ten or fifteen minutes and began every school day with a reprimand.

Even though Saul, for seven years, turned over every penny of his earnings to his aunt, he never felt he contributed enough money, and began to set unattainable goals of how much he had to earn each day. Any failure to meet these goals was punished by denying himself part or all of his dinner. To that end he learned to chew slowly, to "cheek" his food, or to rearrange it on his plate so that it appeared diminished. If forced to swallow by the gaze of his aunt or uncle (not that he believed they cared about his nutrition), he learned to vomit quietly in the bathroom after meals. Just as he once had attempted to buy his way into his family, he was now trying to buy a secure seat at the table of Dr. K. and the Stockholm Institute.

"My children don't need any money. My son earns two thousand dollars for a coronary bypass, and often does two a day. And my daughter's husband has a six-figure salary. I'd rather give the money now to the Stockholm Institute than have one of my ex-wives snatch it later. I've decided on a fifty-thousand-dollar gift. Why not? I can afford it. My Social Security and my university pension pay me far more than I need to live on. I'll make it anonymous. I can keep the money-order receipt and, if the worst happens, I can always produce the evidence that I returned the money. If none of this is necessary, then it's still all right. It's for a good cause—the best that I know."

"It's not the decision but how and when you make it that's important. There's a difference between *wanting* to do something and *having* to do it (to avoid some danger). I believe you're operating in the 'having to' mode right now. If giving fifty thousand dollars is a good idea, it will still be a good idea a month from now. Trust me, Saul, it's best not to make irreversible decisions when you're highly stressed and not functioning (as you yourself have noted) entirely rationally. I'm only asking for time, Saul. Just delay the gift for the time being, until the crisis has passed, till the letters have been opened."

Once again he nodded assent. Once again I began to suspect that he had already sent the fifty thousand dollars and was unwilling to tell me. That would not be uncharacteristic of him. In the past he had so much difficulty sharing potentially embarrassing material that I instituted, in the last fifteen minutes of each hour, a designated "secrets" time, when I explicitly asked him to take a leap and share the secrets he had sheltered over the earlier part of the therapy hour.

Saul and I proceeded in this manner for several sessions. I arrived at his house early in the morning, entered through the door, mysteriously left ajar, and conducted therapy by the side of Saul's bed, where he lay flattened by an ailment we both knew was fictitious. But the work seemed to be going well. Although I was less engaged with him than in the past, I was doing what therapists are traditionally supposed to do: I illuminated patterns and meanings; I helped Saul understand why the letters struck him as so fateful, how they not only represented some current professional misfortune but symbolized a lifetime's search for acceptance and approval. His search was so frantic, his need so pressing, that he defeated himself. In this instance, for example, if he hadn't been desperate for Dr. K.'s approval, he would have avoided the whole problem by doing what any collaborator does—simply keep one's co-author informed about all developments in their joint work.

We traced out the earlier developments of these patterns. Certain scenes (the child who was always "last to sleep, first to rise"; the adolescent who would not swallow his food if he had not sold enough newspapers; the aunt shrieking, "This orphan needs medical attention") were condensed images—*episthèmes*, Foucault has called them—that represented in crystalline form the patterns of an entire life.

But Saul, failing to respond to conventionally correct therapy, sank deeper, with each hour, into despair. His emotional tone flattened, his face grew more frozen, he volunteered less and less information—and he lost all humor and sense of proportion. His self-depreciation took on Gargantuan dimensions. For example, during one hour when I was reminding him of how much gratuitous teaching he had given to the Stockholm Institute fellows and junior faculty, he stated that, as a result of what he had done to these bright young students, he had set the field back twenty years! I had been contemplating my nails as he spoke, and smiled as I looked up, expecting to see an ironic, playful expression on his face. But I was chilled to learn there was no play: Saul was deadly serious.

More and more frequently he rambled on interminably about the research ideas he had stolen, the lives he had ruined, the marriages destroyed, the students unjustly failed (or promoted). The scope and expansiveness of his badness was, of course, evidence of an ominous grandiosity which, in turn, overlay a deeper sense of worthlessness and insignificance. During this discussion I recalled one of the first patients I had been assigned during my residency—a red-faced, sandy-haired, psychotic farmer who insisted that he had started the Third World War. I hadn't thought of this farmer—I've forgotten his name—for over thirty years. That Saul's behavior brought him to my mind was itself a portentous diagnostic sign.

Saul had severe anorexia; he began to lose weight rapidly, his sleep was deeply disrupted, and incessant self-destructive fantasies ravaged his mind. He was now crossing that critical boundary that separates the troubled, suffering, anxious person from the psychotic. The ominous signs were multiplying rapidly in our relationship: it was losing its human qualities; Saul and I no longer related as friends or allies; we stopped smiling together or touching each other—either psychologically or physically.

I began to objectify him: Saul was no longer a person who was depressed but was instead a "depression"—specifically, in terms of the *Diagnostic and Statistical Manual of Mental Disorders*, a "major" depression of a severe, recurrent, melancholic type, with apathy, psychomotor retardation, loss of energy, appetite and sleep disturbance, ideas of reference, and paranoid and suicidal ideation. I wondered what medication I should try, and where I should hospitalize him.

I have never liked to work with those who cross the boundary into psychosis. More than anything else, I place high value on the therapist's presence and engagement in the therapy process, but now I noted that the relationship between Saul and me was full of concealment—mine no less than his. I colluded with him in the fiction about his back injury. If, indeed, he were bedridden, who was helping him? Feeding him? But I never asked since I knew such inquiries would drive him further away. It seemed best to act without consulting him, and to inform his children of his condition. I wondered what position I should take about the fifty thousand dollars? If Saul had already sent the money to the Stockholm Institute, should I not advise them to return the gift? Or at least put a temporary hold on it? Did I have the right to do that? Or the responsibility? Was it malpractice *not* to do that?

I still thought often about the letters (though Saul's condition had grown so grave that I had less confidence in my surgical "draining the abscess" analogy). As I walked through Saul's house on my way to his bedroom, I glanced around trying to locate that desk in which they were stored. Should I remove my shoes and tiptoe about—all shrinks have a bit of the sleuth in them—till I found them, rip them open, and restore Saul to sanity with their contents?

I thought of how, when I was eight or nine, I had developed a large ganglion on my wrist. The kindly family doctor held my hand gently as he examined it—then suddenly, with a heavy book he was holding surreptitiously in his other hand, he slammed my wrist, bursting my ganglion. In one blinding instant of pain, the treatment was over and an extensive surgical procedure averted. Is there ever a place in psychiatry for such benevolent despotism? The results were excellent, and my ganglion was cured. But it was many years before I was ever willing to shake hands with a doctor again!

My old teacher, John Whitehorn, taught me that one can diagnose "psychosis" by the character of the therapeutic relationship: the patient, he suggested, should be considered "psychotic" if the therapist no longer has any sense that he and the patient are allies who are working together to improve the patient's mental health. By that criterion, Saul was psychotic. No longer was my task to help him open those three sealed letters, or be more assertive, or treat himself to a noonday stroll: instead, it was to keep him out of the hospital and prevent him from destroying himself.

Such was my dilemma when the unexpected occurred. The evening before one of my visits, I received a message from Saul that his back had improved, that he was now able to walk again, and would meet me in my office for our appointment. Within seconds after seeing him, before he said a word, I was aware that he had profoundly changed: the old Saul was suddenly back with me. Gone was the man who had been awash in despair, stripped of his humanity, his laugh, and self-awareness. For weeks he had been encased in a psychosis, on whose windows and walls I had been frantically rapping. Now, unexpectedly, he had broken out and casually rejoined me.

Only one thing could have done this, I thought. The letters!

Saul did not keep me long in suspense. The day before, he had received a phone call from a colleague asking him to review a grant application. During their conversation the friend asked, *en passant,* whether he had heard the news about Dr. K. Apprehensive, Saul replied that he had been confined to bed and out of touch with everyone for the past few weeks. His colleague said that Dr. K. had suddenly died of a pulmonary embolus, and proceeded to describe the circumstances around the death. Saul could barely restrain himself from interrupting and exclaiming, "I don't care who was with him, how he died, where he was buried, who spoke at the memorial service! I don't care about any of these things! Just tell me *when* he died!" Eventually Saul obtained the exact date of death and, through some fast arithmetic, established that Dr. K. must have died before the journal could have reached him, and thus could not have read Saul's article. He had not been found out! The letters instantly lost their terror for him, and he fetched them from the desk and opened them.

The first letter was from a Stockholm Institute postdoctoral fellow asking Saul to write a letter supporting his application for a junior faculty position at an American university.

The second letter was a simple announcement of Dr. K.'s death and schedule of memorial services. It had been mailed to all past and present fellows and faculty of the Stockholm Research Institute.

The third letter was a short note from Dr. K.'s widow, who wrote that she assumed that Saul had by now heard of Dr. K.'s death. Dr. K. had always spoken highly of Saul, and she knew he would have wanted her to send this unfinished letter that she found on Dr. K.'s desk. Saul handed me the brief handwritten note from the dead Dr. K.:

Dear Professor C.,

I'm planning a trip to the United States, my first in twelve years. I'd like to include California in my itinerary, provided that you'll be in residence and be willing to see me. I've very much missed our chats. As always, I feel isolated here—professional colleagueship is scarce at the Stockholm Institute. We both know our joint venture may not have been our finest effort but, for me, the important thing is it afforded the opportunity to know you personally after knowing and respecting your work for thirty years.

One further request——

Here the letter broke off. Perhaps I read too much into it, but I imagined that Dr. K. was looking for something from Saul, something just as crucial for him as the affirmation Saul sought from him. But that conjecture aside, this much was certain: all of Saul's apocalyptic forebodings were disconfirmed; the tone of the letter was unmistakably accepting, even affectionate and respectful.

Saul did not fail to register this, and the salubrious effect of the letter was immediate and profound. His depression with all its ominous "biological" signs disappeared within minutes, and he now began to regard his thinking and behavior of the past few weeks as ego-alien and bizarre. Furthermore, he rapidly reinstituted our old relationship: he once again felt warmly toward me, thanked me for sticking with him, and expressed regret at having given me such a hard time the last few weeks.

His health restored, Saul was ready to terminate immediately but agreed to come in twice more—the following week and one month hence. During these sessions we tried to make sense of what had happened, and mapped out a strategic response to future potential stress. I explored all the aspects of his functioning that had troubled me—his self-destructiveness, his grandiose sense of badness, his insomnia and anorexia. His recovery appeared remarkably solid. After that, there seemed to be no further work we could do, and we parted.

Later it occurred to me that, if Saul had so badly misjudged Dr. K.'s sentiments, then he probably misinterpreted my feelings as well. Did he ever realize how much I cared for him, how much I wanted him to forget his work from time to time and enjoy the leisure of an afternoon stroll on Union Street? Did he ever realize how much I would have liked to join him, perhaps have a quick cappuccino together?

But, to my regret, I never said those things to Saul. We did not meet again; and three years later, I learned he had died. Shortly afterward, at a party, I met a young man who had just returned from the Stockholm Institute. During a long conversation about his year's fellowship, I mentioned that I once had a friend, Saul, who also had a rewarding stay there. Yes, he had known Saul. In fact, in a curious way, his fellowship was due partly to "the good will Saul established between the university and the Stockholm Institute." Had I heard that, in his will, Saul had left the Stockholm Institute a bequest of fifty thousand dollars?

# 9

##### ❧❧❧

# Therapeutic Monogamy

*"I'm nothing. Garbage. A creep. A cipher. I slink around on the refuse dumps* outside of human camps. Christ, to die! To be dead! Squashed flat on the Safeway parking lot and then to be washed away by a fire hose. Nothing remaining. Nothing. Not even chalked words on the sidewalk saying, 'There was the blob that was once named Marge White.'"

Another one of Marge's late-night phone calls! God, I hated those calls! It wasn't the intrusion into my life—I'd learned to expect that: it goes with the territory. A year ago when I first accepted Marge as a patient, I knew there'd be calls; as soon as I saw her, I sensed what was in store for me. It didn't take much experience to recognize the signs of deep distress. Her sagging head and shoulders said "depression"; her gigantic eye pupils and restless hands and feet said "anxiety." Everything else about her—multiple suicide attempts, eating disorder, early sexual abuse by her father, episodic psychotic thinking, twenty-three years of therapy—shouted "borderline," the word that strikes terror in the heart of the middle-aged comfort-seeking psychiatrist.

She had told me she was thirty-five, a lab technician; that she had been in therapy for ten years with a psychiatrist who had just relocated to another city; that she was desperately alone; and that sooner or later, it was just a matter of time, she would kill herself.

She smoked furiously during the session, often taking two or three drags before angrily snuffing out the cigarette, only minutes later to light up another. She could not sit for the session but three times stood and paced up and down. For a few minutes she sat on the floor at the opposite corner of my office and curled up like a Feiffer cartoon character.

My first impulse was to get the hell away, far away—and not see her again. Use an excuse, any excuse: my time all filled, leaving the country for a few years, embarking on a full-time research career. But soon I heard my voice offering her another appointment.

Perhaps I was intrigued by her beauty, by her ebony hair in bangs framing her astonishingly white, perfectly featured face. Or was it my sense of obligation to my career as a teacher? Recently I had been asking myself how, in all good faith, I could go on teaching students to do psychotherapy and at the same time refuse to treat difficult patients. I guess I accepted Marge as a patient for many reasons; but, more than anything, I believe it was shame, shame at choosing the easy life, shame at shunning the very patients who needed me the most.

So I had anticipated desperation calls like this. I had anticipated crisis after crisis. I had expected that I would need to hospitalize her at some point. Thank God I had avoided that—the dawn meetings with the ward staff, the writing of orders, the public acknowledgment of my failure, the trudging over to the hospital every day. Huge chunks of time devoured.

No, it wasn't the intrusion or even the inconvenience of the calls I hated: it was *how* we talked. For one thing, Marge stuttered on every word. She always stuttered when she grew distraught—she stuttered and distorted her face. I could picture her with one side of her handsom face horridly disfigured by grimaces and spasms. During quiet, settled times, Marge and I talked about the facial spasms and decided that they were an attempt to make herself ugly. An obvious defense against sexuality, they occurred when there was a sexual threat from without or within. Much good the interpretation did—like throwing pebbles at a rhino: the mere utterance of the word *sex* was enough to summon the spasms.

Her stutter always annoyed me. I knew she was in pain, but still I had to restrain myself from saying, "Come on, Marge! Get on with it! What's the next word going to be?"

But the worst thing about the calls was my ineptitude. She put me to the test, and I was always found wanting. I must have had twenty such calls from her in the past year, and not once had I found a way to give her the help she needed.

The problem that night was that she had seen a feature article on my wife in the *Stanford Daily*. After ten years, my wife was leaving her position as the administrative head of the Stanford Center for Research on Women, and the campus newspaper had eulogized her extravagantly. To make matters worse, that evening Marge had gone to a public lecture given by an extremely articulate and attractive young woman philosopher.

I have met few people with as much self-hatred as Marge. These feelings never disappeared but during her best times merely receded to the background, awaiting a suitable cue to return. There was no cue more powerful than the publicly acclaimed success of another woman of her own age: then Marge's self-hatred washed over her, and she began to consider, more seriously than usual, suicide.

I fumbled for words of comfort. "Marge, why are you doing this to yourself? You talk about having done nothing, having accomplished nothing, not being fit to exist, but we both know that these ideas are a state of mind. They've nothing to do with reality! Remember how great you felt about yourself two weeks ago? Well, nothing has changed in the external world. You're exactly the same person now as you were then!"

I was on the right track. I had her attention. I could hear her listening, and continued.

"This business of comparing yourself unfavorably to others is always self-destructive. Look, give yourself a break. Don't choose to compare yourself with Professor G., who may be the most brilliant speaker in the whole university. Don't choose my wife on the one day in her life when she's being feted. It's always possible, if you want to torment yourself, to find someone to compare yourself with unfavorably. I know the feeling, I've done the same thing.

"Look, why not just one time pick someone who may not have what you have? You've always shown compassion for others. Think about your volunteer work with the homeless. You never give yourself credit for that. Compare yourself with someone who doesn't give a damn about others. Or why not compare yourself with, say, one of the homeless people you've helped? I'll bet they all compare themselves unfavorably with you."

The click of the telephone being hung up confirmed what I instantly realized: I had made a colossal mistake. I was well enough acquainted with Marge to know exactly what she would do with my blunder: she would say that I had let my true feelings out, that I think she's so hopeless that the only persons with whom she might compare favorably would be the most hapless souls on earth.

She did not pass up the opportunity and began our next regular therapy hour—fortunately the following morning—by expressing that very sentiment. She then continued in chilling voice and staccato cadence to give me the "real facts" about herself.

"I am thirty-five years old. I have been mentally ill all my life. I have seen psychiatrists since I was twelve years old and cannot function without them. I shall have to take medicine the rest of my life. The most I can hope for is to stay out of a mental hospital. I have never been loved. I will never have children. I have never had a long-term relationship with a man nor any hope of ever having one. I lack the capacity to make friends. No one calls me on my birthday. My father, who molested me when I was a child, is dead. My mother is a crazy, embittered lady, and I grow more like her every day. My brother has spent much of his life in a mental hospital. I have no talents, no special abilities. I will always work in a menial job. I'll always be poor and will always spend most of my salary for psychiatric care."

She stopped. I thought she had finished, but it was hard to tell since she spoke like a simulacrum—with uncanny stillness, with nothing moving but her lips, not her breath, or her hands, or her eyes, or even her cheeks.

Suddenly she began again, like a key-wound mechanical toy that still had one remaining spasm of energy: "You tell me to be patient. You tell me I'm not ready—not ready to stop therapy, not ready to get married, not ready to adopt a child, not ready to stop smoking. I've waited. I've waited my whole life away. Now it's too late, it's too late to live."

I sat unblinking through this litany and, for a moment, felt ashamed for being unmoved. But it was not callousness. I had heard it before and remembered how unsettled I was the first time she delivered it when, stricken with empathy and grief, I became what Hemingway has referred to as a "wet-thinking Jewish psychiatrist."

Worse yet, much worse (and this is hard to admit), *I agreed with her.* She presented her "true case history" so poignantly and convincingly that I was fully persuaded. She *was* severely handicapped. She probably *would never* marry. She *was* a misfit. She *did* lack the capacity to be close to others. She probably *would* need therapy for many, many years, perhaps always. I was drawn so deeply into her despair and pessimism that I could easily understand the allure of suicide. I could scarcely find a word of comfort for her.

It took me a week, until our next session, to realize that the litany was depression-spawned propaganda. It was her depression speaking, and I was foolish enough to be persuaded by it. Look at all the distortions, look at what she had *not* said. She was an exceptionally intelligent, creative, highly attractive woman (when she was not distorting her face). I looked forward to seeing her and being with her. I had respect for the way that, despite her suffering, she had always given to others and maintained her commitment to community service.

So now, hearing the litany again, I pondered how to shift her from this state of mind. On similar occasions in the past, she had settled heavily into a depression and stayed there for several weeks. I knew that by acting immediately I could help her avoid a great deal of pain.

"That's your depression talking, Marge, not you. Remember that every time you've sunk into a depression, you've climbed out again. The one good—the *only* good—thing about depression is that it always ends."

I walked over to my desk, opened her file, and read aloud parts of a letter she had written only three weeks earlier when she was feeling exhilarated about life:

" . . . It was a fantastic day. Jane and I walked down Telegraph Avenue. We tried on 1940s evening dresses at old clothes' stores. I found some old Kay Starr records. We jogged across the Golden Gate Bridge, brunched at Greens restaurant. So there's life after all in San Francisco. I only give you the bad news—I'd thought I'd share some of the good stuff. See you Thurs.———"

But though warm spring breezes were wafting through the open window, it was winter in my office. Marge's face was frozen. She stared at the wall and seemed hardly to hear me. Her response was icy: "You think I'm nothing. Look at your comment asking me to compare myself with the homeless. That's what you think I'm worth."

"Marge, I apologize for that. My batting average for being useful on the phone isn't great. It was a clumsy effort on my part. But, believe me, my intentions were to be helpful. As soon as I said that, I knew it was a mistake."

That seemed to help. I heard her exhale. Her tight shoulders relaxed, her face loosened, her head turned ever so slightly toward me.

I edged an inch or two closer. "Marge, you and I have been through crises before, times when you've felt just as awful as you do right now. What's helped in the past? I remember times you've walked out of the office feeling much better than when you entered. What made the difference? What did you do? What did I do? Let's figure it out together."

Marge couldn't answer this question at first, but she showed interest in it. More signs of thawing: she snapped her neck and sent her long black hair flying to one side and then combed her fingers through it. I nagged her with the same question several times, and eventually we became co-investigators, working on it together.

She said that it was important to her to be listened to, that she had no one else but me and nowhere else but my office to express her pain. She also knew that it helped when we carefully examined the incidents that precipitated a depression.

Soon we were going through, one by one, all the unsettling events of the week. In addition to the stresses she had described to me on the phone, there had been others. For example, in an all-day meeting of the university laboratory where she worked, she had been pointedly ignored by the professional and academic staff. I empathized with her and told her that I had heard many others in her situation—including my wife—complain of similar treatment. I confided that my wife had been irritated by Stanford's tendency to accord non-faculty staff limited privileges and little respect.

Marge returned to the topic of her lack of success and how much more accomplished was her thirty-year-old boss.

"Why do we," I mused, "pursue these unfavorable comparisons? It's so self-punishing, so perverse—like grinding an aching tooth." I had also, I told her, compared myself unfavorably with others on many occasions. (I did not give specific details. Perhaps I should have. That would have been treating her like an equal.).

I used the metaphor of a thermostat regulating self-esteem. Hers was malfunctioning: it was located too close to the surface of her body. It did not keep her self-esteem stable but instead fluctuated wildly according to external events. Something good happened, and she felt great; one criticism from someone, and she was down for days. It was like trying to keep your house heated with a furnace thermostat placed too close to the window.

By the time the hour ended, she did not have to tell me how much better she felt: I could see it in her breathing, in her walk, and in her smile as she left the office.

The improvement held. She had an excellent week, and I received no crisis phone calls. When I saw her a week later, she seemed almost ebullient. I've always believed that it's as important to find out what makes one better as it is to determine what makes one worse, so I asked her what had made the difference.

"Somehow," Marge said, "our last hour turned things around. It is almost miraculous how you, in such a short time, pulled me out of that funk. I'm really glad you're my psychiatrist."

Though charmed by her ingenuous compliment, I was made uncomfortable by both thoughts: the mysterious "somehow," and the vision of me as a miracle worker. As long as Marge thought in those terms, she would not get better because the source of help was either outside of herself or beyond comprehension. My task as a therapist (not unlike that of a parent) is to make myself obsolete—to help a patient become his or her own mother and father. I didn't want to make her better. I wanted to help her take the responsibility of making herself better, and I wanted the process of improvement to be as clear to her as possible. That's why I felt uncomfortable with her "somehow," and so set about exploring it.

"What precisely," I asked, "was helpful to you in our last hour? At what moment did you begin to feel better? Let's track it down together."

"Well, one thing was the way you handled the crack about the homeless. I could have used that to keep punishing you—in fact, I know I've done that with shrinks in the past. But when you stated in such a matter-of-fact way what your intentions were and that you had been clumsy, I found I couldn't throw a tantrum about it."

"Sounds like my comment allowed you to stay connected to me. Since I've known you, the times you've been most persistently depressed are the times you've broken your connections to everyone and been really isolated. There's an important message in there—about keeping your life peopled." I asked what else helpful had happened during the hour.

"The main thing that turned me around—in fact, the moment the calm set in—was when you told me that your wife and I had similar problems at work. I feel I'm so icky, so creepy and your wife so holy that we couldn't both be mentioned in the same breath. Confiding to me that she and I had some of the same problems *proved* you had some respect for me."

I was about to protest, to insist I have always had respect for her, but she intercepted me. "I know, I know—you've often *told* me you respected me, and *told* me you liked me, but it was just words. I never really believed it. This time it was different, you went beyond words."

I was very excited by what Marge said. She had a way of putting her finger on vital issues. Going "beyond words," *that* was what counted. It was what I *did*, not what I said. It was actually *doing* something for the patient. Sharing something about my wife was doing something for Marge, giving her a gift. *The therapeutic act, not the therapeutic word!*

I was so stimulated by this idea that I could hardly wait until the hour was over so I could think more about it. But now I returned my attention to Marge. She had more to tell me.

"It also helped a lot when you kept asking me what had helped me in the past. You kept putting the responsibility onto me, making me take charge of the session. That was good. Usually I sulk in a depression for weeks, but you had me, within minutes, working to figure out what happened.

"In fact, *just asking the question,* 'What helped in the past?' was helpful because it assured me that there was a way I could get better. Also, it helped that you didn't get into your role of the wizard letting me guess about questions you know the answers to. I liked the way you admitted you didn't know and then invited me to explore it together with you."

Music to my ears! Throughout my year of work with Marge, I had only a single real rule in my work—treat her as an equal. I had tried not to objectify her, to pity her, or to do anything that created a gulf of inequality between us. I followed that rule to the best of my ability, and it felt good now to hear that it had been helpful.

The project of psychiatric "treatment" is fraught with internal inconsistencies. When one person, the therapist, "treats" another, the patient, it is understood from the beginning that the treatment pair, the two who have formed a therapeutic alliance, are not equals or full allies; one is distressed and often bewildered, while the other is expected to use professional skills to disentangle and examine objectively issues that lie behind that distress and bewilderment. Furthermore, the patient pays the one who treats. The very word *treat* implies non-equality. To "treat" someone as an equal implies an inequality which the therapist must overcome or conceal by behaving as though the other were an equal.

So, in treating Marge as an equal, was I merely pretending to her (and to myself) that we were equals? Perhaps it is more accurate to describe therapy as treating the patient as an adult. This may seem like scholastic hairsplitting, yet something was about to happen in Marge's therapy that forced me to be very clear about how I wanted to relate to her or, for that matter, to any patient.

About three weeks later, three weeks after my discovery of the importance of the therapeutic act, an extraordinary event occurred. Marge and I were in the midst of an ordinary hour. She had had a rotten week and was filling me in on some of the details. She seemed phlegmatic, her skirt was wrinkled and twisted, her hair unkempt, and her face lined with discouragement and fatigue.

In the middle of her dirge, she suddenly closed her eyes—not in itself unusual since she often went into an autohypnotic state during the session. I had long before decided not to take the bait—not to follow her into the hypnoidal state—but instead would call her out of it. I said, "Marge," and was about to utter the rest of the sentence, "Will you please come back?" when I heard a strange and powerful voice come out of her mouth: "You don't know me."

She was right. I didn't know the person who talked. The voice was so different, so forceful, so authoritative, I looked around the office for an instant to see who else might have entered.

"Who are you?" I asked.

"Me! Me!" And then the transformed Marge jumped up and proceeded to prance around the office, peering into bookcases, straightening pictures, and inspecting my furniture. It was Marge, but it was not Marge. Everything but the clothing had changed—her carriage, her face, her self-assurance, her walk.

This new Marge was vivacious and outrageously, but enjoyably, flirtatious. The strange, full contralto voice pronounced: "As long as you're going to pretend to be a Jewish intellectual, you might as well furnish your office like one. That sofa cover belongs at the Goodwill store—if they'd take it—and that wall hanging is decaying rapidly—thank God! And those shots of the California coast. Spare me any more psychiatrists' home photos!"

She was savvy, willful, very sexy. What a relief to have a break from Marge's droning voice and relentless whining. But I was beginning to feel uneasy; I enjoyed this lady too much. I thought of the Lorelei legend, and though I knew it would be dangerous to tarry, still I visited awhile.

"Why have you come?" I asked. "Why today?"

"To celebrate my victory. I've won, you know."

"Won what?"

"Don't play dumb with me! I'm not her, you know! Not every thing you say is maaaaaarvelllous. You think you're going to help Marge?" Her face was wonderfully mobile, her words delivered with the broad sneer one would expect from the villain of a Victorian melodrama.

She continued in a derisive, gloating manner: "You could have her in therapy for thirty years, but I'd still win. I can tear down a year's work in a day. If necessary, I could have her step off a curb into a moving truck."

"But why? What do you get out of it? If she loses, you lose." Perhaps I was staying longer with her than I should. It was wrong to talk to her about Marge. It was not fair to Marge. Yet this woman's appeal was strong, almost irresistible. For a brief time I felt a wave of eerie nausea, as though I were peering through a rent in the fabric of reality, at something forbidden, at the raw ingredients, the clefts and seams, the embryonic cells and blastulas that are, in the natural order of things, not meant to be seen in the finished human creature. My attention was riveted to her.

"Marge is a creep. You know she's a creep. How can you stand to be with her? A creep! A creep!" And then, in the most astounding theatrical performance I have ever seen, she proceeded to imitate Marge. Every gesture I had witnessed over the months, Marge's every grimace, every action, passed in front of me in chronological order. There was Marge timidly meeting me for the first time. There she was curled up in the corner of my office. And there with large, panic-filled eyes, pleading with me not to give up on her. There she was in an autotrance, eyes closed, flickering eyelids covering frenetic REM-like activity. And there with her face in spasm, like Quasimodo's, horribly distorted, barely able to talk. There she was cowering behind her chair as Marge was wont to do when frightened. There she was complaining melodramatically and mockingly of a dreadful stabbing pain in her womb and breast. There she was ridiculing Marge's stutter and some of her most familiar comments. "I'm soooooooo g-g-g-g-glad you're my psychiatrist!" On bended knee: "D-d-d-o-o-o you like me, D-D-D-Doctor Yalom? D-d-d-don't leave m-m-m-me, I d-d-d-d-d-disappear when you're not here."

The performance was extraordinary: like watching the curtain call of an actress who has played several roles in an evening and amuses the audience by briefly, perhaps for just a few seconds, slipping back into each of them. (I forgot for a moment that in this theater the actress was not really the actress but only one of the roles. The real actress, the responsible consciousness, remained concealed backstage.)

It was a virtuoso performance. But also an unspeakably cruel performance by "Me" (I didn't know what else to call her). Her eyes blazed as she continued to defile Marge who, she said, was incurable, hopeless, and pathetic. Marge, "Me" said, should write her autobiography and entitle it (here she began to chuckle) "Born to Be Pathetic."

"Born to Be Pathetic." I smiled despite myself. This Belle Dame sans Merci was a formidable woman. I felt disloyal to Marge for finding her rival so attractive, for being so bemused by her mimicry of Marge.

Suddenly—presto!—it was over. "Me" closed her eyes for a minute or two and, when she opened them, she had vanished and Marge was back, crying and terrified. She put her head between her knees, breathed deeply, and slowly regained her composure. For several minutes she sobbed and then finally talked about what had happened. (She had good recall of the scene that had just occurred.) She had never before split off—oh yes, there had been one time, a third personality named Ruth Anne—but the woman who came today had never appeared before.

I felt bewildered by what had happened. My one basic rule—"Treat Marge as an equal"—was no longer sufficient. Which Marge? The whimpering Marge in front of me or the sexy, insouciant Marge? It seemed to me that the important consideration was my relationship with my patient—the betweenness (one of Buber's endless store of awkward phrases) of Marge and me. Unless I could protect and remain faithful to that relationship, any hope of therapy was lost. It was necessary to modify my basic rule, "Treat the patient as an equal," to "Be faithful to the patient." Above all, I must not permit myself to be seduced by that other Marge.

A patient can tolerate the therapist's being unfaithful outside of the hour that is the patient's own. Though it is understood that therapists embrace other relationships, that there is another patient waiting in the wings for the hour to end, there is often a tacit agreement not to address that in therapy. Therapist and patient conspire to pretend that theirs is a monogamous relationship. Both therapist and patient secretly hope that the exiting and the entering patients will not meet one another. Indeed, to prevent that from happening, some therapists construct their office with two doors, one for entering, one for exiting.

But the patient has a right to expect fidelity *during* the hour. My implicit contract with Marge (as with all my patients) is that when I am with her, I am wholly, wholeheartedly, and exclusively with her. Marge illuminated another dimension of that contract: that I must be with her most central self. Rather than relating to *this* integral self, her father, who abused her, had contributed to the development of a false, sexual self. I must not make that error.

It was not easy. To be truthful, I wanted to see "Me" again. Though I had known her for less than an hour, I had been charmed by her. The drab backdrop of the dozens of hours I had spent with Marge made this engaging phantom stand out with a dazzling clarity. Characters like that do not come along often in life.

I didn't know her name and she didn't have much freedom, but we each knew how to find the other. In the next hour she tried several times to come to me again. I could see Marge flicker her eyelids and then close them. Only another minute or two, and we would have been together again. I felt foolish and eager. Balmy bygone memories flooded my mind. I recalled waiting at a palm-edged Caribbean airport for a plane to land for my lover to join me.

This woman, this "Me," she understood me. She knew that I was weary, weary of Marge's whimpering and stuttering, that I was weary of her panics, her curling up in corners and hiding under desks, and weary of her thready childlike voice. She knew I wanted a real woman. She knew that I only pretended to treat Marge as an equal. She knew we were not equals. How could we be when Marge acted so crazy and I patronized her by tolerating her craziness?

"Me's" theatrical performance, in which she regurgitated all those snippets of Marge's behavior, convinced me that both she and I (and *only* she and I) understood what I had gone through with Marge. She was the brilliant, beautiful director who had created this film. Though I could write a clinical article about Marge or tell colleagues about the course of therapy, I could never really convey the essence of my experience with her. It was ineffable. But "Me" knew. If she could play all those roles, she must be the concealed, guiding intelligence behind them all. We shared something that was beyond language.

But fidelity! Fidelity! I had promised myself to Marge. If I consorted with "Me," it would be catastrophic for Marge: she'd become a bit player, a replaceable character. And that, of course, is precisely what "Me" wanted. "Me" was a Lorelei, beautiful and intriguing, but also lethal—the incarnation of all Marge's rage and self-hatred.

So I stayed faithful and, when I sensed "Me" approaching—for example, when Marge closed her eyes and began to enter a trance—I was quick to jar her awake by shouting, "Marge, come back!"

After this happened a few times, I realized that the final test still lay ahead: "Me" was inexorably gathering strength and desperately trying to return to me. The moment demanded a decision, and I chose to stand by Marge. I would sacrifice her rival to her, pluck her feathers, pull her asunder, and, bit by bit, feed her to Marge. The feeding technique was to repeat one standard question, "Marge, what would 'she' say if she were here?"

Some of Marge's answers were unexpected, some familiar. One day when I saw her timidly scanning the objects in my office, I said, "Go ahead, speak, Marge. Speak for 'her.'"

Marge took a deep breath and revved up her voice. "If you're going to pretend to be a Jewish intellectual, why not furnish your office like one?"

Marge said this as though it were an original thought, and it was apparent that she had not remembered *everything* "Me" had said. I couldn't help smiling: I was pleased that I and "Me" shared some secrets.

"All suggestions are welcome, Marge."

And, to my surprise, she offered several good ones. "Put a partition, perhaps a hanging fuchsia plant, perhaps a standing screen, to separate your cluttered desk from the rest of the office. Get a quiet dark brown frame for that beach picture—if you must have it—and above all, get rid of that ratty tapa-cloth wall hanging. It's so busy that it gives me a headache. I've been using it to hypnotize myself."

"I like your suggestions, Marge, except that you're being tough on my wall hanging. It's an old friend. I got it thirty years ago in Samoa."

"Old friends may feel more comfortable at home than the office."

I stared at her. She was so quick. Was I really talking to Marge?

Since I hoped to establish a confederacy or fusion of the two Marges, I was careful to stay on the positive side of each. If I antagonized "Me" in any way, she would simply take her revenge on

Marge. So I took pains, for example, to tell Marge (I assumed "Me" heard everything) how much I enjoyed "Me's" insouciance, vitality, brashness.

But I had to steer a tight course. If I were too honest, Marge would see how much I preferred the other Marge. Probably "Me" had already taunted Marge with it, but I saw no evidence. I was certain that "Me," the other Marge, was in love with me. Perhaps she loved me enough to change her behavior! Surely she must know that I would be repelled by wanton destructiveness.

Now that's a facet of psychotherapy we don't learn about in training: have a romance with your patient's worst enemy, and then, when you are sure the enemy loves you, use that love to neutralize her attacks upon your patient.

Over the next several months of therapy, I continued faithful to Marge. Sometimes she would try to tell me about Ruth Anne, the third personality, or slip into a trance and regress to an earlier age, but I refused to be seduced by any of these enticements. More than anything else, I resolved to be "present" with her, and I immediately called her back whenever she started to leave my presence by slipping away into another age or another role.

When I first began to work as a therapist, I naively believed that the past was fixed and knowable; that if I were perspicacious enough, I could discover that first false turn, that fateful trail that has led to a life gone wrong; and that I could act on this discovery to set things right again. In those days I would have deepened Marge's hypnotic state, regressed her in age, asked her to explore early traumas—for example, her father's sexual abuse—and urged her to experience and discharge all the attendant feelings, the fear, the arousal, the rage, the betrayal.

But over the years I've learned that the therapist's venture is not to engage the patient in a joint archeological dig. If any patients have ever been helped in that fashion, it wasn't because of the search and the finding of that false trail (a life never goes wrong because of a false trail; it goes wrong because the main trail is false). No, a therapist helps a patient not by sifting through the past but by being lovingly present with that person; by being trustworthy, interested; and by believing that their joint activity will ultimately be redemptive and healing. The drama of age regression and incest recapitulation (or, for that matter, any therapeutic cathartic or intellectual project) is healing only because it provides therapist and patient with some interesting shared activity while the real therapeutic force—the relationship—is ripening on the tree.

So I devoted myself to being present and faithful. We continued to ingest the other Marge. I mused aloud, "What would she have said in that situation? How would she have dressed or walked? Try it. Pretend you're her for a minute or two, Marge."

As the months passed, Marge grew plump at the other Marge's expense. Her face grew rounder, her bodice fuller. She looked better, dressed better; she sat up straight; she wore patterned stockings; she commented upon my scuffed shoes.

At times I thought of our work as cannibalistic. It was as though we had assigned the other Marge to a psychological organ bank. Now and then, when the receptor site was well prepared, we withdrew some part of "Me" for transplantation. Marge began to treat me as an equal, she asked me questions, she flirted a bit. "When we finish, how will you get along without me? I'm sure you'll miss my little late-night calls."

For the first time, she began asking me personal questions. "How did you decide to get into this field? Have you ever regretted it? Do you ever get bored? With me? What do you do with *your* problems?" Marge had appropriated the bold parts of the other Marge as I urged her to do, and it was important that I be receptive and respectful to each of her questions. I answered each one as fully and honestly as possible. Moved by my answers, Marge grew ever bolder but gentler in her talks with me.

And that other Marge? I wonder what's left of her now? A pair of empty spike heels? An enticing, bold glance that Marge has not yet dared to appropriate? A ghostly, Cheshire cat smile? Where is the actress who played Marge with such brilliance? I'm sure *she's* gone: that performance required great vital energy, and by now Marge and I have sucked all that juice out of her. Even though we continued our work together for many months after the hour "Me" appeared, and though Marge and I eventually stopped talking about her, I have never forgotten her: she flits in and out of my mind at unexpected times.

Before we began therapy, I had informed Marge that we could meet for a maximum of eighteen months because of my sabbatical plans. Now the time was up, our work at an end. Marge had changed: the panics occurred only rarely; the phone calls were a thing of the past; she had begun to build a social life and had made two close friends. She had always been a talented photographer and now, for the first time in years, had picked up her camera and was once again enjoying this form of creative expression.

I felt pleased with our work but was not deluded into thinking that she had finished therapy, nor was I surprised, as our final session approached, to see a recrudescence of her old symptoms. She retreated to bed for entire weekends; she had long crying jags; suicide suddenly seemed appealing again. Just after our last visit, I received a sad letter from her containing these lines:

> I always imagined that you might write something about me. I wanted to leave an imprint on your life. I don't want to be "just another patient." I wanted to be "special." I want to be something, anything. I feel like nothing, no one. If I left an imprint on your life, maybe I would be someone, someone you wouldn't forget. I'd exist then.

Marge, please understand that though I've written a story about you, I do not do it to enable you to exist. You exist without my thinking or writing about you, just as I keep existing when you aren't thinking of me.

Yet this *is* an existence story—but one written for the other Marge, the one who no longer exists. I was willing to be her executioner, to sacrifice her for you. But I have not forgotten her: she avenged herself by burning her image into my memory.

# 10

❧❧❧

# In Search of the Dreamer

*"Sex is at the root of everything. Isn't that what you fellows always say? Well,* in my case you may be right. Take a look at this. It'll show you some interesting connections between my migraines and my sex life."

Drawing a thick scroll from his briefcase, Marvin asked me to hold one end, and carefully unrolled a three-foot chart upon which was meticulously recorded his every migraine headache and every sexual experience of the past four months. One glance revealed the complexity of the diagram. Every migraine, its intensity, duration, and treatment, was coded in blue. Every sexual rush, colored red, was reduced to a five-point scale according to Marvin's performance: premature ejaculations were separately coded, as was impotence—with a distinction made between inability to sustain an erection and inability to have one.

It was too much to absorb in a glance. "That's an elaborate piece of work," I said. "It must have taken you days."

"I liked doing it. I'm good at it. People forget that we accountants have graphic skills that are never used in tax work. Here, look at the month of July: four migraines and each one preceded by either impotence or a grade-one or -two sexual performance."

I watched Marvin's finger point to the blips of migraine and impotence. He was right: the correlation was impressive, but I was growing edgy. My timing had been thrown off. We had only just begun our first session, and there was much more I wanted to know before I would feel ready to examine Marvin's chart. But he pressed it before me so forcefully that I had no option other than to watch his stubby finger trace out the love leavings of last July.

Marvin at sixty-four had suddenly, six months ago, for the first time in his life, developed disabling migraine headaches. He had consulted a neurologist, who had been unsuccessful in controlling Marvin's headaches and then referred him to me.

I had seen Marvin for the first time only a few minutes earlier when I went out to my waiting room to fetch him. He was sitting there patiently—a short, chubby, bald man with a glistening pate and owl eyes which never blinked as they peered through oversized, gleaming chrome spectacles.

I was soon to learn that Marvin was particularly interested in spectacles. After shaking hands with me, his first words, while accompanying me down the hall to my office, were to compliment me on my frames and to ask me their make. I believe I fell from grace when I confessed ignorance of the manufacturer's name; things grew even more awkward when I removed my glasses to read the brand name on the stem and found that, without my glasses, I could not read it. It did not take me long to realize that, since my other glasses were now resting at home, there was no way that I could give Marvin the trivial information he desired, so I held out my spectacles for him to read the label. Alas, he, too, was farsighted, and more of our first minutes together were consumed by his switching to his reading glasses.

And now, a few minutes later, before I could proceed to interview him in my customary way, I found myself surrounded by Marvin's meticulous red-and-blue-penciled chart. No, we were not off to a good start. To compound the problem, I had just had a poignant but exhausting session with an elderly, distraught widow whose purse had recently been stolen. Part of my attention was still with her, and I had to spur myself to give Marvin the attention he deserved.

Having received only a brief consultation note from the neurologist, I knew practically nothing about Marvin and began the hour, after we completed the opening eyeglass ritual, by asking "What ails?" That was when he volunteered that "you fellows" think "sex is at the root of everything."

I rolled up the chart, told Marvin I'd like to study it in detail later, and attempted to restore some rhythm to the session by asking him to tell me the whole story of his illness from the beginning.

He told me that about six months ago he, for the first time in his life, began suffering from headaches. The symptoms were those of classical migraine: a premonitory visual aura (flashing lights) and a unilateral distribution of excruciating pain which incapacited him for hours and often necessitated bedrest in a darkened room.

"And you say you have good reason to believe that your sexual performance touches off the migraine?"

"You may think it strange—for a man of my age and position—but you can't dispute the facts. There's the proof!" He pointed to the scroll now resting quietly on my desk. "Every migraine of the last four months was preceded within twenty-four hours by a sexual failure."

Marvin spoke in a deliberate, pedantic manner. Obviously he had rehearsed this material beforehand.

"For the last year I have been having violent mood swings. I pass quickly from feeling good to feeling that it's the end of the world. Now don't jump to conclusions." Here he shook his finger at me for greater emphasis. "When I say I feel good, I do *not* mean I'm manic—I've been down that road with the neurologists who tried to treat me for manic-depressive disease with lithium—didn't do a thing except screw up my kidneys. I can see why docs get sued. Have *you* ever seen a case of manic-depression starting at sixty-four? Do *you* think I should have gotten lithium?"

His questions jarred me. They were distracting and I didn't know how to answer them. *Was* he suing his neurologist? I didn't want to get involved with that. Too many things to deal with. I made an appeal to efficiency.

"I'd be glad to come back to these questions later, but we can make best use of our time today if we first hear your whole clinical story straight through."

"Right you are! Let's stay on track. So, as I was saying, I flip back and forth from feeling good to feeling anxious and depressed—both together—and it is *always* in the depressed states that the headaches occur. I never had one till six months ago!"

"And the link between sex and depression?"

"I was getting to that——"

Careful, I thought. My impatience is showing. It's clear he's going to tell it his way, not mine. For Chrissakes stop pushing him!

"Well—this is the part you'll find hard to believe—for the last twelve months my moods have been totally controlled by sex. If I have good sex with my wife, the world seems bright. If not, bingo! Depression and headaches!"

"Tell me about your depressions. What are they like?"

"Like an ordinary depression. I'm down."

"Say some more."

"What's to say? Everything looks black."

"What do you think about in the depressions?"

"Nothing. That's the problem. Isn't that what depression is all about?"

"Sometimes when people get depressed, certain thoughts circle around in their mind."

"I keep knocking myself."

"How?"

"I start to feel that I will always fail in sex, that my life as a man is over. Once the depression sets in, I am bound to have a migraine within the next twenty-four hours. Other doctors have told me that I am in a vicious circle. Let's see, how does it work? When I'm depressed I get impotent, and then because I'm impotent I get more depressed. Yep, that's it. But knowing that doesn't stop it, doesn't break the vicious circle."

"What does break it?"

"You'd think, after six months, I'd know the answer. I'm pretty observant, always have been. That's what good accountants get paid for.

But I'm not sure. One day I have good sex, and everything's all right again. Why that day and not another day? I haven't a clue."

And so the hour went. Marvin's commentary was precise but stingy, slightly abrasive, and larded with cliches, questions, and the comments of other doctors. He remained remarkably clinical. Although he brought up details of his sexual life, he expressed no embarrassment, self-consciousness, or, for that matter, any deeper feelings.

At one point I tried to get beneath the forced "hale fellow" heartiness.

"Marvin, it must not be easy for you to talk about intimate aspects of your life to a stranger. You mentioned you had never talked to a psychiatrist before."

"It's not a matter of things being intimate, it's more to do with psychiatry—I don't believe in psychiatrists."

"You don't believe we exist?" A stupid attempt at a feeble joke, but Marvin did not note my tongue in cheek.

"No, no, it's not that. It's that I don't have faith in them. My wife, Phyllis, doesn't either. We've known two couples with marital problems who saw psychiatrists, and both ended up in the divorce court. You can't blame me for being on guard, can you?"

By the end of the hour, I was not yet able to make a recommendation and scheduled a second consultation hour. We shook hands, and as he left my office I became aware that I was glad to see him go. I was sorry I had to see him again.

I was irritated with Marvin. But why? Was it his superficiality, his needling, his wagging his finger at me, his "you fellows" tone? Was it his innuendoes about suing his neurologist—and trying to draw me into it? Was it that he was so controlling? He took over the hour: first with the silly business of the glasses, and then with his determination to stick that chart in my hands whether I wanted it or not. I thought of tearing that chart to shreds and enjoying every moment of it.

But so much irritation? So Marvin disrupted the pace of the hour. So what? He was up front, he told me exactly what was troubling him as best he could. He had worked hard according to his conception of psychiatry. His chart was, after all, useful. I would have been pleased with it had it been my idea. Perhaps it was more my problem than his? Had I grown so stodgy, so old? Was I so rigid, in such a rut that if the first hour didn't proceed just the way I wished it to, I grew cranky and stomped my feet?

Driving home that evening I thought more about him, the two Marvins—Marvin the man, Marvin the idea. It was the flesh-and-blood Marvin who was irritating and uninteresting. But Marvin the *project* was intriguing. Think of that extraordinary story: for the first time in his life, a stable, if prosaic, previously healthy sixty-four-year-old man who has been having sex with the same woman for forty-one years suddenly becomes exquisitely sensitive to his sexual performance. His entire well-being soon becomes hostage to sexual functioning. The event is *severe* (his migraines are exceptionally disabling); it is *unexpected* (sex never presented any unusual problems previously); and it is *sudden* (it erupted in full force precisely six months ago).

Six months ago! Obviously there lay the key and I began the second session by exploring the events of six months ago. What changes in his life had occurred then?

"Nothing of significance," Marvin said.

"Impossible," I insisted, and posed the same question many different ways. I finally learned that six months ago Marvin had made the decision to retire and sell his accountancy firm. The information emerged slowly, not because he was unwilling to tell me about retirement, but because he attached little importance to the event.

I felt otherwise. The markers of one's life stages are *always* significant, and few markers more so than retirement. How is it possible for retirement *not* to evoke deep feelings about the passage and passing of life, about the meaning and significance of one's entire life project? For those who look inward, retirement is a time of life review, of summing up, a time of proliferating awareness of finitude and approaching death.

Not so for Marvin.

"Problems about retiring? You've got to be kidding. This is what I've been working for—so I *can* retire."

"Will you find yourself missing anything about your work?"

"Only the headaches. And I guess you can say I've found a way to take them with me! The migraines, I mean." Marvin grinned, obviously pleased with himself for having stumbled upon a joke. "Seriously, I've been tired and bored with my work for years. What do you think I'll miss—the new tax forms?"

"Sometimes retirement stirs up important feelings because it is such an important milestone in life. It reminds us of life passages. You've been working for how long? Forty-five years? And now you suddenly stop, you pass on to a new stage. When I retire, I think it will bring home to me more clearly than I've ever known that life has a beginning and an end, that I've been slowly passing from one point to another, and that I am now approaching the end."

"My work is about money. That's the name of the game. What retirement really means is that I've made so much money I don't need to make any more. What's the point of it? I can live on my interest very comfortably."

"But, Marvin, what will it *mean* not to work again? All your life you've worked. You've gotten your meaning out of working. I've a hunch there's something scary about giving it up."

"Who needs it? Now, some of my associates are killing themselves piling up enough money so they can live on their interest's interest. That's what I call crazy—*they* should see a psychiatrist."

*Vorbeireden, vorbeireden:* we talked past each other, past each other. Again and again I invited Marvin to look within, to adopt, even for a moment, a cosmic perspective, to identify the deeper concerns of his existence—his sense of finitude, of aging and decline, his fear of death, his source of life purpose. But we talked past each other. He ignored me, misunderstood me. He seemed pasted to the surface of things.

Weary of traveling alone on these little subterranean excursions, I decided to stay closer to Marvin's concerns. We talked about work. I learned that, when he was very young, his parents and some teachers had considered him a math prodigy; at the age of eight, he had auditioned, unsuccessfully, for the "Quiz Kids" radio show. But he never lived up to that early billing.

I thought he sighed when he said this, and asked, "That must have been a big wound for you. How well did it heal?"

He suggested that perhaps I was too young to appreciate how many eight-year-old boys auditioned unsuccessfully for the "Quiz Kids."

"Feelings don't always follow rational rules. In fact, usually they don't."

"If I would have given in to feelings every time I was hurt, I'd never have gotten anywhere."

"I notice that it is very hard for you to talk about wounds."

"I was one of hundreds. It was no big deal."

"I notice, too, that whenever I try to move closer to you, you let me know you don't need anything."

"I'm here for help. I'll answer all your questions."

It was clear that a direct appeal would be of no value. It was going to take Marvin a long time to share his vulnerability. I retreated to fact gathering. Marvin grew up in New York, the child of impoverished first-generation Jewish parents. He majored in mathematics at a small city college and briefly considered graduate school. But he was impatient to get married—he had dated Phyllis since he was fifteen—and, since he had no financial resources, decided to become a high school teacher.

After six years of teaching trigonometry, Marvin felt stuck. He arrived at the conclusion that getting rich was what life was all about. The idea of thirty-five more years of slender high-school-teacher paychecks was unbearable. He was certain the decision to teach school had been a serious mistake and, at the age of thirty, set about rectifying it. After a crash accountancy course, he said goodbye to his students and colleagues and opened an accounting firm, which ultimately proved to be highly lucrative. With wise investments in California real estate, he had become a wealthy man.

"That brings us up to now, Marvin. Where do you go in life from here?"

"Well, as I said, there's no point in accumulating any more money. I have no children"—here his voice turned gray—"no poor relatives, no desires to give it to good causes."

"You sounded sad when you talked about not having children."

"That's past history. I was disappointed then, but that was a long time ago, thirty-five years ago. I have a lot of plans. I want to travel. I want to add to my collections—maybe they're my substitute for children—stamps, political campaign buttons, old baseball uniforms, and *Reader's Digests*."

Next, I explored Marvin's relationship with his wife which he insisted was extremely harmonious. "After forty-one years I still feel my wife is a great lady. I don't like being away from her, even for one night. In fact, I feel warm inside when I see her at the end of the day. All my tension disappears. Perhaps you could say that she's my Valium."

According to Marvin, their sex life had been wonderful until six months ago: despite forty-one years, it seemed to have retained luster and passion. When Marvin's periodic impotence began, Phyllis had at first shown great understanding and patience but, during the last couple of months, had become irritable. Only a couple of weeks ago, she had grumbled that she was tired of "being had"—that is, being sexually aroused and then left unsatisfied.

Marvin gave much weight to Phyllis's feelings and was deeply troubled when he thought he had displeased her. He brooded for days after an episode of impotence and was entirely dependent upon her to regain his equilibrium: sometimes she brought him around simply by reassuring him that she still found him virile, but generally he required some physical comforting. She lathered him in the shower, she shaved him, she massaged him, she took his soft penis into her mouth and held it there gently until it throbbed into life.

I was struck in the second interview, as in the first, by Marvin's lack of wonderment at his own story. Where was his curiosity that his life had changed so dramatically, that his sense of direction, his happiness, even his desire to live was now entirely dictated by whether he could sustain tumescence in his penis?

It was time now to make a recommendation to Marvin about treatment. I did not think that he would be a good candidate for a deep, uncovering type of psychotherapy. There were several reasons. I've always found it difficult to treat someone with so little curiosity. Although it is possible to assist in the unfolding of curiosity, the subtle and lengthy process would be incompatible with Marvin's wish for a brief and efficient treatment. As I thought back over the two hours, I was also aware that he had resisted every one of my invitations to dig deeper into his feelings. He didn't seem to understand, we talked past each other, he had no interest in the inner meaning of events. He also resisted my attempts to engage him more personally and directly: for example, when I had asked him about his wound or pointed out that he ignored any of my attempts to get closer to him.

I was about to offer my formal recommendation that he begin a course of cognitive behaviorial therapy (an approach based on changing concrete aspects of behavior, especially marital communication and sexual attitudes and practice) when, almost as an afterthought, Marvin mentioned that he had had some dreams during the week.

I had inquired about dreams during the first interview; and, like many other patients, he replied that, though he dreamed every night, he could not recall the details of a single dream. I had suggested he keep a writing pad by his bed to record dreams, but he seemed so little inner-directed that I doubted he would follow through and I neglected to inquire about them in the second session.

Now he took out his notepad and began to read a series of dreams:

*Phyllis was distraught that she hadn't been good to me. She left to go home. But when I followed her there, she was gone. I was afraid I would find her dead in this large castle on a high mountain. Next, I was trying to get into the window of a room where her body might be. I was on a high narrow ledge. I couldn't go any farther, but it was too narrow to turn around and go back. I was afraid that I'd fall, and then I grew afraid that I'd jump and commit suicide.*

*Phyllis and I were undressing to make love. Wentworth, a partner of mine, who weighs two hundred fifty pounds, was in the room. His mother was outside. We had to blindfold him so we could continue. When I went outside, I didn't know what to say to his mother about why we blindfolded him.*

*There was a gypsy camp forming right in the front lobby of my office. All of them were filthy dirty—their hands, their clothes, the bags they were carrying. I heard the men whispering and conspiring in a menacing way. I wondered why the authorities would permit them to camp out in the open.*

*The ground under my house was liquefying. I had a giant auger and knew that I would have to drill down sixty-five feet to save the house. I hit a layer of solid rock, and the vibrations woke me up.*

Remarkable dreams! Where had they come from? Could Marvin have possibly dreamed them? I looked up, half expecting to see someone else sitting across from me. But he was still there, patiently awaiting my next question, his eyes blank behind his gleaming spectacles.

We had only a few minutes left. I asked Marvin whether he had any associations to any aspect of these dreams. He merely shrugged. They were a mystery to him. I had asked for dreams, and he had given them to me. That was the end of it.

The dreams notwithstanding, I proceeded to recommend a course of marital therapy, perhaps eight to twelve sessions. I suggested several options: to see the two of them myself; to refer them to someone else; or to refer Phyllis to a female therapist for a couple of sessions and then for the four of us—Phyllis, Marvin, I, and her therapist—to meet in conjoint sessions.

Marvin listened attentively to what I said, but his facial expression was so frozen that I had no hint of what he felt. When I asked for his reaction, he became strangely formal and said, "I'll take your sugges-tions under consideration and let you know my decision."

Was he disappointed? Did he feel rejected? I couldn't be sure. It seemed to me at the time that I had made the right recommendation. Marvin's dysfunction was acute and would respond, I thought, to a brief cognitive-behavioral approach. Furthermore, I was convinced he would not profit from individual therapy. Everything weighed against it: he was too resistant; in the trade language, he had simply too little "psychological mindedness."

Nonetheless, it was with regret that I passed up the opportunity of working in depth with him: the dynamics of his situation fascinated me. I was certain that my first impression had been close to the mark: that his impending retirement had stoked up much fundamental anxi-ety about finitude, aging, and death, and that he was attempting to cope with this anxiety through sexual mastery. So much was riding on the sexual act that it was overtaxed and, ultimately, overwhelmed.

I believed that Marvin was entirely wrong when he said that sex was at the root of his problems; far from it, sex was just an ineffective means of trying to drain off surges of anxiety springing from more fun-damental sources. Sometimes, as Freud first showed us, sexually in-spired anxiety is expressed through other devious means. Perhaps just as often the opposite is true: *other anxiety masquerades as sexual anxiety.* The dream about the giant auger could not have been more clear: the ground under Marvin's feet was liquefying (an inspired visual image for groundlessness), and he was trying to combat that by drilling, with his penis, sixty-five feet (that is, sixty-five years) down!

The other dreams gave evidence of a savage world beneath Mar-vin's placid exterior—a world seething with death, murder, suicide, anger toward Phyllis, fears of dirty and menacing phantoms erupting from within. The blindfolded man in the room where he and Phyllis were to make love was particularly intriguing. When investigating sex-ual problems it is always important to ask, Are there more than two people present during lovemaking? The presence of others—phantoms of parents, rivals, other lovers—vastly complicates the sexual act.

No, behavioral therapy was the best choice. It was best to keep the lid of this underworld sealed. The more I thought about it, the more pleased I was that I had restrained my curiosity and had acted selflessly and systematically in the best interests of the patient.

But rationality and precision in psychotherapy are rarely rewarded. A few days later, Marvin called and asked for another appointment. I had expected that Phyllis would accompany him, but he arrived alone, looking anxious and haggard. No opening ceremonies that day. He came right to the point.

"This is a bad day. I feel miserable. But first, I want to say that I appreciate your recommendation last week. To be honest, I'd expected you to advise me to come to see you three or four times a week for the next three or four years. I'd been warned that you psychiatrists did that regardless of the problem. Not that I blame you—after all, you guys are running a business and gotta earn a living.

"Your advice about couples therapy made sense to me. Phyllis and I *do* have some communication problems, more than I really told you about last week. Actually, I understated the case to you. I've had some difficulties with sex—not as bad as now—which caused me to flip back and forth in my moods for twenty years. So I decided to take your advice, but Phyllis will not cooperate. She flat out refuses to see a shrink, a marriage therapist, a sex therapist—anyone. I asked her to come in one time today to talk to you, but she has dug in her heels."

"How come?"

"I'll get to that but, first, there are two other things I want to cover today." Marvin stopped. At first I thought it was to catch his breath: he had been racing through his sentences. But he was composing himself. He turned away, blew his nose, and wiped his eyes surreptitiously.

Then he continued. "I'm way down. I had my worst migraine ever this week and had to go to the emergency room night before last for an injection."

"I thought you looked drawn today."

"The headaches are killing me. But to make things worse, I'm not sleeping. Last night I had a nightmare which woke me up about two in the morning, and I kept replaying it all night long. I still can't get it out of my mind."

"Let's go over it."

Marvin started to read the dream in such a mechanical manner that I stopped him and employed the old Fritz Perls device of asking him to begin again and to describe the dream in the present tense, as though he were experiencing it right now. Marvin put aside his notepad and from memory recited:

> *The two men are tall, pale, and very gaunt. In a dark meadow they glide along in silence. They are dressed entirely in black. With tall black stovepipe hats, long-tailed coats, black spats and shoes, they resemble Victorian undertakers or temperance workers. Suddenly they come upon a carriage, ebony black, cradling a baby girl swaddled in black gauze. Wordlessly, one of the men begins to push the carriage. After a short distance he stops, walks around to the front, and, with his black cane, which now has a glowing white tip, he leans over, parts the gauze, and methodically inserts the white tip into the baby's vagina.*

I was transfixed by the dream. The stark images took form immediately in my own mind. I looked up in amazement at Marvin, who seemed unmoved and unappreciative of the power of his own creation, and the notion occurred to me that this was not, could not be, *his* dream. A dream like that could not have sprung from *him*: he was merely the medium through whose lips it was expressed. How could I, I wondered, meet the dreamer?

Indeed, Marvin reinforced that whimsical notion. He had no sense of familiarity with the dream and related to it as though it were some alien text. He still experienced fear as he recited it, and shook his head as though he were trying to get the dream's bad taste out of his mouth.

I focused on the anxiety. "Why was the dream a nightmare? Precisely what part of it was frightening?"

"As I think about it *now,* the last thing—putting the cane in the baby's vagina—is the horrible part. Yet *not when I was having the dream.* It was everything else, the silent footsteps, the blackness, the sense of deep foreboding. The whole dream was soaked in fear."

"What feeling was there *in* the dream about the insertion of the cane into the baby's vagina?"

"If anything, that part seemed almost soothing, as though it quieted the dream—or, rather, it tried to. It didn't really do it. None of this makes any sense to me. I've never believed in dreams."

I wanted to linger with the dream but had to return to the needs of the moment. The fact that Phyllis was unwilling to talk to me, even once, to help her husband, who was now *in extremis,* belied Marvin's account of his idyllic, harmonious marriage. I had to proceed with delicacy here because of his fear (which Phyllis obviously shared) that therapists snoop out and fan marital problems, but I had to be certain that she was inexorably opposed to couples therapy. Last week I had wondered if Marvin hadn't felt rejected by me. Perhaps this was a ploy to manipulate me into seeing him in individual therapy. How much of an effort had Marvin really made to persuade Phyllis to participate with him in treatment?

Marvin assured me that she was very set in her ways.

"I told you she doesn't believe in psychiatry, but it goes far beyond that. She won't see *any* doctor, she's not had a GYN exam in fifteen years. It's all I can do to get her into the dentist when she's got a toothache."

Suddenly, when I asked for other examples of Phyllis being set in her ways, some unexpected things came pouring out.

"Well, I might as well tell you the truth. No sense of spending good money and sitting here and lying to you. Phyllis has her problems. The main thing is that she's afraid of going out of the house. That has a name. I've forgotten it."

"Agoraphobia?"

"Yeah, that's it. She's had it for years and years. She rarely leaves the house for any reason unless"—Marvin's voice grew hushed and conspiratorial—"it's to escape another fear."

"What other fear?"

"The fear of people visiting the house!"

He went on to explain that they had not entertained guests at home for years—indeed, for decades. If the situation demanded it—for example, if family members visited from out of town—Phyllis was willing to entertain them in a restaurant: "An inexpensive restaurant, since Phyllis hates to spend money." Money was another reason, Marvin added, that she opposed psychotherapy.

Moreover, Phyllis did not permit Marvin to entertain at home either. A couple of weeks ago, for example, some out-of-town guests called to ask if they could view his collection of political buttons. He said he didn't bother to ask Phyllis: he knew she'd raise hell. If he tried to force the issue, it would be, he said, "a month of Sundays" before he "got laid again." Consequently, as he had done many times before, he spent the better part of a day packing up his whole collection to exhibit it in his office.

This new information made it even more clear that Marvin and Phyllis very much needed marital therapy. But there was a new twist now. Marvin's first dreams had so teemed with primitive iconography that, the week before, I had feared individual therapy might break the seal of this seething unconscious and thought marital therapy would be safer. Now, however, with this evidence of severe pathology in their relationship, I wondered whether couples therapy might also unleash demons.

I reiterated to Marvin that, all things considered, I still believed the treatment of choice to be behaviorally oriented couples therapy. But couples therapy requires a couple, and if Phyllis was not yet willing to come in (as he immediately reaffirmed), I told him I would be willing to see him in a trial of individual therapy.

"But be forewarned, individual treatment will most likely require many months, even a year or longer, and it will not be a rose garden.

Painful thoughts or memories may emerge which will temporarily make you more uncomfortable than you are right now."

Marvin stated that he *had* thought about it during the last few days, and wished to begin immediately. We arranged to meet twice weekly.

It was apparent that both he and I had reservations. Marvin continued to be skeptical about the psychotherapeutic enterprise and showed little interest in an inner journey. He agreed to therapy only because the migraine had brought him to his knees and he had nowhere else to turn. I, for my part, had reservations because I was so pessimistic about treatment: I agreed to work with him because I saw no other viable therapy option.

But I could have referred him to someone else. There was another reason—that voice, the voice of that being who had created those astonishing dreams. Buried somewhere within Marvin's walls was a dreamer tapping out an urgent existential message. I drifted back into the landscape of the dream, back into the silent, dark world of the gaunt men, the black meadow, and the black-gauzed baby girl. I thought of the incandescent tip of the cane and the sexual act that was not sex but merely a futile attempt to dispel the dread.

I wondered, If disguise were unnecessary, if the dreamer could speak to me without guile, what might he say?

> "I am old. I am at the end of my life's work. I have no children, and I approach death full of dread. I am choking on darkness. I am choking on the silence of death. I think I know a way. I try to pierce the blackness with my sexual talisman. But it is not enough."

But these were my reflections, not Marvin's. I asked him to associate to the dream, to think about it, and to say anything that came to mind. Nothing came. He merely shook his head.

"You shake your head no almost instantaneously. Try again. Give yourself a chance. Take any part of the dream and let your mind wander with it."

Nothing whatsoever.

"What do you make of the white-tipped cane?"

Marvin smirked. "I was wondering when you'd get around to that! Didn't I say earlier that you fellows see sex at the root of everything?"

His accusation seemed particularly ironic because, if there were one conviction I had about him, it was that sex was *not* the source of his difficulty.

"But it's *your* dream, Marvin. And your cane. You created it, what do you make of it? And what do you make of the allusions to death—undertakers, silence, blackness, the whole atmosphere of dread and foreboding?"

Given the choice of discussing the dream from the perspective of death or of sex, Marvin, with dispatch, chose the latter.

"Well, you might be interested in something sexual that happened yesterday afternoon—that would be about ten hours before the dream. I was lying in bed still recovering from my migraine. Phyllis came over and gave me a head and neck massage. She then kept on going and massaged my back, then my legs, and then my penis. She undressed me and then took off all her clothes."

This must have been an unusual event: Marvin had told me he initiated sex almost all of the time. I suspected that Phyllis wanted to expiate her guilt for refusing to see a couples therapist.

"At first, I wouldn't respond."

"How come?"

"To tell you the truth, I was scared. I was just getting over my worst migraine, and I was afraid I'd fail and get another migraine. But Phyllis started sucking my cock and got me hard. I've never seen her so persistent. I finally said, 'Let's go, a good lay might be just the thing to get rid of some of this tension.'" Marvin paused.

"Why do you stop?"

"I'm trying to think of her exact words. Anyway, we started making love. I was doing pretty well, but just as I was getting ready to come, Phyllis said, 'There are other reasons for making love than to get rid of tension.' Well, that did it! I lost it in a second."

"Marvin, did you tell Phyllis exactly how you felt about her timing?"

"Her timing is not good—never has been. But I was too riled up to talk. Afraid of what I'd say. If I say the wrong thing, she can make my life hell—turn off the sexual spigot altogether."

"What sort of thing might you say?"

"I'm afraid of my impulses—my murderous and sexual impulses."

"What do you mean?"

"Do you remember, years ago, a news story of a man who killed his wife by pouring acid on her? Horrible thing! Yet I've often thought about that crime. I can understand how fury toward a woman could lead to a crime like that."

Christ! Marvin's unconscious was closer to the surface than I thought. Remembering I hadn't wanted to take the lid off such primitive feelings—at least not this early in treatment—I switched from murder to sex.

"Marvin, you said you're frightened also by your sexual impulses. What do you mean?"

"My sex drive has always been too strong. I've been told that's true of many bald men. A sign of too much male hormone. Is that true?"

I didn't want to encourage the distraction. I shrugged off the question. "Keep going."

"Well, I've had to keep it under rein all my life because Phyllis has got strong ideas about how much sex we will have. And it's always the same—two times a week, some exceptions for birthdays and holidays."

"You've got some feelings about that?"

"Sometimes. But sometimes I think restraints are good. Without them I might run wild."

That was a curious comment. "What does 'running wild' mean? Do you mean extramarital affairs?"

My question shocked Marvin. "I've never been unfaithful to Phyllis! Never will be!"

"Well, what *do* you mean by 'running wild'?"

Marvin looked stumped. I had a sense he was talking about things he had never discussed before. I was excited for him. It had been one hell of an hour's work. I wanted him to continue, and I just waited.

"I don't *know* what I mean, but at times I've wondered what it would have been like to have married a woman with a sex drive like mine, a woman who wanted and enjoyed sex as much as me."

"What do you think? Your life would have been very different?"

"Let me back up a minute. I shouldn't have used the word *enjoy* a few minutes ago. Phyllis enjoys sex. It's just that she never seems to *want* it. Instead, she . . . what's the word? . . . dispenses it—if I'm good. These are the times when I feel cheated and angry."

Marvin paused. He loosened his collar, rubbed his neck, and rolled his head around. He was getting rid of tension, but I imagined him to be looking around the room, as though to assure himself no one else was listening.

"You look uncomfortable. What are you feeling?"

"Disloyal. Like I shouldn't have been saying these things about Phyllis. Almost like she'll find out about it."

"You give her a lot of power. Sooner or later we're going to need to find out all about that."

Marvin continued to be refreshingly open during the first several weeks of therapy. All in all, he did far better than I had expected. He was cooperative; he relinquished his pugnacious skepticism about psychiatry; he did his homework, came prepared for the sessions, and was determined, as he put it, to get a good return on his investment. His confidence in therapy was boosted by an unexpected early dividend: his migraines mysteriously almost disappeared as soon as he started treatment (although his intense sex-spawned mood swings continued).

During this early phase of therapy, we concentrated on two issues: his marriage and (to a lesser extent, because of his resistance) the implications of his retirement. But I was careful to tread a fine line. I felt like a surgeon preparing the operative field but avoiding any deep dissection. I wanted Marvin to explore these issues, but not too searchingly—not enough to destabilize the precarious marital equilibrium he and Phyllis had established (and thus drive him immediately out of therapy) and not enough to evoke any further death anxiety (and thus ignite further migraines).

At the same time as I was conducting this gentle, somewhat concrete therapy with Marvin, I was also engaged in a fascinating discourse with the dreamer, that vastly enlightened homunculus housed—or, one might say, jailed—by Marvin, who was either ignorant of the dreamer's existence or allowed him to communicate with me in a spirit of benign indifference. While Marvin and I strolled and casually conversed on superficial levels, the dreamer drummed out a constant stream of messages from the depths.

Perhaps my discourse with the dreamer was counterproductive. Perhaps I was willing to permit Marvin a slower pace because of my encounter with the dreamer. I remember beginning every hour not with excitement about seeing Marvin, but with anticipation about my next communiqué from the dreamer.

Sometimes the dreams, like the first ones, were frightening expressions of ontological anxiety; sometimes they foreshadowed things to come in therapy; sometimes they were like subtitles to therapy, providing a vivid translation of Marvin's cautious statements to me.

After the first few sessions, I began to receive hopeful messages:

*The teacher in a boarding school was looking around for children who were interested in painting on a large blank canvas. Later I was telling a small, pudgy boy—obviously myself—about it, and he got so excited he began to cry.*

No mistaking that message:

"Marvin senses he's being offered an opportunity by someone—undoubtedly you, his therapist—to start all over again. How exciting—to be given another chance, to paint his life all over again on a blank canvas."

Other hopeful dreams followed:

*I am at a wedding, and a woman comes up and says she is my long-forgotten daughter. I'm surprised because I didn't know I had a daughter. She's middle-aged and dressed in rich brown colors. We had only a couple of hours to talk. I asked her about the conditions of her life, but she couldn't talk about that. I was sorry when she left, but we agreed to correspond.*

The message:

"Marvin, for the first time, discovers his daughter—the feminine, softer, sensitive side of himself. He's fascinated. The possibilities are limitless. He considers establishing ongoing communication. Perhaps he can colonize the newfound islets of himself."

Another dream:

*I look out the window and hear a commotion in the shrubbery. It is a cat chasing a mouse. I feel sorry for the mouse and go outside to it. What I find are two baby kittens who have not yet opened their eyes. I run to tell Phyllis about it because she's so fond of kittens.*

The message:

"Marvin understands, he really understands, that his eyes have been closed, and that he is finally preparing to open them. He is excited for Phyllis, who is also about to open her eyes. But be careful, he suspects you of playing a cat-and-mouse game."

Soon I received more warnings:

*Phyllis and I are having dinner in a ramshackle restaurant. The service is very poor. The waiter is never there when you want him. Phyllis tells him he is dirty and poorly dressed. I am surprised that the food is so good.*

The message:

"He is building up a case against you. Phyllis wants you out of their lives. You are highly threatening to both of them. Be careful. Do not get caught in a crossfire. No matter how good your food, you are no match for a woman."

And then a dream providing specific grievances:

*I'm watching a heart transplant. The surgeon is lying down. Someone is accusing him of being involved only in the transplantation process and being uninterested in all the messy circumstances of how he got the heart from the donor. The surgeon admits that was true. There was an operating room nurse who said she didn't have this privilege—she had to witness the whole mess.*

The message:

"The heart transplant is, of course, psychotherapy. [Hats off to you, my dear dreamer friend! "Heart transplant"—what an inspired visual symbol for psychotherapy!] Marvin feels you're cold and un-involved and that you've taken little personal interest in his life—in how he got to be the person he is today."

The dreamer was advising me how to proceed. Never have I had a supervisor like this. I was so fascinated by the dreamer that I began to lose sight of his motivation. Was he acting as Marvin's agent to help me to help Marvin? Was he hoping that if Marvin changed, then he, the dreamer, would gain his release through integration with Marvin? Or was he chiefly acting to alleviate his own isolation by taking pains to preserve the relationship he had with me?

But regardless of his motivation, his advice was sagacious. He was right: I was not truly engaged with Marvin! We stayed on such a formal level that our use of first names seemed ungainly. Marvin took himself very seriously: he was practically my only patient with whom I could never joke or banter. I tried often to focus on our relationship, but aside from some barbs in the first couple of sessions (of the "you fellows think sex is at the root of everything" genre), he made no reference to me whatsoever. He treated me with such respect and deference and generally responded to my inquiries about his feelings toward me with statements to the effect that I must know what I'm doing since he continued to remain free of migraines.

By the time six months had gone by, I cared somewhat more about Marvin, yet still had no deep fondness for him. This was very strange since I adored the dreamer: I adored his courage and his scorching honesty. From time to time, I had to prod myself to remember that the dreamer *was* Marvin, that the dreamer provided an open channel to Marvin's central nucleus—that whorl of the self which possesses absolute wisdom and self-knowledge.

The dreamer was correct that I had not plunged into the messy details of the origin of the heart to be transplanted: I had been far too inattentive to the experiences and patterns of Marvin's early life. Consequently, I devoted the following two sessions to a detailed examination of his childhood. One of the most interesting things I learned was that, when Marvin was seven or eight, a cataclysmic secret event shattered his family and resulted in his mother banishing his father permanently from her bedroom. Though the nature of the event was never revealed to Marvin, he now believes, on the basis of a few stray comments by his mother, that his father had either been unfaithful or a compulsive gambler.

After his father's exile, it fell upon Marvin, the youngest son, to become his mother's constant companion: it was his job to escort her to all her social functions. For years he endured his friends' jibes about dating his mother.

Needless to say, Marvin's new family assignment did not increase his popularity with his father, who became a thin presence in the family, then a mere shadow, and soon evaporated forever. Two years later, his older brother received a postcard from their father saying he was alive and well and was sure the family was better off without him.

Obviously, the foundation was in place for major oedipal problems in Marvin's relations with women. His relationship with his mother had been exclusive, overly intimate, prolonged in its closeness and had disastrous consequences for his relationship with men; indeed, he imagined he had, in some substantial way, contributed to his father's disappearance. It was not surprising, then, to learn that Marvin had been wary of competition with men and inordinately shy of women. His first real date, with Phyllis, was his last first date: Phyllis and he kept steady company until their marriage. She was six years younger, equally shy and equally inexperienced with the opposite sex.

These anamnestic sessions were, to my mind, reasonably productive. I grew acquainted with the characters who peopled Marvin's mind, and identified (and shared with him) certain important repetitive life patterns: for example, the way he had re-created part of his parents' pattern in his own marriage—his wife, like his father's wife, wielded control by cutting off sexual favors.

As this material unfolded, it was possible to understand Marvin's current problems from each of three very different perspectives: the *existential* (with a focus on the ontological anxiety that had been evoked by passing a major life milestone); the *Freudian* (with an emphasis on oedipal anxiety which resulted in the sexual act being welded to primitive catastrophic anxiety); and the *communicational* (with an emphasis on how the marital dynamic equilibrium had been unsettled by recent life events; more about this was to emerge shortly).

Marvin, as always, worked hard to produce the necessary information, but, though his dreams had requested it, he soon lost interest in past origins of current life patterns. He commented once that these dusty events belonged to another age, almost another century. He also wistfully noted that we were discussing a drama in which every character, save himself, was dead.

The dreamer soon gave me a series of messages about Marvin's reaction to our historical forays:

> *I saw a car with a curious shape, like a large, long box on wheels. It was black and patent-leather shiny. I was struck by the fact that the only windows were in the back and were very askew—so that you could not really look through them.*

*There was another vehicle with problems with the rear-vision mirror. It had rear windows with a kind of filter that slid up and down but it was stuck.*

*I was giving a lecture with great success. Then I started having trouble with the slide projector. First, I couldn't get a slide out of the projector to put in another. It was a slide of a man's head. Then I couldn't focus the slide. Then people's heads kept getting in the way of the screen. I moved all over the auditorium to get an unobstructed view, but I could never see the whole slide.*

The message I believed the dreamer was sending me:

"I try to look back but my vision fails. There are no rear windows. There is no rear-vision mirror. A slide with a head in it obstructs the view. The past, the true story, the chronicle of real events, is unrecoverable. The head in the slide—my head, my vision, my memory—gets in the way. I see the past only filtered through the eyes of the present—not as I knew and experienced it at the time, but as I experience it now. Historical recall is a futile exercise in getting the heads out of the way.

"Not only is the past lost forever, but the future, too, is sealed. The patent-leather car, the box, my coffin, has no front windows either."

Gradually, with relatively little prompting from me, Marvin began to wade into deeper waters. Perhaps he overheard scraps of my discourse with the dreamer. His first association to the car, the curious black box on wheels, was to say, "It is not a coffin." Noticing my raised eyebrows, he smiled and said, "Was it one of you fellows who said you give yourself away by protesting too much?"

"The car has no front windows, Marvin. Think about that. What comes to you?"

"I don't know. Without front windows you don't know where you're heading."

"How would that apply to you, by what you're facing ahead of you in your life now?"

"Retirement. I'm a little slow, but I'm beginning to get it. But I don't worry about retirement. Why don't I *feel* anything?"

"The feeling is there. It seeps into your dreams. Maybe it's too painful to feel. Maybe the pain gets short-circuited and put onto other things. Look how often you've said, 'Why should I get so upset about my sexual performance? It doesn't make sense.' One of our main jobs is to sort things out and restore the feelings to where they belong."

Soon he reported a series of dreams with explicit material about aging and death. For example, he dreamed of walks in a large, unfinished, underground concrete building.

One dream, in particular, affected him:

*I saw Susan Jennings. She was working in a bookstore. She looked depressed, and I went up to her to offer my sympathy. I told her I knew others, six others, who felt the same way. She looked up at me, and her face was a hideous mucous-filled skull. I woke up extremely frightened.*

Marvin worked well with this dream.

"Susan Jennings? Susan Jennings? I knew her forty-five years ago in college. I don't think I've thought of her once till now."

"Think about her now. What comes to mind?"

"I can see her face—round, pudgy, large glasses."

"Remind you of anyone?"

"No, but I know what *you'd* say—that she looks like me: the round face and oversized spectacles."

"What about the 'six others'?"

"Oh, there's something there, all right. Yesterday I was talking to Phyllis about all our friends who have died and also about a newspaper article about people who die immediately after retirement. I told her that I had read an alumni bulletin and noted that six persons in my college class have died. That must be the 'six others who felt the same way' in the dream. Fascinating!"

"There's a lot of fear of death there, Marvin—in this dream and in all the other nightmares. Everyone's afraid of death. I've never known anyone who wasn't. But most people work on it over and over throughout the years. With you it seems to have exploded all at once. I feel strongly that it's the thought of retirement that's ignited it."

Marvin mentioned that the strongest dream of all was that first dream, six months ago, of the two gaunt men, the white cane, and the baby. Those images kept drifting back into his mind—especially the image of the gaunt Victorian undertaker or temperance worker. Perhaps, he said, that was a symbol for him: he had been temperate, too temperate. He'd known for a couple of years that he had deadened himself all his life.

Marvin was beginning to astonish me. He was venturing into such depths that I could scarcely believe I was talking to the same person. When I asked him what had happened a couple of years ago, he described an episode he had never shared before, not even with Phyllis. As he was flipping through a copy of *Psychology Today* in a dentist's office, he was intrigued by an article suggesting that one attempt to construct a final, meaningful conversation with each of the important vanished people in one's life.

One day when he was alone, he tried it. He imagined telling his father how much he had missed him and how much he would have liked to have known him. His father didn't answer. He imagined saying his final goodbye to his mother, sitting across from him in her familiar bentwood rocker. He said the words, but no feelings came with them. He gritted his teeth and tried to force feelings out. But nothing came. He concentrated on the meaning of *never*—that he would *never, never* see her again. He remembered banging his fist on his desk, forcing himself to remember the chill of his mother's forehead when he kissed her as she lay in her casket. But nothing came. He shouted aloud, "I will *never* see you again!" Still, nothing. *That* was when he learned that he had deadened himself.

He cried in my office that day. He cried for all that he had missed, for all the years of deadness in his life. How sad it was, he said, that he had waited until now to try to come alive. For the first time I felt very close to Marvin. I clasped his shoulder as he sobbed.

At the end of this session, I was exhausted and very moved. I thought we had finally broken through the impenetrable barrier: that finally Marvin and the dreamer had fused and spoken with one voice.

Marvin felt better after our session and was highly optimistic until, a few days later, a curious event occurred. He and Phyllis were just commencing sexual intercourse when he suddenly said, "Maybe the doctor is right, maybe all my sexual anxiety *is* really anxiety about death!" No sooner had he finished this sentence, than— whoooosh!—he had a sudden, pleasureless premature ejaculation. Phyllis was understandably irritated by his selection of topics for sexual small talk. Marvin immediately began to berate himself for his insensitivity to her and for his sexual failure and toppled into a profound depression. Soon I received an urgent, alarmed message from the dreamer:

> *I had been bringing new furniture into the house, but then I couldn't close the front door. Someone had placed a device there to keep the door open. Then I saw ten or twelve people with luggage outside the door. They were evil, awful people, especially one toothless old crone whose face reminded me of Susan Jennings. She also reminded me of Madame Defarge in the movie* A Tale of Two Cities*—the one who knitted at the guillotine as heads were lopped off.*

The message:

"Marvin is very frightened. He has become aware of too much, too fast. He knows now that death is waiting for him. He has opened the door of awareness; but now he fears that too much has come out, that the door is jammed, that he will never be able to close it again."

Frightening dreams with similar messages followed rapidly:

*It was night, I was perched high on the balcony of a building. I heard a small child crying below in the darkness, calling for help. I told him I would come because I was the only one who could help, but as I started down into the darkness, the stairwell grew more and more narrow and the flimsy banister came off in my hands. I was afraid to go farther.*

The message:

"There are vital parts of me that I have buried all my life—the little boy, the woman, the artist, the meaning-seeking part. I know that I deadened myself and have left much of my life unlived. But I cannot descend now into these realms. I cannot cope with the fear and the regret."

And yet another dream:

*I am taking an examination. I hand in my blue book and remember that I haven't answered the last question. I panic. I try to get the book back, but it is past the deadline. I make an appointment to meet my son after the deadline.*

The message:

"I realize now that I have not done what I might have done with my life. The course and the exam is over. I would have liked to have done it differently. That last question on the exam, what was it? Maybe if I had taken a different turn, to have done something else, to have become something else—not a high school teacher, not a rich accountant. But it is too late, too late to change any of my answers. The time has run out. If only I had a son, I might through him spew myself into the future past the death line."

Later, the same night:

*I am climbing a mountain trail. I see some people trying to rebuild a house at night. I know that it can't be done, and I try to tell them but they can't hear me. Then I hear someone calling my name from behind. It is my mother trying to overtake me. She said she has a message for me. It is that someone is dying. I know that it is me who is dying. I wake up in a sweat.*

The message:

"It is too late. It is not possible to rebuild your house at night—to change the course you have set, just as you are preparing to enter the sea of death. I am now my mother's age when she died. I am overtaking her and realize that death is inevitable. I cannot alter the future because I am being overtaken by the past."

These messages from the dreamer drummed louder and louder. I had to heed them. They forced me to take my bearings and to review what had been happening in therapy.

Marvin had moved fast, too fast perhaps. At first he was a man without insight: he could not, would not, direct his sight inward. In the relatively short period of six months, he had made enormous discoveries. He learned that his eyes, like those of a newborn kitten, had been closed. He learned that deep inside there is a rich teeming world which, if confronted, brings terrible fear but also offers redemption through illumination.

The surface appearance of things no longer compelled him: he was less captivated by his collections of stamps and the *Reader's Digest*. His eyes open now to the existential facts of life, he was grappling with the inevitability of death and with his powerlessness to save himself.

Marvin awakened more quickly than I had expected; perhaps he listened, after all, to the voice of his own dreamer. At first he was eager to see, but soon enthusiasm gave way to a powerful sense of regret. He grieved for his past and his impending losses. Most of all, he grieved for the vast empty spaces of his life: the unused potential within him, the children he had never had, the father he had never known, the house that had never brimmed with family and friends, a life work that might have contained more significance than the accumulation of too much money. Finally, he grieved for himself, for the imprisoned dreamer, for the little boy crying for help in the darkness.

He knew he had not lived the life he really wanted. Perhaps it could still be done. Perhaps there was still time to paint his life anew on a large blank canvas. He began to twist the knobs of secret doors, to whisper to an unknown daughter, to wonder where vanished fathers go.

But he had overstepped himself. He ventured farther than his supply lines could reach, and now was assailed from all sides: the past was dusky and irretrievable; the future, blocked. It was too late: his house had been built, his final examination turned in. He had flung open the sluice gates of awareness, only to be inundated with death anxiety.

Sometimes death anxiety is dismissed as trivial in its universality. Who, after all, does not know and fear death? Yet it is one thing to know about death in general, to grit one's teeth and stoke up a shudder or two; it is quite another to apprehend one's own death and to experience it in the bones and sockets of one's being. Such death awareness is a terror that comes rarely, sometimes only once or twice in a lifetime—a terror that Marvin now experienced night after night.

Against this dread, he lacked even the most common defenses: childless, he could not be comforted by the illusion of immortal germ cells; he had no sustaining religious belief—neither of a consciousness-preserving afterlife nor of an omnipresent, protective personal deity; nor did he have the satisfaction of knowing that he had realized himself in life. (As a general rule, the less one's sense of life fulfillment, the greater one's death anxiety.) Worst of all, Marvin could foresee no end to his anxiety. The dream image was graphic: the demons had escaped the room of his mind and were in full, menacing view. He could neither escape nor reincarcerate them by closing the jammed door.

So Marvin and I had reached a crucial point, a juncture to which full awareness inevitably leads. It is the time when one stands before the abyss and decides how to face the pitiless existential facts of life: death, isolation, groundlessness, and meaninglessness. Of course, there are no solutions. One has a choice only of certain stances: to be "resolute," or "engaged," or courageously defiant, or stoically accepting, or to relinquish rationality and, in awe and mystery, place one's trust in the providence of the Divine.

I didn't know what Marvin would do, nor did I know how else to help. I remember looking forward to each session with more than a little curiosity about the choices that he would make. What would it be? Would he flee his own discovery? Would he find a way, once more, to pull the comforter of self-deception over his head? Would he ultimately embrace a religious solution? Or would he find strength and shelter in one of the *Lebens*-philosophical solutions? Never have I felt so keenly the dual role of the therapist as participant-observer. Although I was now emotionally engaged and cared deeply about what would happen to Marvin, at the same time, I remained aware that I was in a privileged position to study the embryology of belief.

Though Marvin continued to feel anxious and depressed, he gamely continued to work in therapy. My respect for him grew. I had thought that he would have terminated therapy long before. What kept him coming?

Several things, he said. First, he was still migraine-free. Second, he remembered my warning to him, the first time we met, that there were going to be times in therapy when he would feel worse; he trusted my word that his current anxiety was a stage in therapy and would ultimately pass. Furthermore, he was persuaded that something significant must be happening in therapy: he'd learned more about himself in the past five months than in his previous sixty-four years!

And something else totally unexpected had happened. His relationship to Phyllis had begun to undergo a perceptible shift.

"We've been talking more frequently and more honestly than ever before. I'm not sure when it started. When you and I first began to meet, we had a brief flurry of talking. But that was a false alarm. I think Phyllis was only trying to persuade me that we could talk without having to see a therapist."

"But over the last few weeks, it's been different. We are *really* talking now. I've been telling Phyllis what you and I talk about every hour. In fact, she waits at the door for me to return home from the sessions and gets annoyed if I delay—for example, if I suggest we wait until dinner because it gives us such interesting table conversation."

"What types of things seem most important to her?"

"Almost everything. I told you Phyllis doesn't like to spend money—she loves sales. We've been joking that we've gotten a two-for-the-price-of-one therapy bargain."

"That's the kind of bargain I'm glad to give."

"I think the thing that meant the most to Phyllis was when I told her about our discussions about my work, about how disappointed I am with myself for not having done more with my abilities, for having devoted myself only to money, for never having considered what I might have given to the world. That hit her very hard. She said that, if it were true for me, it was true in spades for her—that she had led a totally self-centered life, that she's never given anything of herself."

"She's given you a great deal."

"I reminded her of that. At first she thanked me for saying it, but later, after thinking about it more, she said she's not so sure—maybe she's helped me, but she said that in some ways she may have stood in my way."

"How so?"

"She mentioned all the things I talked to you about: the way she's barred others from our home; the way she's discouraged me from making friends who might have wanted to visit our home; the way she's refused to travel and discourages me from traveling—did I ever tell you about that? Most of all, she regrets her childlessness and her refusal many years ago to see a fertility doctor."

"Marvin, I'm amazed. This openness, this honesty! How are you two doing it? These are tough things to talk about, really tough."

He went on to say that Phyllis had paid a price for her insights—she had become very agitated. One night he couldn't sleep and heard some whispering from her room. (They slept in separate bedrooms because of his snoring.) He tiptoed in and saw Phyllis kneeling by her bed, praying, chanting the same phrase over and over: "The mother of God will protect me. The mother of God will protect me. The mother of God will protect me. The mother of God will protect me."

Marvin was very affected by this scene though it was hard for him to put it into words. I think he was overcome with pity—pity for Phyllis, for himself, for all small, helpless people. I think he realized that her chanting that phrase was a magical incantation, a wafer-thin protection against the terrible things we all have to face.

He finally got back to sleep and later that night had a dream:

*There was a statue of a female god on a pedestal in a large crowded room. It looked like Christ but was wearing a flowing orange pastel dress. On the other side of the room there was an actress with a long white dress. The actress and the statue traded places. Somehow they traded dresses, and the statue got down and the actress climbed up on the pedestal.*

Marvin said he finally understood a dream: the dream meant that he had turned women into goddesses and then believed he would be safe if he could appease them. That was why he had always dreaded Phyllis's anger, and that was why, when he was anxious, she could offer such relief by soothing him sexually.

"Especially oral sex—I think I told you that when I'm in panic, she takes my penis in her mouth and my bad feelings just melt away. It's not sex—you've been saying that all along, and now I know you're right—my penis can be completely soft. It's just that she accepts me totally and takes me into her. It's like I've become a part of her."

"You *do* grant her magical powers—like a goddess. She can heal you with just a smile, an embrace, or by taking you inside her. No wonder you take great pains not to displease her. But the problem is that sex is turned into something medicinal—no, that's not strong enough—sex becomes a life or death proposition, and your survival depends on merging with this woman. No wonder sex has been difficult. It should be a loving, joyful act, not protection from danger. With that view of sex, anyone—certainly including me—would have problems with potency."

Marvin took out his notepad and wrote down a few lines. I had been irritated weeks ago when he first started taking notes, but he made such good use of therapy that I had learned to respect any of his mnemonic aids.

"Let's see if I have this right. Your theory is that what I call sex is often not sex—at least not good sex—but instead is a way of protecting myself against fear, especially fear of aging and death. And when I'm impotent, it is not because I fail sexually as a man but because I'm asking sex to do things that sex can't do."

"Exactly. And there's a lot of evidence for this. There's the dream of the two gaunt undertakers and the white-tipped cane. There's the dream of the liquefying ground under your house which you try to cure by drilling with your giant auger. There's the feeling you just described of being soothed by a physical connection with Phyllis which masquerades as sex but isn't, as you noted, sex at all."

"So there are two issues. First, I'm asking sex to do something beyond its power. Second, I'm giving almost supernatural power to Phyllis to heal me or protect me."

"And then everything fell apart when you overheard her plaintive, repetitive chant."

"That was when I realized how frail she is—not Phyllis in particular, but *all* women. No, not just women, but everybody. What I've been doing was exactly what Phyllis was doing—depending on magic."

"So you depend on her power for protection, and she, in turn, pleads for protection by a magical chant—look where that leaves you.

"There's something else that's important. Consider things now from Phyllis's side: if she, in her love for you, accepts the role of goddess that you assign her, think of what that role does to her own possibilities for growth. In order to stay on her pedestal, she was never able to talk to you about *her* pain and *her* fears—or not until very recently."

"Slow down! Let me get this down. I'm going to have to explain all this to Phyllis." Marvin was scribbling away furiously now.

"So in a sense she was following your unspoken wishes by not openly expressing her uncertainties, by pretending to be stronger than she felt. I have a hunch that's one of the reasons she wouldn't come into therapy when we started—in other words, she picked up your wish that she *not* change. I also have a hunch that if you ask her now, she might come."

"God, we are really on the same wavelength now. Phyllis and I have already discussed it, and she is ready to talk to you."

And that was how Phyllis entered therapy. She arrived with Marvin for the next hour—a handsome, graceful woman who, by sheer will, overcame her timidity and in our three-way session became boldly self-revealing.

Our conjectures about Phyllis had been close to the mark: she often had to swallow her own feelings of inadequacy in order not to agitate Marvin. And, of course, she had to be particularly solicitous when he was in distress—which meant, recently, that she had to be solicitous almost all the time.

But her behavior was not entirely reactive to Marvin's problems. She was also struggling with many personal issues, particularly her painful sensitivity about her lack of education and her belief that she was intellectually inferior to most people, especially Marvin. One of the reasons she dreaded, and avoided, social events was that someone might ask her, "What do you do?" She avoided lengthy conversations because it might become evident that she had never attended college. Whenever she compared herself with others, she invariably concluded that they were better informed and more clever, socially adept, self-confident, and interesting.

"Perhaps," I suggested, "the only area where you can maintain power is sex. That's one place where Marvin needs you and can wield no control over you."

Phyllis responded hesitantly at first, and then the words began to pour out of her. "I guess I had to have *something* that Marvin wanted. In most other ways he is very self-sufficient. Often I feel I don't have much else to offer. I wasn't able to have children, I'm afraid of people, I've never worked outside the home, I have no talents or skills." She paused, wiped her eyes and said to Marvin, "See, I *can* cry if I put my mind to it."

She turned back to me. "Marvin's told you that he tells me about the things the two of you have been discussing. I've been in therapy once removed. Some of the topics shook me up, they apply more to me than to him."

"For example?"

"For example, regret. That idea really hit home. I have a lot of regret about what I've done with my life or, better, what I haven't done."

My heart went out to Phyllis at that moment, and I desperately wanted to say something helpful. "If we stare too hard into the past, it's easy to be overcome with regret. But now the important thing is to turn toward the future. We've got to think about change. What must *not* occur is that five years from now you look back with regret over the way you've lived these coming five years."

Phyllis responded after a short pause, "I started to say that I'm too old to do things differently. I felt that way for thirty years. Thirty years! My whole life's gone by feeling it was too late. But watching Marvin change over the last several weeks has been impressive. You may not realize it, but the mere fact that I'm here today, in a psychiatrist's office, talking about myself is in itself a big, big, step."

I remember thinking how fortunate it was that Marvin's change had spurred Phyllis to change. Often therapy doesn't work that way. In fact, not uncommonly therapy places strain on a marriage: if a patient changes and the spouse stays locked in the same position, then the dynamic equilibrium of the marriage often disintegrates. The patient has either to forego growth or to grow and jeopardize the union. I was very grateful that Phyllis demonstrated so much flexibility.

The last thing we discussed was the timing of Marvin's symptoms. I had satisfied myself that the symbolic meaning of retirement—the existential anxiety underlying this important life marker—was sufficient explanation for the onset of his symptoms. But Phyllis supplied additional explanations for "Why now?"

"I'm sure you know what you're talking about and that Marvin must be more upset than he knows at the idea of retiring. But, frankly, *I'm* disturbed at the idea of his retirement—and when I get upset, upset about anything, Marvin gets upset. That's the way our relationship works. If I worry, even if I keep it completely silent, he senses it and gets upset. Sometimes he gets so upset, he takes my upsetness away from me."

Phyllis said all this with such facility that I forgot for a moment the great strain she was under. Earlier she had been glancing at Marvin every couple of sentences. I wasn't certain whether it was to obtain his support or to reassure herself that he could tolerate what she had to say. But now she was engrossed in her own words, holding her body and her head absolutely still as she talked.

"What about Marvin's retirement disturbs you?"

"Well, for one thing, he feels retirement means travel. I don't know how much he has told you about me and traveling. I'm not proud of it, but I'm having a lot of trouble leaving the house, let alone traveling halfway around the world. Also, I'm not looking forward to Marvin's 'taking over' the house. For the last forty years he's run the office and I've run the house. Now, I know that it's his house, too. It's his house mainly, you could say—his money bought it. But it's very upsetting to hear him talk about remodeling rooms so he can display his various collections. For example, right now he's trying to get someone to build a new glass dining-room table which will display his political campaign buttons. I don't want to eat on top of political buttons. I just fear we're heading toward trouble. And——" She stopped.

"You were going to say something else, Phyllis?"

"Well, this is the hardest thing to say. I feel ashamed. I'm afraid that when Marvin begins staying home, he will see how little I do each day and lose respect for me."

Marvin simply took her hand. It seemed the right thing to do.

In fact, throughout the session he remained deeply empathic. No distracting questions, no jocular clichés, no struggling to stay on the surface. He reassured Phyllis that travel was important to him, but not so important that he couldn't wait until she was ready. He told her explicitly that the most important thing in the world to him was their relationship, and that he had never felt closer to her.

I met with Phyllis and Marvin as a couple for several more sessions. I reinforced their new, more open mode of communication and instructed them in some fundamentals of sexual functioning: how Phyllis could help Marvin sustain his erection; how she could help him avoid premature ejaculation; how Marvin could approach sex less mechanically; and how he could, if he lost his erection, bring Phyllis to orgasm manually or orally.

She had been housebound for years and now rarely ventured forth alone. It seemed to me that the time was ripe to interrupt that pattern. I believed that the meaning, or at least one meaning, of her agoraphobia was now obsolete and could be influenced by paradox. I first obtained Marvin's agreement to help Phyllis overcome her phobia by promising to follow any suggestions I gave him. I then instructed him to say to her, punctually every two hours, phoning her if he were at work, these words precisely: "Phyllis, please don't leave the house. I need to know you are there at all times to take care of me and prevent me from being frightened."

Phyllis's eyes widened. Marvin looked at me incredulously. Could I possibly be serious?

I told him that I knew it sounded crazy, but persuaded him to follow my instructions faithfully.

They both giggled the first few times Marvin told Phyllis not to leave the house: it seemed ridiculous and artificial; she had not left the house in months. But soon irritation replaced the giggle. Marvin was irritated with me for making him promise to keep repeating the same stupid statement. Phyllis, even though she knew Marvin was following my instructions, grew irritated with him for ordering her to stay at home. After a few days she went to the library alone, then shopping, and in the next few weeks ventured farther than she had for years.

I rarely employ such manipulative approaches in therapy; usually the price is too high—one must sacrifice the genuineness of the therapeutic encounter. But paradox can be effective in those instances where the therapeutic foundation is solid and the prescribed behavior explodes the meaning of the symptom. In this case, Phyllis's agoraphobia was not *her* symptom but *their* symptom, and it served to maintain the marital equilibrium: Phyllis was eternally there for Marvin; he could venture forth into the world, provide for their security, yet feel secure in the knowledge that she was always there waiting for him.

There was a certain irony in my use of this intervention: an existential approach and a manipulative paradox ordinarily make bizarre bedfellows. Yet here the sequence seemed natural. Marvin had applied to his relationship with Phyllis the insights he had obtained from a confrontation with the deep sources of his despair. Despite the discouragement (depicted in his dreams by such symbols as being unable to rebuild a house at night), he had nonetheless proceeded upon a radical reconstruction of his relationship to his wife. Both Marvin and Phyllis now cared so much for the other's growth and being that they could genuinely collaborate in the process of wrenching a symptom from its socket.

Marvin's change initiated an adaptive spiral: liberated from a restricting role, Phyllis underwent enormous change in the space of a few weeks and continued and solidified that improvement in individual therapy with another therapist over the next year.

Marvin and I met only a few more times. Pleased with his progress, he had realized, as he put it, a good yield on his investment. The migraines, his reason for seeking therapy, had never returned. Though his mood swings still occurred (and were still dependent on sex), their intensity had diminished considerably. Marvin estimated that the mood swings were now approximately the same as they had been for the previous twenty years.

I, too, felt satisfied with our work. There is always more that can be done, but overall we had accomplished far more than I could have anticipated at our initial session. The fact that Marvin's anguished dreams had stopped was also reassuring. Though I had received no messages from the dreamer for the last several weeks, I had not missed them. Marvin and the dreamer had fused, and I spoke to them now as to a single person.

I next saw Marvin one year later: I always schedule patients for a one-year follow-up session—both for their benefit and for my own edification. I also make it a practice to play for the patient a tape recording of part of our initial session. Marvin listened to ten minutes of our initial interview with great interest, smiled at me, and said, "Who is that jerk, anyway?"

Marvin's quip has a serious side. Having heard the same reaction from many patients, I have come to regard it as a valid marker of change. Marvin, in effect, was saying, "I'm a different person now. I hardly recognize that Marvin of a year ago. Those things I used to do—refusing to look at my life; trying to control or intimidate others; trying to impress others with my intelligence, my charts, my thoroughness—they're gone. I don't do that any more."

These are no minor adjustments: they represent basic modifications in personhood. Yet they are so subtle in character that they generally elude most research-outcome questionnaires.

With his usual care, Marvin had come prepared with one-year follow-up notes which reviewed and assessed the tasks we had addressed in therapy. The verdict was mixed: in some areas he had maintained his changes; in others he had done some backsliding. First, he informed me that Phyllis was doing well: her phobia about leaving the house remained much improved. She had joined a women's therapy group and was working on her fear of attending social functions. Perhaps most impressive was her decision to address adaptively her concern about her lack of education—by enrolling in several college extension courses.

As for Marvin? He had no further migraines. His mood swings persisted but were not disabling. He was still periodically impotent but brooded about it less. He had changed his mind about retirement and was now working part-time, but had switched fields and was doing more real estate development and management—work that he found more interesting. He and Phyllis still related very well, but at times he found himself aggrieved at her newfound activities and felt ignored by her.

And my old friend, the dreamer? What of him? Did he have a message for me? Although Marvin had had no nightmares or powerful dreams, he knew there were nocturnal rumblings. The night before our meeting, he had had a short dream which was full of mystery. It seemed to be trying to tell him something. Perhaps, he suggested, I could understand it.

*My wife is in front of me. She is naked and standing with her legs spread apart. I am looking through the triangle of her legs off into the distance. But all I can see, far away on the horizon, is my mother's face.*

My final message from the dreamer:

"My vision is bounded by the women of my life and imagination. Nonetheless, I can still see far into the distance. Perhaps that is sufficient."

# AFTERWORD

## On Rereading *Love's Executioner* at Age Eighty

※2C※

*When I agreed to write a postscript for* Love's Executioner, *I had no idea of the* emotional adventure ahead of me. I wrote this book twenty-five years ago and, since then, had not once read it in its entirety. This view backward to the writing of an earlier self was thrilling and poignant, but also dismaying and embarrassing. The flush of pride I first experienced quickly gave way to a sense of deflation: "This guy writes a lot better than I can."

At first I thought I would be encountering myself as a very young man, but a bit of arithmetic led to the realization that I was no sapling when I wrote this book: I was in my mid-fifties! That was surprising since the writer seems so youthful, energetic, and often unrestrained and sophomoric. And outrageously active—often charging at a patient's defenses with a battering ram! I wish I could have supervised him and settled him down.

And yet there are so many things I like about this younger self. I like the way he avoided diagnosis or categorization. It was as though he were seeing for the very first time each particular set of complaints and personality characteristics, as though he truly believed each individual was unique and required a unique therapy approach. And I liked his willingness to put up with uncertainty and to undertake the laborious task of inventing a different therapy for each patient. I felt sorry for the discomfort he experienced in each course of therapy. He lacked the confidence provided by an established school of thought, a professional home such as a Freudian, a Jungian, a Lacanian, an Adlerian, or a cognitive-behavioral one with an all-embracing explanatory system. But I was pleased he never believed he knew unknowable things.

And such audacity. His amount of self-disclosure was outrageous twenty-five years ago and set most therapists' teeth on edge. And still it seems outrageous. I personally feel shocked. How dare he disclose so many of my private matters? My secret cache of love letters, my compulsive work habits, my inexcusably unkind, judgmental attitudes toward obese people, my love obsession that prevented me from being fully present at a family beach vacation. Despite such behavior, I am nonetheless proud of his putting nothing in the way of forging a true therapy encounter; I would do exactly the same today. I remain convinced that a therapist's judicious self-disclosure facilitates the course of therapy.

*Love's Executioner* was a pivotal turning point for me. During my first several years as a member of the Stanford University Medical School faculty, I had been heavily involved in psychotherapy teaching, research, and publishing in professional journals. I developed a specialty in group therapy and, during my first sabbatical, embarked on writing a textbook on group therapy. After finishing this book, I turned to another interest that had long been percolating under the surface—the role of existential concerns in human life and human distress. After a decade of study and research, I wrote a textbook, *Existential Psychotherapy*, intending not to establish a new field but to make all therapists more aware of existential issues. Four major existential concerns— death, meaning in life, isolation, and freedom—play a crucial role in the inner life of every human being and constitute the thrust of that book.

Once this book was finished, I continued to develop new ideas about the utilization of these existential concerns in therapy, but gradually came to the conclusion that such ideas are best expressed through the narrative form. It did not escape me that the ideas of some of the most important existential thinkers—for example, Camus and Sartre—are most vivid and compelling in their stories and novels rather than in technical philosophic works.

Nor did it escape me that narrative played a vital, if covert, role in my textbooks. I have heard from many teachers and students that the numerous tales—some a few pages long, some merely a paragraph or two—I had interspersed in both *The Theory and Practice of Group Psychotherapy* and *Existential Psychotherapy* vastly increased each book's effectiveness. Students have told me they were more willing to plod through dry theory knowing there would likely be an interesting tale just around the bend.

And so I gradually developed the notion that the best way I could convey my ideas to students, and enhance an existential sensibility, was through narrative. In 1987, I took the plunge and resolved to write a different kind of book, a book in which I would put story first and theoretical discussion second. In no way was I deviating from my role as a teacher of psychotherapy—I was simply going about it in a different fashion. *Love's Executioner* was meant to be a collection of teaching stories aimed (like all my subsequent stories and novels) at the young psychotherapist and all other people, including patients, interested in psychotherapy. The mother book fueling the ideas for the stories was *Existential Psychotherapy*.

There was yet another component in this decision. I had always wanted to be a storyteller. As long as I can remember, I've been a voracious reader and somewhere in early adolescence I began yearning to be a real writer. That desire must have been percolating on the back burner as I pursued my academic career, for as I began writing these ten stories, I sensed I was on the way to finding myself.

Books and places are bonded together in my memory. Whenever I reread or even think about a book I've read, I immediately visualize the place where I first read it. Rereading *Love's Executioner* evoked a stream of delicious memories that began in 1987 when my youngest child left home for college, and my wife and I set off around the world for a year's sabbatical. First, we became acquainted with Japanese culture, as I taught for two weeks in Tokyo; then, two weeks of travel in China where my wife, a feminist scholar, lectured to university students and teachers. On my last day in China, I spent an afternoon alone wandering through the back streets of Shanghai and came upon a handsome but entirely deserted Catholic church. After making certain I was alone, I entered the confessional booth (appropriating the priest's seat) and meditated upon the generations of priests who had heard confessions in this box. I envied their ability to pronounce, "You are forgiven." What therapeutic power! While sitting in that seat of power, I had an extraordinary writerly experience. For an hour, I slipped into a reverie in which the entire plot of "Three Unopened Letters" came to me. I scribbled the essentials of the story on the only paper available to me: the blank pages of my passport.

It was in Bali that I began to write in earnest. We settled into a two-month stay in Kuta on Bali in an exotic house that had a high wall around the large lush garden property but no interior walls other than hanging shades. Needing no reference books for my writing, I traveled light and had only a stack of my session notes for about fifty patients. The atmosphere was exotic and otherworldly. Birds in iridescent colors boldly perched in the intricately twisted trees of the garden and caroled strange melodies. The perfume of unfamiliar blossoms intoxicated me where I sat in the garden reading all my notes over and over again. As memories of my sessions flowed through my mind over the days, a story would, almost without my noticing it, take root and develop such energy as to compel me to put aside all other notes and devote myself to that particular story. As I started writing, I had no idea where a story would lead or what shape it would take. I felt myself almost a bystander as I watched it develop organically. I had often heard writers say a story writes itself, but it was only then that I understood what they meant as one after another of my stories wrote itself. After two months, I had an entirely new and deep appreciation of an old anecdote I had heard in high school about the nineteenth-century English novelist William Makepeace Thackeray: in it, as he came out of his study, his wife asked how the day's writing had gone. He responded, "Oh a terrible day! Pendennis [one of his characters] made a fool of himself today and I couldn't stop him." Soon I became used to hearing my characters talk to one another. I eavesdropped all the time—even after finishing the day's writing, when I was strolling arm in arm with my wife on one of the endless buttery sand Balinese beaches.

Soon I was to have another writerly experience, one of the peak experiences of my life. At some point while deep into a story, I observed my fickle mind flirting with another story, one that appeared to be slowly taking shape beyond my immediate perception. I understood that as a signal—an uncanny one—to myself from myself that the story I was writing was coming to an end, with another on the way.

I had written all my previous books with pencil and paper with the help of my Stanford secretary, who typed them out. But it was now 1987—time to modernize and switch to a computer and printer. I taught myself to type on the flight overseas by means of a video game in which, when letters attacked my spaceship, my only defense was to punch an attacking letter before it detonated my ship. The computer was one of the earliest and still unreliable portable models, and the printer even more unreliable, giving up the ghost after one month in Bali. Alarmed at the prospect of my work disappearing without a trace into the computer's innards, I sought help. There turned out to be only one printer in Denpasar, the major city of Bali, and it was located in a computer school. From it, through either begging or bribing (I've forgotten which), I obtained a precious hard copy of my work to date.

Inspiration came quickly in Bali. I had no distractions (in those halcyon days before e-mail) and have never written better or more quickly. While there, I wrote the title story of *Love's Executioner,* as well as "In Search of the Dreamer" and "If Rape Were Legal . . . ," and transcribed the notes I had made in my passport in the confessional for "Three Unopened Letters." I wrote "Two Smiles" and "Do Not Go Gentle" in Hawaii and the remaining stories in Paris, most of them in a café down the street from the Pantheon.

My initial plan was to follow each story with a few paragraphs discussing the theoretical points it illustrated. I soon found this plan unwieldy and instead put all the theoretical material into a fifty-page epilogue in which I explained in depth what my book was really about. Shortly after I had sent the manuscript to my publisher, I was contacted by Phoebe Hoss, an editor from hell (but also from heaven), with whom I was to have a long, ferocious struggle. She was absolutely persuaded that no theoretical explanation whatsoever was needed, and that I should let my stories speak for themselves. We battled for months. I submitted one version after another; each one was returned to me considerably shortened until, after several months, she had reduced my fifty-page prologue to about ten pages. As I reread the book now, I am reminded once again that she was absolutely right.

Though I feel proud of this book, I have regrets about one story—"Fat Lady." Several obese women have e-mailed me that my words seriously offended them, and today I would probably not be so insensitive. Nonetheless, though I have put myself on trial several times and found myself guilty, let me take advantage of this opportunity to state my defense. I am the main character in this story, not the patient. It is a story about countertransference—that is, irrational, often shameful, feelings a therapist experiences toward a patient that constitute a formidable obstacle in therapy. My negative feelings about obese people prevented me from achieving the deep engagement that I believe is necessary for effective therapy. While I struggled internally with these feelings, I had not expected my patient to perceive them. She had, nonetheless, accurately sensed my feelings, as she recounts at the end of the story. The story depicts my struggle to work through these unruly feelings in order to relate to the patient at a human level. However I may deplore those feelings, I can take pride in the denouement expressed in the story's final words: "I could get my arms all the way around her."

I end this retrospective with an observation my younger self would have found surprising: namely, that the view from eighty is better than expected. Yes, I can't deny that life in the later years is just one damn loss after another; but, even so, I've found far greater tranquility and happiness in my seventh, and eighth and ninth decades than I ever imagined possible. And there's one additional bonus to aging: *reading your own work can be more exciting!* I have found that the memory loss that no one escapes has some advantages. As I turned the pages of "Three Unopened Letters," "Love's Executioner," "The Wrong One Died," among other stories, I felt myself burning with delicious curiosity. I had forgotten how they ended!